BACKROADS & BYWAYS OF
WISCONSIN

BACKROADS & BYWAYS OF
WISCONSIN

Drives, Day Trips
& Weekend Excursions

Kevin Revolinski

The Countryman Press
Woodstock, Vermont

We welcome your comments and suggestions.
Please contact Editor
The Countryman Press
P.O. Box 748, Woodstock
VT 05091, or e-mail countrymanpress@wwnorton.com

ISBN 978-0-88150-816-1

Book design, map, and composition by Hespenheide Design
Cover and interior photos by the author unless otherwise specified

Published by The Countryman Press, P.O. Box 748, Woodstock, VT 05091

Distributed by W. W. Norton & Company, Inc., 500 Fifth Avenue, New York, NY 10110

Printed in the United States of America

10 9 8 7 6 5 4 3

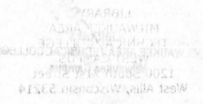

To my grandfather, Louie Girga: the drive was fine.
The last ten miles or so were downhill
and so I didn't have to push.

Map of Wisconsin

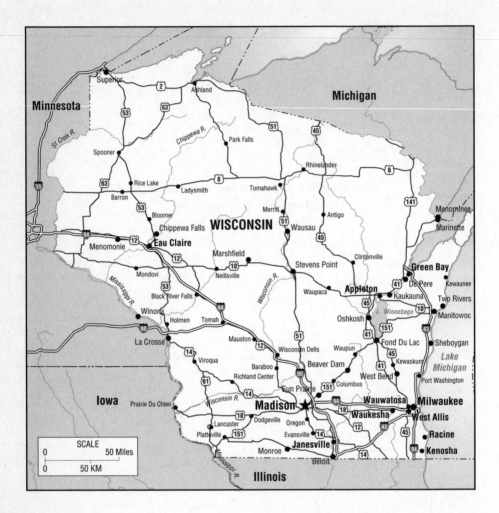

Contents

Acknowledgments

There is no way to thank everyone who has contributed in some way to this guidebook. Putting a book like this together is amassing a mountain of tiny details and all of this comes from a thousand helpful souls who drop a name, share a secret, or point a finger in the right direction.

Thanks goes out to Kim Grant for her editorial guidance, understanding and pep talks. I owe much to Matt Forster and Lisa Sacks for their careful editing. I am forever a fan of the State Parks of Wisconsin and all the marvelous people who manage and care for them. Cheers to Kristin, Erica, and Marty for the occasional Google hotline. Who needs a Blackberry anyhow? Thanks to Peung for being the occasional copilot or at least phoning it in, and to Marty Statz for additional copilot duties and a true appreciation for those roads less traveled. Thanks to Traci, Rob, Michelle, L.A., Andrea, and of course Debbie for making Door County seem less like work and more like the fun and games we all (wrongly) imagine travel writing to be. Hats off to Jon Jarosh for being the walking encyclopedia of Door County and for capturing in photos my attempts to drop kick my camera for being uncooperative. Couch providers for this journey include Erica, Alexandra, and Veronica, as well as Riz, Risa, Sidra, and Nina—the latter actually gave up her room for the cause, and I am humbled by her seven-year-old's generosity. I'm grateful to Tom Huhti for commiseration and advice, Andy Larsen and Sarah Soczka for their help with places to stay and many good recommendations, and Burt DeHaven for his Minocqua knowledge. Blessed are the cheesemakers (or the makers of dairy products in general) whose curds kept back hunger when the clock didn't want me to take time for lunch, and a nod to DeLorme for making a pretty darn good road atlas. I have my parents to thank for my appreciation of local attractions; those family vacations in faraway destinations and big cities such as Wausau and Green Bay will always make me smile.

And lastly I want to express my unending gratitude and admiration for my late grandfather, Louie Girga. His door was always open when I needed a place to stay, and we were never short on bacon. The questionable conditions of my cars over the years were also a great source of amusement for the both of us. As far back as my very earliest memories, all backroads and byways have lead to the farm in Moquah. As he was fond of saying of others he admired, so I will say of him: "He was a real prince of a guy." He will be sorely missed.

Introduction

The beauty of Wisconsin has been a long time coming. The landscape is a geological symphony consisting in part of rock outcrops and lava flows over a billion years old, layers of sediments laid down when a warm sea covered the land millions of years ago, and thousands of years of grinding glaciers, the last advance of which only melted away about 10,000 years ago. The many lakes and rivers, the sculpted hills and gorges and the rocky deposits such as the moraines are the beneficiaries of the Ice Age; the lands untouched by ice this last time around, known as the Driftless Area, show no lakes, but rolling hills and towering bluffs. All across this spreads a mix of farmland, prairie, wetlands, forest, and savanna giving a home to a cornucopia of flora and fauna much of which remains today or has been restored.

The area was inhabited even before the last glacier started its retreat and shows evidence of human occupation before 8000 B.C. in such places as the rock shelter at Natural Bridge State Park. Other cultures followed including mound builders—whose effigy mounds are spread throughout the state—and a variety of other Woodland Indians. Today six native nations remain in Wisconsin including the Ojibwe, Ho-Chunk (Winnebago), and Potawatomi.

The French were the first Europeans to arrive, and they explored the lakes and riverways and set up a fur trade with Native Americans. Great waterways such as the Fox, Wisconsin, and Mississippi functioned as the main thoroughfares connecting the Great Lakes to the Gulf of Mexico. Both the Wisconsin and Mississippi function as backbones of two of this guidebook's chapters.

Wisconsin didn't become a state until 1848, but saw a rush of miners just before that, and lumberjacks not long after. In the nineteenth century a wide variety of European pioneers brought with them their own customs and culture and created communities that reminded them of the home they left behind. Thus we have the Swiss communities in Green County, the Cornish heritage of Mineral Point, and in many places the German tradition of beer.

Within these pages are twelve routes through some of the loveliest portions of the state, and each one of them offers a different look. Anyone who has never seen the Great Lakes will immediately recognize that Lakes Superior and Michigan are not rowboat fishing holes but rather great northern seas; many a ship has suffered the wrath of lake storms, and their tragic wrecks are chronicled in museums or by lakeside memorials. The Great Lake shorelines are pure and beautiful, and the colors and character of the waters can shift suddenly with each lake's moody temperament.

Mineral Point may be the quintessential nineteenth-century town, but there are many other towns and villages around the state that have preserved or restored portions of the architecture and ambience of their yesteryear heydays. Strolls down Main Streets put the traveler in touch with the simple life of the small town.

The work of the glaciers is something to behold. The entire Kettle Moraine Scenic Drive in chapter six is a tribute to the massive moving of earth and stone, but there are plenty of outwash plains and scattered moraines in other areas, and the various segments of the thousand-mile Ice Age National Scenic Trail gives hikers a tour of the edge of the last stopping point of the glaciers. The bluffs of Devil's Lake and the Baraboo Hills are reminders of the power of stone; even the Wisconsin River and the glaciers had to work around them.

Wisconsin is fortunate to have fertile lands that hold forth a varied harvest like few others. You can still find the silos and red barns of family farms set amid idyllic green pastures. Cherries grow in Door County; apples abound in the Bayfield Peninsula (and so many other places); and growers produce blueberries, raspberries, strawberries, and more throughout the summer. Some regions even give root to grapevines, and so a wine industry has sprung up here in the land more commonly associated with beer (there are more than seventy breweries) and milk. The latter, of course, is the source of the Dairy State's tradition of cheesemaking. Local products abound, from honey and maple syrup to homemade jams and pies, and you can't visit Wisconsin without at least trying a cheese curd.

Roadside attractions such as the World's Largest Musky, Dr. Evermor's Forevertron, or the Dickeyville Grotto are quirky cultural counterpoints to picturesque waterfalls, scenic overlooks, fields of wildflowers, and verdant forest reserves. Rustic taverns with furry hunting trophies mounted on the walls might be just down the road from eclectic art galleries or a gourmet coffee shop. Friday night fish fries are rivaled by prime rib Saturdays, but you never know when you'll come across a certified authentic Italian pizza or a traditional Cornish pasty. Meals such as a fiery Door County fish boil are as much of an event as a meal.

Finally, Wisconsin is a friendly state. One of the old tourism slogans was "You're Among Friends," and this gets to the spirit of the land that La Crosse's former brewer G. Heileman once advertised as "God's country." People will help you find your way when you're turned around and will generally give you a hand when you need one.

Throughout my childhood, my family never strayed outside Wisconsin's borders for vacation. I always enjoyed where we went, but I'm not sure I ever really appreciated how magnificent my own backyard was. I do now. I remember taking some serious backroads—the kind of sand and gravel and no road signs—with my Grandpa Louie in his truck. We'd head up into the Barrens of Moquah to go blueberry picking in the summer and just take a turn around the now reforested hills. Despite all my world travels, I think it's telling that those memories of Wisconsin always bring me back to these backroads and byways to seek some more.

The Four Seasons

What's the best season to travel? That depends on your tastes. Winter can get harsh. Some years we get buried by snow, while other years the lakes don't even freeze over (rare). But it is also one of the loveliest times of the year. The patterns of frost on the window panes, fine layers of snow on tree branches, and a cozy bed and breakfast with a fireplace make winter travel worth considering—as do snowmobiling, skiing, snowshoeing, ice skating, and ice fishing. In Wisconsin we don't hunker down and hide from Old Man Winter; we just bundle up and continue with alternative activities. That said, make sure the businesses along your byway haven't taken on an alternative activity such as taking these months off. Some do. Summer is an obvious choice, but winter is the only time you can drive on an ice highway (to Madeline Island), watch eagles congregate over open water on the Wisconsin River, or see the ice caves along Lake Superior.

Spring of course brings wildflowers and blossoms. Temperatures can vary from very mild 60s and 70s down to hey-didn't-they-say-winter-was-over? Pasque flowers start to poke up through the snow in April; fishing season traditionally begins the first Saturday in May. Far up north this season may be stubborn about getting started sometimes waiting well into May. Elsewhere April is nice jacket weather and air simply tingles in your lungs as winter gets left behind. Migrating birds make their way back north at this time.

Summer brings the full green and temperatures range from the sixties and seventies in June to the eighties or more in July or August. These are not promises. Pack a light jacket for the evenings and anytime you are traveling near one of the Great Lakes. "Cooler by the lake" isn't a cliché for nothing. Mosquitoes can be a nuisance, and humidity might surprise you. Thunderstorms can make for awesome displays of Nature's power, but be aware of the dangers of lightning, and take tornado warnings seriously.

Fall has, of course, the advantage of colors starting in late September up north and gradually working their way south through October. If you don't want to miss the optimal time to see them, watch for the fall color report at TravelWisconsin.com or sign up to receive e-mailed updates (www.travelwisconsin.com/fallcolor_report.aspx). The air gets chilly in the fifties and sixties (though we still get some gorgeous days in the seventies), and the mosquitoes go away. Migration makes this a great time for birders.

State Parks

Wisconsin can be proud of its wonderful state park system. Whether you aim to just stop for a scenic view, take a hike, have a picnic, go fishing, or even camp for the night, there is a state park that will fit the bill. State Park stickers are a great idea if you plan on doing more than one or two state park visits throughout the year. The sticker is available at any state park with a park attendant and is good for the given calendar year. You can also order them online at Friends of Wisconsin State Parks at www.fwsp.org. Annual fees are $25 for Wisconsin residents and $35 for nonresidents. Daily fees at the parks are $7, and one-hour passes are $5. Some parks have self-pay stations in cases where there is no park attendant or when the park office is closed. Most county parks are free; notable exceptions are those in Marinette County in chapter eleven.

Rustic Roads

The state of Wisconsin celebrates its own backroads and byways with a list—at 107 and growing—of country drives designated as State Rustic Roads. Each is numbered and marked with a brown and yellow sign with an outline of the state on it. I have tried to include at least one of these roads within each chapter. In some cases they veer off the main route, but in any case make a worthy diversion through some classic Wisconsin scenery. The Department of Transportation maintains a free guide booklet, and a map of these special roads is online at www.dot.state.wi.us/travel/scenic/ rusticroads.htm.

Road Hazards and Warnings

We often joke that there are two seasons in Wisconsin: winter and road construction. The humor has a point: the first often causes the latter. Harsh winters and their frost heaves combined with the three other seasons makes for some wear and tear on the roads. Before heading out on your trip, it is wise to check for detours and impasses. The Department of Transportation maintains a printer friendly map online at www.dot.state.wi.us/travel/ road/workzones.htm or you can call 1-800-ROADWIS (1-800-762-3947) for the latest construction updates or winter road conditions.

Winter means snow and ice, so be aware of slippery roads. But be especially aware of the phenomenon known as black ice. When temperatures are hovering around freezing or even just above, you may see patches of road that are a bit darker and duller than the rest of the surface. When a wet road surface refreezes, you can't always detect the ice. If you should hit a patch of ice and start to skid, remember to always turn in the direction of a skid and never slam on the brakes. Maintaining a safe following distance is a good idea at any time, but even more critical in winter.

Potholes can be a bother, especially on the roads less traveled, and though most roads are paved, this book will alert you to a few rustic crushed-gravel lanes.

I don't mean to be alarmist, but do be careful when driving through the Wisconsin countryside: It's a zoo out there. Nearly 45,000 deer are struck each year by vehicles, and these collisions can be extremely damaging to both car and passengers, and in some cases even deadly. Deer can move at any time of day, but be especially careful at dusk and in the middle of the night. Road kill is a macabre reality, and inevitably you will see (and in the case of skunks, smell) the unfortunate raccoons, possums, squirrels, and deer that didn't look both ways.

Natural Annoyances

At the top of the list is the state bird, the mosquito. Never mind the jungles of the Amazon, the northern Midwest is mosquito country. Pack repellent or wear loose, long-sleeved, light-colored clothing. (A bit of Vick's VapoRub on a bite often stops the itch!) The mosquitoes generally appear in June and start to peter out in early September on into October. A rainy period can really stir things up. Mostly they are annoying; however, there have been some cases of the West Nile virus over the years.

If you are hiking, you should be aware of some additional annoyances. Ticks can get in your clothes and attach to your skin if you are walking through grass and brush. Deer ticks, the size of the E on a dime, are the ones that can carry Lyme disease. The best protection is covering yourself and being sure to check for ticks after your hike. Also along the trail you may find poison ivy, poison oak, or poison sumac. The simple advice is to stay on the trail.

Campers, be aware of raccoons with sticky fingers and, in the far north, the black bear that knows you have a candy bar in the tent or saw you leave the cooler outside.

CHAPTER

1

Cheese Country

Estimated length: 65 miles
Estimated time: 1.5 hours

Getting There: From Madison, take US 18/151 west to WI 69 and start south.

Highlights: The town of New Glarus, with its strong Swiss heritage, may make you think you've driven to Europe. The abundance of cheese factories, such as **Edelweiss Creamery** and **Alp and Dell**, and two breweries—**New Glarus** and **Minhas Craft Brewery**—will reassure you what state you're in. This is also a good route for fall colors.

Much of this byway passes through Green County. Untouched by the last advance of glaciers during the Ice Age, the landscape shows bluffs and valleys and meandering rivers across a canvas of green farmland, prairies, and forests. This loop can be taken easily in a day's drive, but it makes a great two-day sojourn.

The first milking cows were brought to Wisconsin in 1838 at a time when wheat production was the focus of agriculture. Many Swiss immigrants settled in and around New Glarus and Monroe in the 1840s, and when the profits and viability of wheat production started to decline, their knowledge of cheesemaking proved to be a boon for the area. It used to be

EATING YOUR CURDS AND WHEY

Cheese curds are a classic Wisconsin delicacy. The bite-sized chunks, most commonly of cheddar, are only good when fresh and best at room temperature, when they will squeak in your teeth as you eat them. They are made when milk curdles and separates from the cast-off liquid known as whey. Normally these curds are then pressed into a form and aged to make the more familiar cheese wheels and blocks. Cheese factories, or the stores close to them, are the best place to buy. Eat yesterday's curds only when you're desperate. A few seconds in a microwave might bring back the squeak. Deep-fried curds are popular at many restaurants and bars.

that you could find a cheese factory at every crossroads in Green County, and in 1910 the number of producers topped two hundred. Nowadays there are only around twenty, but the demand for cheese is still great.

The first stop along the route is the village of Paoli. Set on the Sugar River, Paoli centers on an old mill and mill pond in the midst of rolling farmland. The village's restored buildings and an unlikely collection of art galleries and eateries have made this a pleasant stop for travelers and weekenders.

At the four-way stop at Paoli you could go right on CR PB to bypass Paoli and Belleville. Otherwise go left to get to Paoli Road, where you will find several galleries. Artisan Gallery, in a 1920s glazed-stone creamery, displays arts and crafts from more than 150 local and national artists. Inside there is also a café. **Paoli Local Foods** is an organic grocery that emphasizes food produced locally or even on the owner's own farm. Organic sandwiches, fresh cheese curds, and some very interesting options you won't find just anywhere—buffalo and ostrich burgers, chicken brats—make this a worthy stop. You can carry out and eat in the small park across the street. The five-meat, five-cheese lasagna is very popular. They even churn their own butter.

Continue through town over the Sugar River and take a right on Diane Avenue to WI 69. Go left and follow the river about 5 miles to Belleville. On your way you'll pass the road to **Cameo Rose Bed and Breakfast**, just 0.7 mile east from WI 69 on Henry Road. The lovely five-guest-room property is set on 120 acres crossed by a segment of the Ice Age National Scenic Trail. The Badger State Trail is also close by.

When you reach Belleville, you'll see the dam-made Lake Belle just inside town with a park, picnic area, and restrooms. Crab apple blossoms are gorgeous here in the spring, and Canada geese stop by during migration periods.

Take a right on WI 69 at the intersection in town and you'll pass Bleoni's on your left, a very down-home breakfast place.

Just about 7 miles outside of Belleville, you'll pass a roadside bluff showing exposed rock—evidence that the last advance of the Ice Age's glaciers never reached here—as you cross the Green County line. A sign reading "Wilkommen" hints at what is to come. The next town, New Glarus, is known as America's Little Switzerland. A group of 108 pioneers from—as you might guess from the name—Glarus, a canton of Switzerland, settled here in 1845. As you enter the town there is little doubt of its ethnic heritage. Swiss flags, characteristic chalet-style architecture, and business names with a Swiss twist all reflect the town's commitment to preserving that heritage.

The first and only traffic lights are at Sixth Avenue/WI 39. Go right and you are in the heart of Switzerland. Antique and gift shops are abundant, and the restaurants lean toward Swiss cuisine. **Puempel's Olde Tavern** has a fascinating collection of money thrown against the ceiling and some 1913 Austrian murals. Lunch soup-and-sandwich specials are good here, and local beer is on tap. Certainly the cheese at **Maple Leaf Cheese and Chocolate Haus** is worth the stop, but they are just as famous for their fudge. Stock up for the drive.

The Swiss are famous for fondue so of course New Glarus has it on the menu. The two best places to dip for cheese are The **New Glarus Hotel Restaurant**, which also serves specialties like weiner schnitzel and deep-fried cheese curds, and **Glarner Stube**, another Swiss-themed eatery that also has a pretty good Friday fish fry.

If you are looking for souvenirs you can eat, the maple syrup at **Bramble Patch** has been regarded as world's best. The shop's various jams, jellies, gourmet mustards, and other foods are no less delicious.

The local brewery has added fame to the New Glarus name, but beer is not the only locally made beverage. **New Glarus Primrose Winery**

HOW NOW, BROWN COW?

The Brown Swiss cow is a star of the dairy industry. Its milk is prized as the best for making cheese with a high fat-to-protein ratio. Brown Swiss are long-lived and produce large amounts of milk. Maple Leaf Cheese in New Glarus offers cheese produced from this high quality milk. As you head south on WI 69 toward Monticello, you'll see Voegeli Farm on the left. Founded in 1854, the family farm first brought Brown Swiss to their herd in 1895.

The copper brew tanks at New Glarus come all the way from Germany.

produces over a dozen handcrafted fruit wines using Wisconsin-grown fruits and berries.

For the history buffs, just up the hill on Seventh Avenue is the **Swiss Historical Village**, a collection of fourteen buildings that recreate life in the nineteenth century. An exhibit also traces Native American history before the arrival of these European pioneers. Tours operate throughout the day, and the gift shop has a nice assortment of Swiss gifts, including a locally produced cookbook and imported Schabziger (Sap Sago), a hard cheese and herb concoction unique to the canton of Glarus.

The **Chalet of the Golden Fleece** on 618 Second Street has a collection of artifacts brought to the area by immigrants, but can only be toured by appointment and with a group of at least five. Call New Glarus Tourist Information.

South out of town, past CR H and across from a trail kiosk for the Sugar River Trail, look for a farm on the hill up to the left. This is actually the **New Glarus Brewery**, home of a very popular handcrafted beer called Spotted Cow and a whole variety of other great microbrews. What's better than a brewery? Two breweries. The farm you see here is a tremendous expansion on the brewery's smaller facility on the north end of town. The old site will still brew smaller specialty batches; the new facility houses a gift shop and an indoor/outdoor beer garden/sampling room. Self-guided tours and samples are available (and highly recommended). Follow the gravel road that will take you on a gradual curling route up to the backside of the brewery.

State Rustic Road 81 is just 3.5 miles west of town. If you are interested in New Glarus Brewery, you might take this short detour first as it brings you back to the south side of town. Head 3.5 miles west on WI 39 and go left on Marty Road, which weaves through farmland and rolling hills; no shoulders, not even a dotted line, but a smooth ride. At the southern end go left on CR H back to New Glarus or take a right off of CR H when you get to CR N and another quick left on CR NN to pass through **New Glarus Woods State Park**. Be aware that to stop at the park does require a park pass (available at the kiosk or office), which can be purchased for the day or the year. The 411-acre park is a remainder of a much larger forest, much of which fell to the axes of pioneers who came to farm the land. CR NN, which ends at WI 69, has history. Native Americans used this path because it ran along the ridge and gave them better views for hunting. It became known as the Old Lead Road as the pioneers followed it years later to haul lead ore in ox carts. At WI 69 you can go left to get to New Glarus Brewery (be careful not to use the shipping entrance, but rather the entry lane at the bottom of the hill) or go right to continue along the byway.

Travelers choosing to stay the night in New Glarus might consider **Chalet Landhaus Inn**, which was built in the rustic Swiss chalet style and offers an indoor pool and some suites with Jacuzzis. A homier option is the **New Glarus Farm House** west of town on the Rustic Road.

Continue south on WI 69 until Monticello. European settlers dammed the Little Sugar River here to make a mill pond. By the mid-1850s, Monticello was grinding grist from as far away as New Glarus and continued to do so until the 1930s. The mill pond was also a source of refrigeration. In winter workers would cut blocks of ice and store them under

Swiss immigrants came to Green County to farm.

LIMBURGER

Let's just call it an acquired taste. This infamously odiferous cheese originated in Belgium, but a Swiss immigrant first produced it in Green County in 1867. A cheese factory started production a year later, and Limburger became quite popular alongside a mug of cold beer. Someone in Monroe once made a big stink over whether it was acceptable or *not* to deliver Limburger via the postal service. It was determined that the cheese had not gone bad, and postal workers were forced to hold their tongues . . . and noses. By the way, the fresher the cheese, the less powerful the odor—so say Limburger fans.

sawdust in icehouses. Then in summer the ice would be sold to local households. When the state of Wisconsin decided to run Highway 69 past Monticello, the "lake" was lost. This still left some low-lying soggy areas, which in 1966 were turned into the present Lake Montesian. It's a nice pull-off for a picnic, and a small stone there is dedicated to the Green County men who died in the Vietnam War.

As you turn east into Monticello on CR F, you pass the lake. In the spring this short road into town is lined with blossoming crab apple trees. On Main Street go left to find the mom-and-pop **M & M Café**. The homemade pies are exceptional. The small Monticello Historical Museum is just down the street from here, and if you go to the end of the street and turn right, you'll find Swiss Heritage Cheese where you can get several varieties including baby Swiss, queso fresco, and Polish honey cheese.

Take CR C out of Monticello heading west 3 miles to the corner of CH N and CH C to find **Edelweiss Creamery**. This is one of the few places to get a personalized tour of a cheese factory. Though there is no cheese store per se, you *can* buy cheese here. Bruce Workman is the only cheesemaker in the country who produces the giant-wheel Swiss. His Gouda and Havarti are other excellent options; he is a certified expert in seven different cheeses, in fact. Most of his cheese is produced with milk from grass-fed cows—no silage—and the difference is remarkable. It's a good idea to call for a tour and you must wear closed-toe shoes.

From Edelweiss, take CR N south toward Monroe to find another important cheese producer. Dating back to 1885, **Chalet Cheese Co-op** is the oldest operating cheese cooperative in Wisconsin and the only factory in the United States that makes Limburger cheese. You can stop by to purchase cheese and sample Limburger; go the southern end of the factory and around the corner to find the cheese store door. The original factory is a round building down the hill near the side of the road.

A Wisconsin welcome awaits at Monroe's depot turned Historic Cheesemaking Center.

Not to be completely outdone by New Glarus's Swiss pride, Monroe is known as the Swiss Cheese Capital of the USA. Where CR N meets WI 81, go left and your first stop on the right is **Alp and Dell**, the cheese store for Roth Käse cheese factory. Try to get there in the morning if you want to have a look through the two viewing windows to see cheese being made and packaged. All the cheeses you can imagine are here and many can be sampled.

Two traffic lights from Alp and Dell, go left on Business 11/69 and pass under the railroad viaduct to 16th Avenue. Turn right and you will come to the nicest town square in this corner of the state. Shops center on the restored 1891 Green County Courthouse and its four-faced clock tower. A couple of murals adorn the walls of the courtroom upstairs, which you can see when court is not in session.

The pride of Wisconsin.

TURNER HALLS

Turner Halls are common in Wisconsin thanks to the state's rich German heritage. In 1853 a group of German-Americans founded the Turners in Milwaukee. The name comes from the German word for gymnast as the group, famous for its interest in social reform, was also keen on physical education, gymnastics in particular. Turner Hall in Monroe is unique in that it is considered the only surviving Turner Hall of Swiss origin.

One of the culinary and cultural highlights on the square is **Baumgartner's Cheese Store and Tavern**. A Swiss cheese sandwich should not be missed, but if you are daring go for the Limburger and onion or braunschweiger (liverwurst) sandwich. A cold beer on the side is recommended.

One block north of the town square on Ninth Street is a Civil War–era church that now houses the Green County Historical Museum. Stop by to see some local history and a one-room country schoolhouse next door.

Just over a block south off the square, Turner Hall has a fine rathskeller that serves a variety of Swiss-influenced dishes for lunch and dinner, as well as a classic Wisconsin Friday-night fish fry. The current 1938 building replaced the original structure, which was built in 1868 but was lost to a fire in the mid-1930s.

Take a stroll around the Romanesque Green County Courthouse in Monroe.

Baumgartner's is a good place to get a cheese sandwich for the road.

CHEESE DAYS

The Green County Cheese Days celebration occurs in Monroe the third weekend in September of the even years. The tradition dates back to 1914 when locals impressed by a sauerkraut festival in Illinois, decided they could also celebrate their local product. Nine days later they brewed up 200 pounds of coffee and served 3,000 cheese sandwiches made up in the garage at the Blumer Brewery (now Minhas Craft Brewery). Even with such short notice they hosted an estimated crowd of nearly 4,000 attendees. Two years later that was 25,000, and nowadays numbers pass 100,000! Enjoy a parade, tractor pull, arts and crafts fair, polka music, yodeling, and, of course, plenty of cheese and beer. Go to Cheesedays.com for more information.

Beer has a long tradition in Monroe. **Minhas Craft Brewery** is the current name of what is the second longest continuously operating brewery in the country. Formerly Joseph Huber, and in 1845 founded as Blumer Brewery, the beer maker continues to make popular brews and a sensational line of sodas. Minhas still produces Huber as well as Berghoff under contract, but the new owners' flagship beer is Lazy Mutt Farmhouse Ale. The museum and gift store are free; $10 tours (which include samples and eight-bottle gift packs) are available at limited times on Fridays and Saturdays and require reservations.

The **Historic Cheesemaking Center** makes its home in an old depot, which you can find on the right heading south out of Monroe on WI 69. Inside is a fine collection of artifacts from the industry as well as a collection of free Wisconsin tourism pamphlets and maps.

Keep driving south to find a bit of a throwback for people who hate to leave their cars. Since 1954, the Goetz family has operated the Sky-Vu Drive-In, just one mile south of Monroe on WI 69. The sound for the films is transmitted via FM signal. The snack bar has outstanding foot-long hot dogs and uses real cheese on top of the nachos and pizzas. The double-feature films are generally family-friendly blockbusters. If you plan to spend the night in Monroe, stick with the cheese theme and check out an 1890's cheesemaker's home, **Victorian Garden Bed and Breakfast**.

As you head northwest out of Monroe on WI 81, you can take a small detour through State Rustic Road 94. Go north on CR J 5.7 miles until you come to Skinner Hollow Road on the left. This will lead you 4.5 miles back through prairie, wetlands, and rock outcroppings to WI 81, crossing Skinner Creek and passing an old cheese factory turned residence.

Set the worlds in motion at the Toy Train Barn.

Continue northwest on WI 81 for about 5 miles and look for a bright orange barn on the left. This is the **Toy Train Barn** and will bring out the kid in anyone. Buck Guthrie is an actual train engineer, but the barn that he created with his wife, Jan, is full of American Flyers and other model trains arranged in various miniature landscapes. The trains are activated by old microwave oven power panels, and a lot of the tiny train world's details feature moving displays such as a house fire being put out and a diminutive Superman emerging from a phone booth. Admission is $5 adults, $2.50 children 4–10 and opening hours are 10–5 daily even in winter.

In Argyle you will come to a right turn that puts you on WI 78, heading north. At the corner of this intersection find the 1878 Partridge Hall. Originally a carpenter shop and show hall, it also had a twenty year stint as the Star Theatre, showing silent films. Since its restoration and placement on the National Registry of Historic Places, the hall offers guest rooms on the second floor. Locals come here for the first-floor restaurant's Friday-night fish fry, Saturday prime rib and walleye specials, and Sunday brunch.

If you are around for breakfast any other day, head over to Irma's Kitchen. Go right at the four corners on Milwaukee Street. To your left at the same intersection, the eastern branch of the Pecatonica River flows over a dam. Argyle has had hydroelectric power since 1906, supplying about 210 megawatts per year. Argyle is also the childhood home of "Fighting" Bob La Follette, a former governor, US Senator, and presiden-tial candidate who fought for progressive politics up until his death in 1925. Plans are in the works to open his former home on Main Street to the public.

Continue north out of Argyle on WI 78 toward Blanchardville. This area was settled by Mormons as Zarahemla in the 1840s when they fled Illinois after the death of Joseph Smith. The Mormons came to farm and mine lead. Alvin Blanchard came in 1856 and platted the land, and in 1857 the village took his name. For a place to stay the night, **Inn Heaven**—a bun-galow in the country—is a fine option just south of WI 39 between Blanchardville and New Glarus.

A nice detour west from Blanchardville is **Yellowstone Lake State Park**, an excellent place for hiking, swimming, and bird-watching. CR F—which leads 8 miles to Lake Road where it is another mile to the park—is a nice drive if you have the time. The park concessions stand sells ice cream in season.

One last recommended stop on this route is **Hauge Log Church**, con-structed by Norwegian immigrants in 1852. Just north of Daleyville on WI 78 you will come to CR Z. Go left being careful to remain on CR Z, and the church is a half-mile down on your left set alongside an old cemetery. The church is open daily during daylight hours. This is a nice quiet stop before getting back on WI 78 to return to US 18/151 for the drive east back to Madison.

IN THE AREA

Accommodations

Cameo Rose Bed and Breakfast, 1090 Severson Road, Belleville. Call 608-424-6340. Web site: www.cameorose.com.

Chalet Landhaus Inn, 801 WI 69, New Glarus. Call 608-527-5234. Web site: www.chaletlandhaus.com.

Inn Heaven, N9136 York Center Road, Blanchardville. Call 608-426-0289.

New Glarus Farmhouse, N8497 Marty Road, New Glarus. Call 608-527-2573. Web site: www.newglarusfarmhouse.com.

Victorian Garden, 1720 16th Street, Monroe. Call 608-328-1720.

Attractions and Recreation

Alp and Dell Cheese Store, 657 Second Street, Monroe. Call 608-328-3355. Open Mon. through Fri. 9–6, Sat. 9–5, and Sun. 10–5.

Artisan Gallery, 6858 Paoli Road, Paoli. Call 608-845-6600. Tues. through Sun. 10–5; weekends only in Jan. and Feb. Web site: www.artisangal.com.

Bramble Patch, 526 First Street, New Glarus. Call 608-527-4878. Web site: www.thebramblepatch.biz.

Chalet Cheese Co-op, N4858 County Road N, Monroe. Call 608-325-4343. Open Mon. through Fri. 7–3:30 and Sat. 8–10.

Edelweiss Creamery, W6117 County Road C, Monticello. Call 608-938-4094. Best to visit Mon. through Fri. before 9 for tours, before noon to buy cheese. Web site: www.edelweisscreamery.com.

Goetz Sky-Vu Drive-In, 1936 State Route 69, Monroe. Call 608-325-4545. Web site: www.goetzskyvu.com.

Green County Historical Museum, 1617 Eighth Street, Monroe. Open Fri. 12–6, Sat. 9–5, and Sun. 9–1. Fee.

Historic Cheesemaking Center, 2108 Seventh Avenue, Monroe. Call 608-325-4636. Daily 9–4. Closed from Dec. through Feb.

Minhas Craft Brewery, 1208 14th Avenue, Monroe. Call 608-325-3191. There's a fee for tour, but not the museum. Tours on Fri. and Sat. Call for an appointment. Web site: www.minhasbrewery.com.

New Glarus Primrose Winery, 226 Second Street, New Glarus. Call 608-527-5053.

New Glarus Woods State Park, W5446 County Road NN, New Glarus. Call 608-527-2335.

Swiss Heritage Cheese, Inc., 114 East Coates Avenue, Monticello. Call 608-938-4455. Open Mon. through Thurs. 8–3, Fri. 8–1, and Sat. 9–1.

Swiss Historical Village, 612 Seventh Avenue, New Glarus. Call 608-527-2317. There's a fee. Open daily 10–4, from May 1 through Oct. 31. Web site: www.swisshistoricalvillage.org.

Toy Train Barn, West 9141 Highway 81, Argyle. Call 608-966-1464. There's a fee. Web site: www.whrc-wi.org/trainbarn.

Dining

Baumgartner's Cheese Store and Tavern, 1023 16th Avenue, Monroe. Call 608-325-6157. Open daily 8–close.

Glarner Stube, 518 First Street, New Glarus. Call 608-527-2216.

Irma's Kitchen, 336 East Milwaukee Street, Argyle. Call 608-543-3703. Open Mon.–Sat. 5–3.

M&M Café, 126 North Main Street, Monticello. Call 608-938-4890. Open Mon.–Fri. 6–2 and Sat. 7–2.

New Glarus Hotel Restaurant, 100 Sixth Avenue, New Glarus. Call 608-527-5244. Open Mon. through Thurs. 11–2 and 5–8:30; Fri. and Sat. 11–9:30; Sunday 10–8. Closed Tues. from Nov. to Apr. Web site: www.newglarushotel.com.

Paoli Local Foods, 6895 Paoli Road, Paoli. Call 608-845-3663.

Partridge Hall, 200 South Main Street, Argyle. Call 608-543-3960. Web site: www.partridgehall.com.

Turner Hall Ratskeller, 1217 17th Avenue, Monroe. Call 608-325-3461. Open Tues. through Sat. for lunch and dinner, Sun. 9–2 for breakfast. Hours change seasonally, so it's best to call ahead. Web site: www .turnerhallofmonroe.org.

Other

Green County Tourism, N3150 B, Highway 81, Monroe. Call 1-888-222-9111. Web site: www.greencounty.org.

New Glarus Tourist Information. Call 608-527-2095. Web site: www.swisstown.com.

Religion and patriotism meet at the Dickeyville Grotto.

CHAPTER 2

Mining Towns

Estimated length: 75 miles
Estimated time: 2 hours minimum

Getting There: From Madison, take US 18/151 west to Mineral Point.

Highlights: The historic miner cottages of **Pendarvis**; the **National Brewery Museum**; the **Dickeyville Grotto**; picturesque, historical and artsy **Mineral Point**; the **mining museums** in Platteville and Potosi.

Wisconsin was nicknamed the Badger State not because of an excessive population of the fierce little creatures, but because of the explosion of the mining industry in the nineteenth century. By 1850 there were over 10,000 hand-dug lead mines in the region. These produced almost the entire supply of lead shot for the Union forces during the Civil War.

Native Americans had been mining lead before the arrival of the Europeans. When the French explorer Nicholas Perrot arrived in 1690, local Ho-Chunk tribe members (formerly known as Winnebago) showed him a cave at the top of one of the bluffs. Various treaties resulted in the tribes losing lands, and after another treaty in 1827, the rush was on as waves of Cornish and Welsh immigrants and East Coast miners came to dig for their fortune.

DRIFTLESS AREA

When the glaciers retreated from Wisconsin during the last period of the Ice Age, they left behind the inevitable debris—rocks, boulders, and sand—that comes with such earthmoving glaciers. This material, often left in formations known as moraines, is referred to as drift. The southwestern corner of Wisconsin was spared in the most recent glaciation and is thus known as the "Driftless Area." The land is characterized by river valleys and rolling hills. There are no natural lakes.

A cholera epidemic in 1848, and the call of a slightly more attractive ore in California, took the wind out of the industry's sails, and lead mining gradually tapered off. But the underground world made a comeback in the late 1850s when zinc became recognized as a profitable metal. The peak of the zinc mining industry was 1917 when 59,000 tons were hauled up from the earth. Gradually, this industry also declined, and the last mine was abandoned in Shullsburg in 1979.

This trip could start or end (or both) in Mineral Point. There are some good stretches of colors in the fall, especially in the Potosi area, but generally speaking this is not a fall colors route.

Entering Mineral Point is like stepping back in time. Few towns have preserved this much history and to this extent. Mineral Point is indeed a state treasure—being at one time the heart of the Wisconsin Territory—but also a national one: the National Historic Trust named this one of the best places to visit.

The name is a hint as to what brought a wave of Cornish immigrant miners here. Evidence of that ethnic heritage remains apparent in some of the food and many of the old buildings. From where it breaks from US 151, take WI 23 left. As you approach Mineral Point watch for the Comfort Inn on the right. Across the highway on your left you will find **Shake Rag Street**. The name comes from the practice of the Cornish miners' wives who waved dishcloths to call their husbands home. Follow Shake Rag and you'll see the town's 1850s brick brewery on your right, which is now **Brewery Pottery Studio**. Just a bit farther down the road is **Pendarvis**, a state historical site. Stop in at the visitor center at the corner of Shake Rag and Spruce Streets.

One of Mineral Point's finest buildings was saved from the wrecking ball for just $800. **Orchard Lawn**, the impressive Italianate home of the Gundry family, was constructed just after the Civil War. At that time it also had a carriage house and barn. When the last of the family in town passed away in 1936, the heirs didn't know what to do with it, so they hired someone to tear it down. Several locals with a vision for the future pooled their

PENDARVIS

Using local limestone, the Cornish immigrants built small cottages reminiscent of the ones they left in England. The lead boom was followed by the zinc boom, and the little community thrived throughout the nineteenth century. When the industry began to wane, however, history started to fade as well. Houses were abandoned, and the unused stones found their way into newer structures. All would have been erased if not for Robert Neal and Edgar Hellum who in 1935 began an effort to save several cottages from oblivion. The first cottage they restored they named Pendarvis after a Cornwall estate. Today even the prairie has been restored, and native flowers and grasses once again adorn the land. Guides dress in period clothing at this historical site.

cash to buy out the demolition contract and created a historical society to preserve it. The home and grounds are still being restored, and the Mineral Point Historical Society makes its home here. During summer months and by appointment, visitors can tour the property.

Mineral Point has become something of an art mecca over the years. At last count there are over **twenty art galleries and studios** in town. The bulk of them are on Commerce and High streets. The town hosts **gallery nights** in April, June, August, and December. Check with the Chamber of Commerce for a calendar of events.

The state's first commercial brewery was in Mineral Point. Brewery Creek Brewpub brings back the tradition.

County Road O is one of the prettier sections of this byway.

For something a bit unusual, visit the studio of **Bruce Howdle.** Howdle is not your typical ceramics potter. His ceramic murals have spanned up to fifty-two feet with the clay weighing in tons. He can show you his work and loves to chat about it. **Johnston Gallery** in town on High Street shows the work of over 150 artists in varying media. The owners also operate the Brewery Pottery Studio which you saw on the way into town. The rustic furniture at **Longbranch Gallery**, made from twigs and branches, is also worth noting. Over fifty artists are represented here as well.

Since 2004, **The Shake Rag Alley Center for the Arts** has been hosting art workshops. Shake Rag Alley is a shaded park with flowers and a stream surrounded by nine historic buildings, including the town's oldest, an 1828 log cabin. Many courses are short and work well for weekend vacations. In summer the outdoor Alley Stage presents original plays from Thursday through Sunday.

Cheese making is arguably an art as well. **Hook's Cheese Company** is perhaps most famous for blue cheese, of which they actually have several versions. But the cheddar (aged up to ten years) and the Colby are outstanding as well and often used by gourmet restaurants. The only time to stop in here is on Fridays. Otherwise you might check in at Five Point Liquor across the street, which carries several varieties of Hook's cheese.

When it's time to eat, you have numerous options. **Old Royal Inn** offers a nice lunch and dinner selection of grilled pizzas, pasta dishes, sandwiches, and full dinner plates. On Friday nights you will generally find live music. The menu at **Café Four** offers locally produced organic salads. A wood-fired Italian oven is the key ingredient to their Neapolitan-style pizzas, and the rest of the entrées are varied but lean toward the Italian.

Gundry and Gray is gift shop on High Street which also happens to serve great sandwiches and salads for lunch.

Brewery Creek Inn and Brewpub is just a stone's throw from the creek of the same name. The inn offers seven rooms of varying sizes, but all

PASTY AND FIGGYHOBBIN
These are not characters from *The Lord of the Rings*, but culinary peculiarities you can find in Mineral Point. A pasty is a self-contained meal, usually meat filling, potatoes, and onions wrapped in a crust pastry. Cornish miners packed them for work, and it is said the thick crust edge was meant as a disposable grasping point for dirty fingers. A figgyhobbin is a rich dessert of a pastry rolled with cinnamon, brown sugar, raisins and nuts, and then covered with caramel and whipped cream or even ice cream. Several places serve them, but a tourist favorite is the classic local diner the Red Rooster Café.

are elegantly appointed and come with double whirlpools. The brewpub serves its own handcrafted beer and upscale pub fare with a tendency toward organic and locally acquired products. Just across the parking lot lies the historic depot. Once part of the Milwaukee Road, this stone building has been restored and is now the **Railroad Depot Museum,** a nice little collection of exhibits tells about the days of rails and other Mineral Point history.

Another place to stay the night is **The Mineral Point Hotel**, a charming four-room hotel right downtown. The owners offer a continental breakfast, which typically consists of homemade organic biscotti and coffee or espresso, in the lobby. **The Coach House**—a former stagecoach stop on Shake Rag Street during the mid-1800s and now within the Shake Rag Alley Center for the Arts—has three upstairs rooms each with a private bath. **The Mousehole** ("mauzel") is a neighboring 1839 stone-and-brick building with two apartments, each with a fully furnished kitchen. **The Cothren House,** a five-minute walk from downtown, gives guests the option of staying in an 1850s stone cottage or an 1835 rustic log cabin, quite possibly the oldest accommodations in Wisconsin.

FIRST CAPITOL

Belmont was the first choice by Henry Dodge as the territorial capitol in 1836. At that time the Wisconsin Territory included Iowa, Minnesota, and parts of the Dakotas, and the population was balanced on either side of the Mississippi River. But the Belmont idea didn't go over so well, and an alternative was sought. After a temporary move to Burlington, John Doty convinced them that Madison was the ideal place. The village of Belmont never survived the jilting. When the railroad was subsequently laid 2 miles to the southeast, all the village's residents picked up and moved to the new Belmont.

Continuing on the byway, get back on US 151 heading southwest. At exit 26, turn right on CR G (toward CH B). Around you is rolling farmland with the occasional tree-covered bluffs. Follow CH G to **Belmont Mound State Park**. This 400-foot bluff is an outlier of the Niagara Escarpment. Facilities consist of shelters, a small playground and picnic area, and a porta-potty. The park lane goes left around the bluff and takes you to the top where you'll find a sixty-four-foot viewing platform. On a clear day you can see three states from here. The mound you see due west is near Platteville.

About 1 mile past the park, continuing on CH G, is a pullover for the memorial for the first capitol.

At the next intersection continue straight on CR B to Platteville through more farmland. As the road curves, you'll come to a right turn, no stop. You'll pass the M & M Group Home on the right. Pay attention here because on the other side of the bluff to your right you will see the **World's Largest M**. It was once the practice of mining schools to build a large M out of rock to designate their school. In 1936 Pat Medley and Alvin Knoerr, two mining engineering students at the University of Wisconsin in Platteville, returned from a mine in Colorado that had a 200-foot tall M. Led by these two students, a group of student moved an estimated 400 tons of limestone to construct this 214-foot-tall letter on this mound east of town. You can climb steps to the top and get a view similar to the one at Belmont Mound.

The University of Wisconsin-Platteville ceased its mining engineering program in the 1990s. As you roll into Platteville on CH B (Broadway Street), the road will take you straight to the **Mining Museum** on Main Street. Find out more about the lead days and the people who came to work underground. A guided tour will take you fifty feet down into an 1845 lead mine. Over two million pounds of lead were mined from here in one year. Extreme claustrophobes beware. Above ground, a 1931 mine locomotive

Visible from miles away, the Giant M of Platteville was constructed by college students in 1936 and is purported to be the world's largest M.

with ore cars offers short rides around the yard during nice weather. A large wooden structure out back houses the head-frame for an old zinc ore mine.

Upstairs from the Mining Museum is **Rountree Gallery**, named for a lead-mine owner and one of the founders of Platteville. The gallery was founded in 1979 as a senior project of a UW-Platteville student. The city and volunteers have since maintained it, and today you can see permanent and temporary exhibits from over seventy regional artists.

Art is not the only collection on hand. Rollo Jamison had a vision of making a museum. He also had an insatiable desire to collect things. The result, the **Rollo Jamison Museum**, shows visitors what life was like fifty to a hundred years ago. His collection of antique furniture, household appliances, tools, and odds and ends is massive, and so displays often rotate in and out. Over 20,000 everyday items are here ranging from carriages and farm tools to music

Items in the Rollo Jamison Museum range from expensive antiques to other, shall we say, oddities?

boxes and old beer bottles. He told his longtime girlfriend that if he ever had to choose between her and the collecting, he would choose the latter, it was that important to him. One look at these sprawling exhibits will tell you how *that* ended.

From the museum continue west on Main Street two blocks to Highway 80. Go left and follow it to Business Highway 151. Across this intersection on the right is **Ed's Café**, a greasy spoon diner popular with the locals. If you're not eating, go left on 151. You can see the giant M again, in the distance to the left. Take a right on CR O. This is a break in scenery and a segment of the byway that is decent for fall colors. You'll pass through forest and farmland and lose the longer looks to the horizon. A couple places along the road show exposed rock. Cornelia is an unincorporated blink of the eyes, but if you keep them open you'll see Mt. Zion United Church of Christ with its tin steeple. The road passes through a shallow valley, and you'll cross a tributary of the Platte River that tumbles over a bit of rock to the left. Not long after that you'll see another tin steeple, that of the 1875 St. Andrew's Church.

When you reach the juncture of CR O and US 61/WI 35, cross the highway to pick up WI 133, which takes you right into **Potosi**, Wisconsin's

Have you had your Good Old Potosi today?

The **National Brewery Museum** is a triumph of the small town's commitment to do big things. Potosi beat out the beer giant cities of Milwaukee and St. Louis to host this museum which showcases the collections of members of the American Breweriana Association (ABA). What is **breweriana**, you might ask? It consists of all those collectibles from the days before the mega-brewers, such as Miller and Anheuser-Busch, when there was a brewer in every town: branded beer glasses, serving trays, neon signs, cans and bottles, lithographs and posters, and much more. The old Potosi Brewery had a run of 150 years ending in 1972. The building fell into decay until locals decided it would make a great site for the museum. They made a pitch to the ABA, and their enthusiasm and a detailed plan for reconstruction and fundraising were convincing. The museum opened in the summer of 2008. A research library inside boasts having records of all the breweries that have ever operated in the United States. It's not just a beer can collection; it offers an interesting angle on American history.

Catfish Capital. Every August the village hosts a **catfish festival** and catfish fry on the Sunday of that weekend.

Potosi was first known as Snake Hollow for the abundance of the slithering reptiles and in fact they used to fall down the mines, perhaps a disconcerting occurrence for miners.

It's hard to imagine when you see the population is 711 on the sign coming into town, that Potosi was once the largest town in the state and an important port on the Mississippi River. But so it was as the beneficiary of the lead mining rush beginning in 1827.

St. John's Mine is a big A-frame building on the right side of the road heading toward the river. The hour-long tour goes *up* into an old mine shaft burrowed into the bluff behind the museum. The town was originally built right around this entrance as the lead rush came on. Willis St. John was one of the settlers who came running when the lead boom began after the Winnebago Peace Treaty in 1827. He staked his claim on Snake Cave and became wealthy. In just two years 450,000 pounds of ore were pulled out of the earth here. Nelson Dewey, the man who would eventually be the state's first governor, and his business partner Henry Massey purchased the mine when St. John's bad investments left him in ruin. If you are looking for a bit more local history, **The Passage Thru Time Museum** on Main Street has some exhibits as well as a self-guided driving tour of the area.

Once the brewery for the town of Mineral Point, now it produces fine pottery.

The complex at the edge of town on the right side of the road is the old **Potosi Brewery**. Included within are the **National Brewery Museum**, the **Great River Road Interpretive Center**, a **transportation museum**, gift shop, and a **restaurant/brewpub**. Several beers are made onsite and the menu is upscale pub fare such as gourmet sandwiches and burgers.

The Great River Road Interpretive Center offers information on Wisconsin's 250-mile segment of this **National Scenic Byway**. An interactive touch-screen allows you to zoom in on communities along the route to find more information. There are also plenty of area maps and brochures to choose from and information on the history and natural beauty of the river area. The Great River Road follows the Mississippi along WI 133 connecting to WI 35, which is in chapter five.

SIDE TRIP

For a nice view of the Mississippi River, follow WI 133 north. The 19-mile drive to Cassville alternatively passes along the river and through bluffs and farmland. The Annual Bald Eagle Days Celebration is held in late January in Cassville. Hundreds of these majestic birds winter in the Cassville area and can be easily spotted from the village's waterfront park. Eagle Roost Resort is a good place to spot eagles as is Nelson Dewey State Park.

The **World's Largest Cone-top** is on your left, across from the Potosi Brewery. This was one of the original grain mills of the brewery but is now painted up like the beer cans of old which were made of tin but capped like a glass bottle.

Presently there are really only two options for lodging in Potosi. The first is **Pine Point Lodge**, a collection of simple cabins just past the brewery complex as you head west out of town on Main Street. The second is for campers at **Grant River Recreation Area**. This park is managed by the Army Corps of Engineers. Archaeological digs have uncovered thousand-year-old burial sites and copper jewelry left by the Woodland tribes. The park is located along the Mississippi River down River Lane Road from WI 133.

Rustic Road 99 offers a 3.4-mile loop through the woods and begins right across Main Street from Potosi Brewery. Follow Brewery Hollow Road to Slazing Road. Go right and you will come to River Lane Road. If you go left here it will take you to Park Lane where a right turn toward the river brings you to Grant

THE GROTTO

Father Matthias Wernerus was the pastor of Holy Ghost Parish from 1918 to 1931. For five years he dedicated himself to the construction of a shrine and grotto dedicated to both God and country. The grotto encloses a statue of the Virgin Mary. Behind this is a series of shrines both religious and patriotic. The materials he used are what make this place most interesting. Upon close inspection visitors see more than just stone and mortar; details show pieces of glass, stones, pottery shards, sea shells, ores, crystals, and myriad other tiny curiosities allegedly from all over the world. Wernerus used no blueprints, but the site took shape over the years and now stands testament to his work. Estimates claim that the grotto receives up to 60,000 visitors each year. A gift shop is on-site, and photos are allowed.

River Recreation Area. Go right and you will complete the Rustic Road loop and come back to WI 133. The views are mostly of forest, and you're likely to see wild animals such as deer or turkeys. This is a must in fall.

Head back on WI 133 to Highway 35 and go south (right) and follow it to Dickeyville to see the famous roadside attraction, the **Dickeyville Grotto.**

If you have the munchies or are looking for a delectable item to take home from this trip, stop at **Hauber's Meats**. The shop sells cheese, syrup, mustard, and other Wisconsin delights, but the beef sticks are the biggest draw. They have even shipped them overseas.

Follow US 151 north to head back toward Mineral Point. The highway passes through some deep cuts in the rock of the Driftless Area. A great way to end this day is a meal or a night's stay in Mineral Point along WI 23 at exit 40.

IN THE AREA

Accommodations

Brewery Creek Inn, 23 Commerce Street, Mineral Point. Call 608-987-3298. Seven guest rooms offer elegant interiors and double whirlpools. The restaurant downstairs is a brewpub with upscale pub fare emphasizing local products. The inn manages two cottages off site as well. Web site: www.brewerycreek.com.

The Coach House at Shake Rag Alley, 18 Shake Rag Street, Mineral Point. Call 608-987-3292. These three upstairs rooms with private baths are located in an historic stage coach stop in the heart of town. Web site: www.mineralpointlodging.com.

Cothren House, 320 Tower Street, Mineral Point. Call 608-987-1522. Guests stay in an historic two-bedroom stone cottage or a rustic log cabin with a fireplace and a loft. A five-minute walk from downtown. Web site: www.cothrenhouse.com.

Grant River Recreation Area. Call 608-763-2140. Open Apr. through Oct. This park has picnic facilities, toilets, and seventy-three campsites. Reservations can only be made online. Web site: www.mvr.usace .army.mil/missriver/campingpage/Grant%20River.htm.

Mineral Point Hotel, 121 Commerce Street, Mineral Point. Call 608-987-3889. This charming small hotel, located right downtown, has four upstairs rooms. Amenities include Wi-Fi, continental breakfast, and pillow-top mattresses. Web site: mineralpointhotel.com.

The Mousehole, 14 Shake Rag Street, Mineral Point. Call 608-987-3292. Choose from two apartments in an 1839 stone-and-brick duplex. They have full kitchens and are located at the heart of town. Web site: www.mineralpointlodging.com.

Pine Point Lodge, 219 South Main Street, Potosi. Call 608-763-2767. These two simple cabins are located just outside of town a short distance from the Mississippi River.

Attractions/Recreation

Belmont Mound State Park, County Road G off US 151, Belmont. Call 608-523-4427. No state park fee required. Open 4 AM–11 PM. The park consists of a small picnic and playground area, shelters, and a porta-potty. At the top is a sixty-four-foot viewing platform offering a tri-state view.

Brewery Pottery Studio, 276 Shake Rag Street, Mineral Point. Call 608-987-3669.This studio/gallery is housed in the town's 1850 brewery. Web site: www.brewerypottery.com.

Dickeyville Grotto and Shrines, 305 West Main Street, Dickeyville. Call 608-568-3119. Check out a massive shrine made of thousands of tiny odds and ends, dedicated to the Virgin Mary and various themes, not just religious, but patriotic as well. Admission is free, but donations encouraged. A gift shop is on site. Web site: www.dickeyville grotto.com.

Hauber's Meats, 125 North Main Street, Dickeyville. Call 608-568-7579. Stop in for some great beef sticks, fresh cheese curds, or even local maple syrup and mustards. They will even ship beef sticks overseas.

Hook's Cheese Company, 320 Commerce Street, Mineral Point. Call 608-987-3259. This company makes award-winning blue cheese, and their Colby and aged cheddars are amazing. They are only open from about 4 AM to 3 PM on Fri. Otherwise stop in at Five Point Liquor across the street for a selection of their cheeses.

Bruce Howdle, 225 Commerce Street, Mineral Point. Call 608-987-3590. You shouldn't miss the ceramic murals of this local artist. His studio hours vary by season and workload; call ahead if you are making a special trip. Web site: www.brucehowdle.com.

Johnston Gallery, 245 High Street, Mineral Point. Call 608-987-3787. Web site: www.johnstongallery.com.

Longbranch Gallery, 203 Commerce Street, Mineral Point. Call 608-987-4499. Representing more than fifty artists, the gallery shows rustic and folk art with some interesting twists. Web site: www.longbranch gallery.com.

Mining Museum and Rollo Jamison Museum, 405 East Main Street, Platteville. Call 608-348-3301. Open May–Oct. 9–5 daily and Nov.–Apr. 9–4 Mon.–Fri. Fee. Find out more about the mining days and tour an old mine. Then check out a collection of everyday items from a century ago. Web site: www.mining.jamison.museum.

Orchard Lawn, 234 Madison Street, Mineral Point. Call 608-987-2884. Call for summer tours of this restored, nineteenth-century, Italianate mansion. Web site: www.mineralpointhistory.org.

Passage through Time Museum, 116 North Main Street, Potosi. Call 608-763-2406. Open May–Sept., Tues.–Sat., noon to 4. See some local historical collections mostly from the nineteenth century, and pick up a map of a local driving tour.

Pendarvis, 114 Shake Rag Street, Mineral Point. Call 608-987-2122. Open May–Oct. Fee. Visit a preserved portion of Cornish mining history where guides are dressed in period costume. Explore old cottages and walk the hill near Merry Christmas Mine. Web site: pendarvis.wisconsinhistory.org.

Potosi Brewery/National Brewery Museum, 209 South Main Street, Potosi. Call 608-763-4002. This complex houses a restaurant/brewpub, two museums, and the Great River Road Interpretive Center. Web site: potosibrewery.com.

Rountree Gallery, 385 East Main Street, Platteville. Call 608-348-6719. Hours vary by season. This free gallery located on the second floor of the Mining Museum houses permanent and temporary exhibits of regional artwork.

St. John Mine, 129 South Main Street, Potosi. Call 608-763-2121. Fee. Take an hour's guided tour up into the mine that was once at the center of this town's boom.

Shake Rag Alley Center for the Arts, 18 Shake Rag Street, Mineral Point. Call 608-987-3292. Take a weekend art workshop here or linger in the shaded park. Original plays are put on in from June–Aug. on the outdoor stage. Web site: www.shakeragalley.com.

Dining/Drinks

Café Four, 20 Commerce Street, Mineral Point. Call 608-987-2030. Closed Mon. Open for lunch and dinner, the restaurant serves a variety of entrées with a tendency toward Italian, including Neapolitan-style pizzas from a wood-fired oven, but also excellent salads made with local, organic foods. Web site: www.fourcafe.com.

Ed's Café, 115 US Business Highway 151, Platteville. Call 608-348-8194. This greasy spoon has been in business a long time, serving unpretentious, hearty breakfasts and lunches.

Gundry and Gray, 215 High Street, Mineral Point. Call 608-987-4444. Closed Tues. This little gift shop is also a great lunch spot. Go here for quality salads and hot and cold sandwiches. Web site: www .historicgundryandgray.com.

Old Royal Inn, 43 High Street, Mineral Point. Call 608-987-4530. Closed Sun. and Mon. Serves grilled pizzas, various sandwiches and pasta plates, and full dinners. Web site: www.theoldroyalinn.com.Red Rooster Café, 158 High Street, Mineral Point. Call 608-987-9936. This is your down-to-earth variety of diner, good for breakfast, and a decent place to find both a pasty and a figgyhobbin.

Other

Great River Road National Scenic Byway (Wisconsin portion). Web site: www.wigreatriverroad.org.

Mineral Point Chamber of Commerce, 225 High Street, Mineral Point. Call 608-987-3201. Web site: www.mineralpoint.com.

Platteville Chamber of Commerce, 275 West Business Highway 151, Platteville. Call 608-348-8888. Web site: www.platteville.com.

Erosion has created an arch out of the sandstone at Natural Bridge State Natural Area.

CHAPTER 3

Through the Hills of Baraboo

Estimated length: 104 miles

Estimated time: 2 hours minimum

Getting There: From Madison, take US 12 northwest to Sauk City.

Highlights: Climb the towering bluffs of **Devil's Lake State Park**; cross the Wisconsin River in the only free car ferry in the state; see an ancient free standing sandstone arch; pick apples at an orchard; sample the wines at the state's oldest winery; visit the **Ringling Brothers Circus Museum**; spot eagles along the Wisconsin River; and enter the bizarre world of Dr. Evermore.

Between the Wisconsin Dells and the Wisconsin River lies the Baraboo Range. This collection of bluffs was once a series of mountains that were buried long ago. What has reemerged is as old as 1.6 billion years, and as such this is one of the oldest outcrops in North America. Much of the hills are formed from pink quartzite and red rhyolite, and the range includes 55,000 acres of forest. The Wisconsin River gets a detour around them bending east a bit before easing west around the southern range.

The Wisconsin Dells are the state's most popular tourist destination and a combination of natural beauty and heavy commercial development,

Wollersheim Winery is a National Historic Site.

especially water parks. The Baraboo Range is just south of the Dells and as such makes a great alternative to the hustle and bustle.

This byway begins on the south side of the range but for those starting from the Dells, you might want to skip ahead to Mirror Lake State Park and the City of Baraboo to pick up the route midway.

As you approach Sauk City on US 12, watch for WI 188 on your right; this is the last right before the bridge that crosses the Wisconsin River into Sauk City. Less than a quarter mile down the road on the left is **Green Acres Restaurant**, a good supper club option if you decide to come back this way at the end of the byway.

Take WI 188 to the right and about two miles down the road you will come to **Wollersheim Winery** on the right. In the 1840s Agoston Haraszthy, a Hungarian count, started vineyards here. He followed the call of gold to California where he continued his viticultural interests, and that state has him to thank for their wine industry. Two generations of the Kehl family, German immigrants, built the buildings and developed the winery until 1899. The winemaking ended until 1972 when Robert and JoAnn Wollersheim bought the aging property and worked to restore the winery and vineyards. Philippe Coquard, originally from the Beaujolais region of France, grew up in a winemaking family and joined the Wollersheims in 1984 (eventually becoming a son-in-law). The winery has several awards, and an expansion completed in 2008 is testament to the winery's continuing success and growth. The winery offers tours and tastings daily.

From the winery continue another mile to WI 60. Go left over the dam into Sauk City's sister city Prairie du Sac. The two cities are often referred to together as Sauk Prairie. To bypass the two towns just go straight across on CR PF.

Sauk City claims August Derleth as one of their own. The prolific writer, arguably Wisconsin's best known, was born here in 1909. His books, photos, and typewriter are on display at the Sauk City Library.

BADGER ORDNANCE WORKS

In October of 1941 farmers on this large glacier outwash plain received the final news. The U.S. government would be taking the land to build what would the largest ammunition plant in the world. The 7,500-acre facility provided housing for employees and their families during World War II. The operation was active during three major wars and closed at the end of the Vietnam War in 1975. The massive use of dangerous chemicals led to contamination, and the facility was put on the list of Super Fund sites for clean up. Today its future is uncertain. Parts of the land may be returned to the native Ho-Chunk who plan to bring bison to graze here.

Canoe trips on the Wisconsin are a great way to see the river. You can hook up with outfitters such as **Sauk Prairie Canoe Rental**, which will provide equipment and pick up/drop off service for trips from one hour up to several days which would include camping on sandbars in the river. **Eagle watching** is extremely popular, especially in winter when the river freezes. At that time the water below the dam remains open, and sometimes more than a couple dozen of the majestic birds congregate in the leafless branches of trees overlooking the fish buffet. Look for the street-side viewing area along Water Street in Prairie du Sac. The third weekend in January is **Eagle Watching Days**.

The **Blue Spoon Creamery Café**, also on Water Street, offers a nice place for breakfast including three types of eggs Benedict and pancakes made with Culver's custard. The lunch menu has a lot of sandwiches and wraps and many other fine choices including gelato. Farther down Water Street in Sauk City, not far from US 12, is the **Cameo Antique Mall**. The

Tower Rock stands along among farmland and bluffs.

building was once a flooring store, and at 8,000 square feet, this is not a tiny collection. If you are looking for something or love to browse, the husband and wife team here really knows their stuff and can help you.

Continuing on the byway after Sauk City/Prairie du Sac, take CR PF west from US 12. The small Sauk Prairie Airport is at this intersection just north of Sauk City. If you are coming straight from the dam along PF, you will be continuing straight across US 12. Those going north on US 12 will go left (west). CR PF takes a scenic route through the farmland tucked among the bluffs.

Just over 8 miles from US 12 watch for Denzer Road on the right (right after Hager Road). When you get here look to your right to see **Tower Rock**, a large sandstone outcrop that overlooks an elementary school and faces a bright red barn. Stay on CR PF about another 4 miles and take a right on CR C. From here you will pass through the village of Leland and arrive at the entry of **Natural Bridge State Natural Area** in just over 1 mile.

People have been coming to this arch for a very long time; in fact, since before 8000 B.C. Next to the impressive sandstone bridge is a rockshelter where archaeologists have found evidence of human occupation dating back to that time. A woodland trail loop with some steps has educational

Just east of Natural Bridge State Park on CR C you will see signs for State Rustic Road 21. These are gravel roads. One branch goes left on Orchard Drive, the other, Slotty Road, is a bit farther down the road and goes right. If you take Orchard Drive, the more forested of the two, follow it to Ruff Road then Denzer Road, always going to the right. It will bring you back to CR C where you would go left to continue east. Slotty Road offers more farmland and connects to Denzer Road as well. Here you go left (north) to CR C and take CR C to the right (east) to remain on the byway.

signage along the way and a scenic overlook. The overlook is to the right, and the shortest trip to the arch is to the left on the loop. As you exit the park go left, continuing east on CR C.

CR C is similar to CR PF, taking right a slightly circuitous route through the rolling farmland to get you back to US 12. At US 12 go left (north). The next roadside attraction requires you to make a U-turn to get on the southbound lane of this divided highway. Continue north watching on the left for a fifteen-foot radiator with a giant key stuck in it and a twenty-foot iron heart with a giant ray gun. At the next left turn, make that turn around and come back to this to see the amazing industrial art that is **Dr. Evermor's Forevertron**. Take the dirt road to the right and pass through a wooden fence. A quick glance might make you think you are entering a junkyard, but once you see the massive metal sculpture constructed of old industrial odds and ends, you'll get out your camera. There's a place to leave donations.

You'll need to make another U-turn through the divided highway to continue north on US 12.

A chance to see Dr. Evermor's Forevertron should not be missed!

Devil's Lake State Park's bluffs are part of the southern Baraboo Range. At the top exposed rocks make excellent viewing platforms of the lake in between the western and eastern bluffs and the glacial moraines at the north and south ends of the lake. What lay between the bluffs was an ancient river bed. During the last advance of glaciers, the Green Bay lobe nestled in between these bluffs, entering from both directions as glacial plugs. When the ice melted, moraines formed at either end thus creating the lake.

The hills are formed of quartzite rock, which consists of grains of sand tightly cemented together. The park has trails throughout, and each bluff can be hiked across its length. Though both are steep strenuous climbs, the west bluff is somewhat easier. The trail from the south shore to the top of the east bluff, however, is the most dramatic. Hikers climb along the broken rock up the exposed bluff face. The views from either side are remarkable, especially during fall colors.

On your right is a large complex of white buildings that is the site of the now defunct Badger Ordnance.

US 12 climbs into the Baraboo Range here, and about 2 miles after you come over the hill past Badger Ordnance Works, look for Ski Hi Road on your right. This is more or less the back door into **Devil's Lake State Park**. On your right, just a quarter mile or so down the road, is **Ski-Hi Fruit Farm**. The farm has been around since 1907. Though you can't pick your own here, you can choose from thirty-five different varieties of apples. Additionally you will find pies and turnovers, cider, and an assortment of non-apple produce such as gourds and potatoes, as well as jams, honey, and maple syrup. Take a self-guided tour of the farm.

Continue past the farm to the end of the road where it meets South Shore Drive. (A left turn would take you out to Park Road. Go right here and it connects to CR DL. The entrance to the north end of the state park, however, is on your right; you'll barely touch CR DL.) But from Ski Hi Road, the byway goes right on South Shore Drive. Stay on this into the park and you will go downhill on a serpentine road which leaves you beneath the western bluff at the southern end of the lake.

To stop in the park requires a state park sticker (daily or annual), which you can get on the other side of the lake on the left or at the north side main office. If you are parking on the right when you first come to the lake, close to the west bluff trail, you should pay that fee first. Continuing on the byway you will drive along the south end of the lake. The next left is the south shore beach area with concessions, changing rooms, and flush

The 500-foot climb on the east bluff at Devil's Lake may leave you breathless, but not as much as the view.

toilets. The trail up the bluff begins at the north end of the lot across the railroad tracks. The park has **three campgrounds** with a total of 407 campsites, all of which are on the north side of the lake. The most secluded and shaded of them are the farthest from the lake at the Ice Age Campground.

South Shore Drive continues past the lake 2 more miles to WI 113. There is prairie on the right that offers hiking amid wildflowers and bluebird houses. You will find another smaller parking lot there. This is also part of the **Ice Age National Scenic Trail**, the 1,000-mile Wisconsin hiking path that follows the line where the last glaciers ended. An 18-mile segment starts in Merrimac, passes through the park here, climbs over both bluffs, and then heads east from the north side campgrounds all the way to Parfrey's Glen.

When you come to WI 113, go left. Just under 2 miles later you CR DL will head left to the main entrance of the park and the camping areas. Just past CR DL on the right is Tower Road, which climbs to **Inn at Wawanissee Point** (see below near Parfrey's Glen). The byway continues north on WI 113 crossing the Baraboo River before entering town.

Baraboo has a pleasant central square that may make you feel as though this is Mayberry. Take a lap around the courthouse. If you're here for lunch, check out **Jen's Alpine Café**, where you can have breakfast at any time, and

THE GREATEST SHOW ON EARTH

Wisconsin was once known as the Mother of Circuses; more than 100 traveling tent shows once made this their home or wintering spot. Baraboo gets the honor of hosting the Circus World Museum, however, because the Greatest Show on Earth once called it home. The five Ringling Brothers emigrated from Germany and founded their circus in Baraboo. The first performance, however, was in Mazomanie. The Ringling Brothers were quite successful, and by 1918 they had bought up their biggest rival, the Barnum and Bailey Show. After the circus days faded, the personal attorney of the brothers returned to Wisconsin to retire and founded the museum. Since 1959 the museum has been owned by the Wisconsin Historical Society.

pick from as many as five homemade soup selections offered daily. The biggest attraction in town is the **Circus World Museum**. The multi-building museum includes history exhibits, a collection of train wagons, and even some circus animals. A video shows the history of the original hometown of the Ringling Brothers Circus, and you can tour some of the original buildings of the Ringling Brothers winter quarters. Check the Web site for a list of daily events.

Baraboo is a nice place to stop for the night either while you are on this byway or if you are visiting the Wisconsin Dells and prefer a quiet evening. Right downtown is **Gollmar Guest House**, a uniquely designed nineteenth-century home once owned by the treasurer of the Gollmar Brothers Circus.

The byway continues north of Baraboo on US 12 to Fern Dell Road/Moon Road, just before you arrive at I-90/94. Two miles to the left is the entrance to the lovely **Mirror Lake State Park**. Central to the park is the lake with waters so still that it merits its name. Surrounding it are bluffs, some fifty-foot cliffs, and wetlands. Trails abound for hiking and

How often do you get to stay at a home designed by Frank Lloyd Wright? The **Seth Peterson Cottage** was one of Wright's last commissions. Oddly enough, the place fell to disrepair and was forgotten until a canoeist Audrey Laatsch happened to see it high on a bluff from where she paddled on Mirror Lake. Following years of fund-raising and restoration it was opened to the public. Each month (second Sunday) there is an open house and an inexpensive tour of the property. Otherwise, this is a rental property and only paying guests are allowed.

RIDE THE RAILS

Get an old school look at the Baraboo Hills by riding the rails at the **Mid-Continent Railway Museum**. Visitors pay to ride seven scenic miles on board refurbished 1915 coach cars. The museum also has a nineteenth-century depot and a large shed full of old engines and coach and freight cars. The railroad ruled this state before the advent of the highway system, and this little museum does a fantastic job of keeping that part of history alive. From Baraboo take WI 136 4 miles to CR PF and go left. CR PF becomes Walnut Street as it turns into North Freedom less than 2 miles later. Stay on this through the four-way stop and you will come to the railroad tracks where the museum depot is.

On tracks that were once part of the Chicago and North Western Railway, the train at the Mid-Continent Railway Museum take a short ride through the Baraboo Hills.

mountain biking in season and snowshoeing and cross-country skiing in winter. The lake is ideal for canoes or kayaks and you can rent them in the park. Three campgrounds offer a combined 151 campsites.

Ishnala means "by itself alone" in the Ho-Chunk language. Not actually part of the park, the **Ishnala Restaurant** is surrounded by state property and thus pretty much has this view to itself as far as businesses go. This supper club has been in operation since a band of brothers opened it in 1953. Prime rib is the specialty. The dining room and bar have fantastic views of Mirror Lake.

The byway continues by heading back to US 12 and going south 1 mile to turn left (east) on Shady Lane Road. Just over a mile away is the **International Crane Foundation**. This is the only place in the world where you can see all fifteen species of cranes, including the greatly endangered whooping crane and the Sarus crane, the tallest flying bird. Their raucous cries may surprise you, and the wetlands viewing area for the whooping crane is a nice place to relax in the shade and observe this remarkable bird.

FLY AWAY HOME

Perhaps you remember the movie starring Jeff Daniels where his child decides to take in orphaned geese, and in the end they must teach the birds to migrate? *Fly Away Home* was based on a true story of a father and daughter from Ontario. In 2001 the same plan was used to show young whooping cranes how to get to Florida for the winter. Trainers dressed up in what looked a bit like white hazmat suits but with one sleeve made to look like a hand puppet of a crane's head. The chicks imprinted on the trainer and after a summer of getting accustomed to the hum of a plane engine, the flock followed an ultralight along a migratory path. A truly "bird-brained" plan, it counted on the cranes' memories to fly back to Wisconsin and repeat the migration the following year. The plan worked, and the recovery of this species continues slowly but surely.

See one of the rarest of the 15 crane species—the whooping crane—at the International Crane Foundation.

When you leave the cranes, continue east on Shady Lane Road just about 4 miles to Van Hoosen Road; turn left and drive less than half a mile to CR U and turn left again (heading east now). Continue on the road for about 5 miles even as it turns and heads south, and then at WI 33 go left (east) again. About 4.5 miles east you will go right (south) on CR W. Let the scenery begin.

CR W twists and turns a bit as you cross through the north range of the Hills of Baraboo. Follow CR W, and just over 3 miles later the road will take a tight right-angle curve left and downhill and then another right-angle turn right (west); *don't* take this second turn. Rather, stay straight and follow Owen Park Road south off of CR W. This takes you right up into the hills. When you get over the hump, look for a wayside on the right.

PARFREY'S GLEN

Though it's not really a secret, not everyone makes it out to this little natural gem. Perhaps it is the bigger Devil's Lake that distracts the traveler. But if you have the chance, don't miss this state natural area. A creek passes through a deep gorge cut into the rock which shows Cambrian-age layers of sand alternating with layers of pebbles and quartzite. Much of the gorge is moist, supporting a verdant layer of moss, and the cool temperatures, even on a hot summer day, support a very different collection of plants. Two threatened birds have been spotted here: the cerulean warbler and the Acadian flycatcher. A boardwalk prevents visitors from trampling on rare plants, and a waterfall waits at the end of the quarter-mile trail. Note: *The flood of June 2008 rerouted the stream and destroyed the boardwalk. Check the Web site for recovery progress.*

From this point you have a marvelous **scenic overlook** of the Baraboo Valley and the southern range of hills and, beyond that, the Wisconsin River. Not a bad place for a picnic.

Continue following Owen Park Road just over a mile downhill to WI 78 and take a right. Just over 2 miles later, CR DL splits to the right. You can take this to Parfrey's Glen or all the way back to Devil's Lake State Park (thus the DL designation).

THE MERRIMAC FERRY

Since 1844 a ferry has been crossing the Wisconsin River at this spot. In the early days it cost anywhere from thirty-five cents to a dollar to go across. If they charged that today, people would protest; the Merrimac ferry has been free, in fact, since 1933. The journey takes a short seven minutes, and if you have to wait at either side, there is an ice cream and snack stand right next to the docks.

The Merrimac Ferry is the only free ferry in Wisconsin and is part of the highway system as a bridge substitute for State Highway 113.

Just above Parfrey's Glen is the most luxurious place to stay on this byway. **Inn at Wawanissee Point** is a four-room bed and breakfast atop one of the highest points in the Baraboo Range offering a complete view of the surrounding hills and the Wisconsin River. Guests consistently rave about service and food, and the design and woodworking in this place are an attraction in themselves. To get there, go right on Bluff Road up the hills to Tower Road where you will go left. If you take Bluff Road south, you will head straight into Merrimac where you can go left a short distance to the ferry landing.

If you have bypassed Parfrey's Glen and remained on WI 78 at its juncture with CR DL, continue just another 4 miles to Merrimac. Look for the ferry landing to your left. (If for some reason the ferry is not running, you can still cross the river by taking WI 78 all the way back to Sauk Prairie. Alternatively, you can backtrack east and take WI 78 to I-90/94.)

From the ferry you can go right on WI 188 back to US 12 or take WI 113 6 miles to Lodi where you can pick up WI 60 going east 4 miles to I-90/94.

IN THE AREA

Accommodations

Gollmar Guest House Bed and Breakfast, 422 Third Street, Baraboo. Call 608-356-9432. The house was built near the end of the nineteenth century in the rare Shingle Style. The attic room has a fireplace and two rooms have two-person whirlpools. Web site: www.gollmar.com.

Inn at Wawanissee Point, E13609 Tower Road, Baraboo. Call 608-355-9899. This new inn takes B&B to luxury-style levels. The four rooms are elegantly appointed, and the architecture and woodwork of the house are exquisite. Gourmet breakfast and evening wine and cheese are included in the rates. The view from here is stunning in all directions. Web site: www.innatwawanisseepoint.com.

Mirror Lake State Park, E10320 Fern Dell Road, Baraboo. Call 608-254-2333. A state park fee applies. Overlooking a beautiful lake surrounded by bluffs and fifty-foot cliffs, the park offers hiking, cross-country skiing, off-road biking, and boating as well as three campgrounds with 151 sites. Bike, boat, canoe, and kayak rentals are available on-site. A cabin and trail are wheelchair accessible. Web site: www.dnr.state.wi.us/org/land/parks/regions/scr/mirrorlake.html.

The Seth Peterson Cottage, E9982 Fern Dell Road, Lake Delton. Call 608-254-6551. Designed by Frank Lloyd Wright in 1958, the cottage sleeps up to four guests. Be aware that this cottage is often booked over a year in advance. Generally a two-night minimum is required though single-night openings occur from time to time. Open-house tours are held the second Sun. of every month from 1–4. Web site: www.seth peterson.org.

Attractions/Recreation

Cameo Antique Mall, 827 Water Street, Sauk City. Call 608-643-8000. This 8,000-square-foot showroom is run by owners who are passionate about antiques and really know their business. Web site: www.cameo antiques.com.

Circus World Museum, 550 Water Street, Baraboo. Call 608-356-8341. Fee. Visit the home site of the original Ringling Brothers Circus. Many of the old buildings of their winter home remain. You can also see restored circus wagons, a documentary about the Ringling Brothers, and some circus animals as well. Find out if they are running the daily Grand Parade. Web site: www.circusworldmuseum.com.

Devil's Lake State Park, S5975 Park Road, Baraboo. Call 608-356-8301. A state park fee applies; the park office is on the north side of the park. Three campgrounds have 407 campsites. The best sites are in the Ice Age campground. The Ice Age National Scenic Trail passes through the park; you can actually hike to Parfrey's Glen from here. Both the north and the south shore have concessions stands. Web site: www.dnr.state.wi .us/org/land/parks/specific/devilslake.

International Crane Foundation, E11376 Shady Lane Road, Baraboo. Call 608-356-9462. There is a fee. Open daily Apr. 15–Oct. 31. Guided tours and audio tours are available. Come see all fifteen world species of cranes, including the very rare whooping crane. Walk the trails through oak savanna and prairies and visit the educational center and a gift shop. Web site: www.savingcranes.org.

Mid-Continent Railway Historical Society, E8948 Diamond Hill Road, North Freedom. Call 1-800-930-1385. Fee. Once in North Freedom, go another .5 mile west on Walnut Street from the four-way stop at the center of town. Ride the rails 7 miles through the hills of Baraboo in restored 1915 coach cars, and then see the other cars and displays inside the Coach Shed. Web site: www.midcontinent.org.

Natural Bridge State Natural Area, 1 mile east of Leland on County Road C, Prairie du Sac. Call Devil's Lake State Park. Open 6 AM–8 PM. A state park fee applies; use the self-pay tube in the parking lot. A loop trail passes a twenty-five-foot sandstone arch and a rockshelter that has evidence of human occupation dating before 8000 BC. Go left on the trail for the shortest distance to the arch.

Parfrey's Glen, located on County Road DL, 2.1 miles east of WI 78 and WI 113. Call 608-356-8301 (Devil's Lake State Park). Open 6 AM– 8 PM. Water and pit toilets on site. A state park fee applies. A creek passes through a gorge of moss-covered sandstone conglomerate. Rare species of plants and animals can be found in this cooled canyon in the forest. No pets allowed. Note: The flood of 2008 destroyed the boardwalk. Confirm that visitors are allowed once again before you visit. Web site: dnr.wi.gov/org/land/er/sna/sna1.htm.

Sauk Prairie Canoe Center, 500 Water Street, Sauk City. Call 608-643-6589. This outfitter has been in business since 1971. Rent canoes or kayaks with return shuttles for trips ranging from one hour to several days including camping on sandbars in the river. Web site: www.spcanoe rentals.com.

Ski-Hi Fruit Farm, E11219A Ski-Hi Road, Baraboo. Call 608-356-3695. Open daily. You can find thirty-five varieties of apples here as well as a whole collection of everything apple: pies, turnovers, cider, etc. Plus there are vegetables, jams and jellies, honey, and maple syrup for sale. Apple season starts at the end of Aug. and goes through Nov. They have self-guided tours but no pick-your-own apples.

Wollersheim Winery, 7876 WI 188, Prairie du Sac. Call 1-800-847-9463. Open year round. The winery charges a nominal fee for its seven daily tours, but tastings are free. Web site: www.wollersheim.com.

Dining/Drinks

Blue Spoon Creamery Café, 550 Water Street, Prairie Du Sac. Call 608-643-0837. Stop in for breakfast for eggs Benedict or Culver's custard pancakes, or for lunch with a full menu of sandwiches, wraps, pizzas, soups, and salads. You can also find gelato here. Web site: www .bluespooncafe.com.

Green Acres Restaurant, 7438 WI 78, Sauk City. Call 608-643-2305. This supper club has a dark interior, but the service keeps it cheery and the food is good and reasonably priced. Web site: www.greenacres restaurant.com.

Ishnala Restaurant, S2011 Ishnala Road, Wisconsin Dells. Call 608-253-1771. Open Memorial Day–mid-Sept. This supper club overlooks beautiful Mirror Lake. If nothing else, have a drink at the Arrowhead Bar. From just east of Mirror Lake State Park entrance, go north on Ishnala Road and watch for the totem pole on the left. Web site: www.ishnala.com.

Jen's Alpine Café, 117 4th Street, Baraboo. Call 608-356-4040. This is the place to go for homemade soups as the restaurant typically offers four or five each day. Open for breakfast and lunch, the café has a varied menu and the setting is a 1930s building. Come on Fri. night for a traditional Wisconsin fish fry. Web site: www.foodspot.com/jensalpine.

Other

Baraboo Area Chamber of Commerce, 600 West Chestnut Street, Baraboo. Call 608-356-8333. Web site: www.baraboo.com.

Merrimac Ferry. The ferry typically begins operating near the beginning of Apr. and runs twenty-four hours per day until winter begins sometime in Nov. Web site: www.dot.wisconsin.gov/travel/water/ merrimac.htm.

Sauk Prairie Area Chamber of Commerce, 421 Water Street # 105, Prairie du Sac. Call 608-643-4168. Web site: www.saukprairie.com.

The trail to the shot tower at Tower Bluff shows the sandstone formed when Wisconsin was under a warm sea over 400,000 years ago.

CHAPTER

4

Along the Wisconsin River

Estimated length: 93 miles
Estimated time: 2 hours minimum

Getting There: From Madison, take US 14 west; from I-94 come south on US 12 and after Sauk City, go south on WI 78 to Mazomanie.

Highlights: Frank Lloyd Wright's **Taliesin** is an example of his unique design philosophy and a contrast to the strange and enigmatic **House on the Rock** nearby; **American Players Theater** puts Shakespeare (and others) in the great outdoors; the Wisconsin River is host to excellent **canoeing**, **camping** and **wildlife viewing**; venture underground at the state's first commercial cavern, **Eagle Cave**.

The state of Wisconsin actually takes its name from the river. When Father Jacques Marquette traveled its waters with Native Americans in 1673, he recorded its name as Meskousing. By 1674 another explorer misread the cursive "M" as "Ou" and it became Ouisconsing. By the mid-nineteenth century, the French-influenced form was lost to its present spelling. Twenty-five hydroelectric plants tap into the power of this mighty 430-mile river that stretches from the state's border with the Upper Peninsula of Michigan all the way to the Mississippi.

Part of this trip follows the Frank Lloyd Wright Memorial Highway, US 14, a tribute to Wisconsin's native son and renowned architect. However, much of the architecture on this route is done by Mother Nature and is what always captivated Wright. The Wisconsin River finishes the last 92 miles from the dam at Prairie du Sac to the Mississippi unimpeded, and the drives along its banks are characterized by forest-covered bluffs and intermittent areas of exposed sandstone once carved by the river itself.

Coming along US 14, the first stop on this route is **Mazomanie**. You will see the steeple of the church over the trees as you approach. In 1844 nearly 700 settlers of the British Temperance and Emigration Society built up a town called Dover just beyond here along the highway. However, when the railroad snubbed them for a place closer to a water source with a better elevation, Dover quickly packed up and followed—buildings and all—settling in present-day Mazomanie; now Dover is merely the stuff of historical landmark waysides.

In 1857 George Lynch and George Walker of Milwaukee built a flouring mill and created Lake Marion as a mill pond. An iron waterwheel provided the power at first, which was later supplied by smaller turbines. The mill exchanged hands a couple times over the following years, and in 1885 a dynamo was installed to produce electricity. From 1888 to 1892 the mill also provided pressurized water to mains for fire protection. Ironically, a fire burnt out the mill on January 1, 1900. Henry Kirch rebuilt it using the remnant walls and the mill went on to operate until 1946. A flood breached the dam in 1950, and Lake Marion was gone forever. Today the Old Feed Mill is home to a restaurant and gift shop.

Mazomanie comes from the Ho-Chunk language for "walking iron." Edward Brodhead, who gave his name to the main street, was a superintendent of the Milwaukee and Mississippi Railroad. He drew up the original plat of the village, which was founded in 1855. The railroad brought growth and notoriety. The Ringling Brothers Classic and Comic Concert Company came here from Baraboo, Wisconsin for their first public performance in 1882. You can see a commemorative plaque on the old Village Store building.

Coming into town on US 14, watch for the second street on your right, Cramer Street. Turn right here, and it will take you past the nice stone St. Barnabas Catholic Church to the **Old Feed Mill**, a fine choice for lunch or dinner in an historical setting.

Cross the old railroad tracks and take a left on Crescent Street. This will lead you into the two-block downtown and its collection of National Historic Register buildings on Brodhead Street. The **Mazomanie Historical Museum,** where the railroad tracks intersect with Brodhead Street, gives you a look into "Mazo's" past. Several arts and crafts shops make Brodhead Street a nice place to linger. One not to miss is the abstract photography of Doris Hembrough at **Hembrough Gallery**.

The **Whistle Stop Café** has ice cream, coffee, baked goods, and serves some great breakfasts and lunches. Just across the street is **Halle's Vintage Shoppe** where you'll find retro fashions and furnishings. **Walter's General Store** is a former hotel and saloon, but now offers a nice assortment of Wisconsin products from sauces, preserves, and beers to guidebooks and crafts.

If you decide to linger here overnight or make this home base, a nice option is the **Walking Iron Bed and Breakfast,** an 1865 brick Victorian Italianate home. Decorated with iron beds and period antiques, the four rooms come with private baths and whirlpools.

Many small communities centered around mills like this one in Mazomanie.

Another great way to see the Wisconsin River is from right on top of it. There are no rapids in the southernmost stretch of the river, and the last dam is in Sauk Prairie, leaving 92 miles of unimpeded water from the dam until where the river meets the Mississippi at Wyalusing State Park. Various outfitters along this route offer rentals complete with pickups and dropoffs, some with meals, guides or overnight excursions involving camping on one of the many sand bars. Trips can be as short as one hour or as long as two days (or more).

Take Brodhead back to the highway. On your right is **Gordon's Drive-In Restaurant**, a nice roadside stop for a sundae, shake, or simple fast food.

The next town down the line is Arena. Right on the highway, **Arena Cheese** is the home of the hybrid Co-Jack, a blend of Monterey Jack and Wisconsin's own Colby. Stop for some fresh cheese curds here or have a look at cheese being made on the other side of a viewing window. Gift boxes are available.

Spring Green lies another 8 miles from Arena. **Peck's Market** on the left hosts a **corn maze** in September and October and fresh produce throughout the growing season. On the other side of Spring Green, there is a second Peck's location along the highway.

There are several attractions just south of Spring Green that are best reached via CR C just before town. If you are planning to check into lodging or get a bite to eat in Spring Green, just stay on US 14 until it intersects WI 23, then go left. Otherwise, prepare for some impressive scenery and attractions.

Go left on CH C (watch for the sign to Tower Hill State Park). The scenery becomes a bit more dramatic with the forest coming up to the road's edge and the path curving around the bluffs. The first stop is **Tower Hill State Park** on your right. This was the site of the village of Helena, a thriving community during the lead-mining days. Troops crossed the river here in pursuit of the warrior Black Hawk on July 28, 1832. Jefferson Davis, Zachary Taylor, and Henry Dodge (the first territorial governor of Wisconsin) were among those troops. The U.S. Army actually tore down most of Helena for wood that was used to build rafts to ferry men and equipment across the water. Camping is allowed here at fifteen sites, and facilities include a canoe launch, picnic area, hiking trails, and pit toilets. The tower and smelter have been reconstructed at the top of the hill, and there is a great view of the river valley. The hike to the top is a bit strenuous but short at 0.2 mile. A slightly longer but more gradual path with

THE SHOT TOWER

From 1833–1861, lead from southwest Wisconsin was formed into shot at what is now Tower Hill State Park. You can see a reconstruction of the smelting house and shot tower at the top of the hill. Daniel Whitney of Green Bay, traveling along the Wisconsin River in 1830, saw business potential in the bluff central to the state park. In 1831 he hired Thomas Bolton Shaunce who spent 187 days of the next two years digging a 120-foot shaft and an accompanying ninety-foot tunnel. A wooden shaft above added sixty feet to make a 180-foot shot tower.

Lead was melted in a smelter at the top, and using a special ladle with holes in it, workers created drops of molten lead which, as they plummeted, formed round pellets. These fell into water at the bottom. When enough lead had amassed below, workers sorted and polished the shot. The process was imperfect, and only perhaps 15 percent of the pellets were usable; the rest were hauled back up the hill again to be thrown back into the smelter.

some stairs begins near campsite #13. Get a park map at the entrance. Pack mosquito spray.

Just past the park entrance, as you continue along CH C, is Golf Course Road on the left. Follow this to get to the **House on the Rock Resort** (*not* to be confused with the House on the Rock) and the **American Players Theatre**. The resort offers rooms overlooking its own eighteen-hole public **golf course** designed by Robert Trent Jones, Sr., a beautiful set of links tucked into the natural contours of the valley. All rooms have balconies or simple terraces. Another nine-hole course is onsite as well.

Continue on CH C past Golf Course Road and just over the guardrail to your right is the mighty river. Just as you arrive at WI 23, you

AMERICAN PLAYERS THEATRE

In 1978 a group of theatre enthusiasts had a mission to find a suitable outdoor venue to perform. The perfect hill to make an amphitheater was found on the Lockwood farm near Spring Green. On July 18, 1980, American Players Theatre staged its first production: Shakespeare's *A Midsummer Night's Dream*. The venue was an immediate hit and over the years has even been nominated for a Tony. Today there are over 1,100 seats in this hallowed hollow, and attendees come early to picnic on the hillside just before the main gate. Over 100,000 theatergoers attend the productions, which adhere to the classics, especially Shakespeare. Try to get your tickets well in advance. If you forgot mosquito spray, don't worry: the theater provides it free of charge.

The Midway Farm barn is another one of Frank Lloyd Wright's creations at Taliesin.

will see the **Frank Lloyd Wright Visitor Center** on your left. Check in here for tours of **Taliesin.** Going right on WI 23 will take you over the Wisconsin River and into Spring Green.

The Frank Lloyd Wright Visitor Center has a comprehensive gift shop and a nice café that serves tea and snacks or full meals for breakfast, lunch, and dinner. In the summer season call well in advance to get on a tour; they fill fast, and it is quite rare that travelers can get on a tour the same day. There are separate tours for the Hillside Studio and Theater and the House at Taliesin. The Highlights Tour gets you through both structures in two hours and emphasizes the architecture. For the juicier bits about Wright and his colorful character, take the House Tour instead. There may be a discount if you purchase both tours. The four-hour Estate Tour is the most comprehensive. Be aware: there are no public restrooms along the tour.

Going south on WI 23 past Taliesin, take a left on CH T. On your right you will see a small churchyard where Frank Lloyd Wright's grave marker is—only he's not under it. On April 9, 1959, Wright passed away after a

THE VENERABLE MR. WRIGHT

Frank Lloyd Wright was born in Richland Center, Wisconsin, on June 8, 1867. Arguably the most famous of American architects, he never attended architecture school. He worked for Louis Sullivan for six years in Chicago before venturing out on his own. His private life and personality were about as unusual and controversial as his designs; he married three times and had seven children.

Some of his most famous works include a dazzling home in Pennsylvania known as Fallingwater, which has a natural waterfall tumbling beneath it, the Imperial Hotel in Tokyo, and the spiraling Guggenheim Museum in New York City. But the hills of Wisconsin always captivated him, and for this he built his experimental home on the estate of Taliesin there. "Nothing picks you up in its arms and so gently almost lovingly cradles you as do these southwestern Wisconsin hills. . . . Every time I come back here it is with the feeling there is nothing anywhere better than this." In 1932 he founded a school of architecture at Taliesin. This prestigious school set in the Hillside Studio has continued to challenge apprentices since his death in 1959.

failed surgery. Wright wanted to be buried near Mamah and Taliesin, but his widow was not a big fan of either. After his wife's death Wright's body was exhumed under cover of darkness and cremated; the ashes of both Wright and his widow were mingled and taken to Taliesin West in Arizona, where they were allegedly built into an undisclosed part of a wall.

If you continue south on WI 23 just about 5 miles from Taliesin, you will come to the strange spectacle that is the **House on the Rock**. Watch for a scenic overlook just before you arrive there. A short walk from the parking lot will offer a peek of the house and its Infinity Room pointing out into space. A pedestrian bridge crosses the highway from the parking lot for northbound traffic.

SCANDAL AND MURDER

Frank Lloyd Wright left his wife and six children in 1909 to travel Europe with Mamah Cheney, the soon-to-be ex-wife of a client. When they returned, Frank and Mamah moved into Taliesin together, creating quite a scandal. However, tragedy brought a bit of sympathy back to Frank when in 1914, a disgruntled servant murdered Mamah and her two visiting children with an axe. He set fire to one wing of Taliesin and killed three of Wright's associates and one of their sons. Wright buried Mamah in the same cemetery as his mother, where he too was later initially laid to rest.

Walk out in the Infinity Room at The House on the Rock.

A DIFFERENT KIND OF ARCHITECTURE

In the 1940s **Alex Jordan** began to build a home high on exposed rock at the top of a towering bluff. The impressive location and the unusual layout drew visitors, and eventually he began charging admission. Jordan was also a fanatic collector of a wide variety of things.

The main house is a tangled maze of rooms, halls, and staircases that follow the contours of the rock. The exhibitions are no less tangled in their layout but astonishing if not bewildering in their extent, from rooms full of antique dolls or guns to an enormous sea battle between full-sized replicas of a whale and a giant octopus. Displays are often accompanied by coin-operated, air-driven music machines. This attraction is anything but ordinary, and some may even walk away hating it. The display of imagination ventures into the surreal, and the world's largest carousel with 20,000 lights and 289 creatures is a sight to behold.

You might not want to tour both Taliesin and the House on the Rock on the same day. To do the entire House on the Rock is about three hours or more depending on how long you linger. There are three self-guided tours, starting with the house tour where you can see the windowed Infinity Room, which juts out 218 feet over a drop of 165 feet. Tours two and three pass through extensive—sometimes amazing, sometimes disturbing—collections of objects ranging from antiques to complex music machines. Bring plenty of quarters to activate the music along the way. There are snack bars along the route, which is reported to be 2.5 miles and growing. The interiors are dark and often musty, so allergy sufferers be advised. Rest assured you will not see anything else like this attraction—for better or for worse.

Not far from here is **Silver Star Country Inn**, a bed and breakfast. Go west on Percussion Rock Road just under a mile north of the scenic overlook of the House on the Rock. The 4-mile drive from WI 23 is quite lovely. Go left down Lakeview Road over a one-lane bridge and continue straight. Take a right on Limmex Hill Road and follow the signs to a field of wildflowers where you'll find the two-story log-built inn.

If you are choosing a less remote stop for the night, **Spring Green** is your best bet . But as this looping trip also ends there, you will read about the town toward the end of this chapter.

The Wisconsin River route continues on CH C heading west from WI 23 south of Spring Green and the river itself. Less than a mile before you come to WI 130 look for Clyde Road. Go left (south) here to visit **Global View**, an unlikely barn full of treasures for sale from Tibet and various other Far Eastern locales. Items range from Buddhist statues to fine tapestries and incense burners.

Continuing on CH C you'll come to WI 130. Turn right and a mile or so

Find a piece of the Far East at Global View.

later you will follow the curve left around the backside of a bluff, where the road runs close to the Wisconsin River. At this point there is a high rock wall to your left and the river full of sandbars to your right. WI 130 and WI 133 cross the river to your right taking you into Lone Rock, but you continue straight on WI 133 South along the southern side of the Wisconsin.

The road leaves the river and puts railroad tracks to your right. This whole region is part of the **Lower Wisconsin State Riverway** and as such is protected land. There are, however, numerous roads along the route where you can drive into these areas to spot wildlife. The paths are typically sand and gravel and can be a bit rough, but odds are good for seeing bald eagles, kingfishers, herons, deer, and various other critters.

Pass some prairie restoration as you enter Avoca. There isn't much here, but you can find a small campground and park by taking a right on Clyde Street and a left on North Eighth Street. Native American mounds can be found here. Pets must be leashed. Campsites with picnic tables and campfire rings are open April 15 to December 1, and several RV sites are shaded by towering pines.

Another 6 miles takes you to Muscoda (MUS-koh-day). Go north on WI 80 here to WI 60 if you want to cut your loop short. As you enter town, look for **Meister Cheese Factory** in the industrial park on the right. Inside the showroom there is a viewing window to the factory, and the shop gives samples and sells a wide assortment of cheeses including a morel mushroom and leek-infused Monterey Jack. Take a right on Wisconsin Avenue (WI 80 and WI 133) to head into downtown. The **Veteran's Park** along the river offers **camping and picnicking** before the bridge. **Vicki's Cozy Café** is a casual breakfast and sandwich eatery located just behind Pierce's IGA grocery store, which can be found left on Iowa Street.

Going west from Muscoda as you continue on WI 133, the railroad tracks are now on your left. The **Muscoda Unit of the Lower Wisconsin Riverway** is on the right just past a sawmill. Look for a gravel road that leads to a wildlife viewing area. Parts of this often bumpy, gravel-and-sand road become a two-tire path with intermittent places to turn around. The brush is often right up to the edge of the road. Some travelers may be reluctant to put their vehicles in here. However, die-hard nature lovers should take their time, drive with care, and give it a go. Be aware that during periods of high water, areas within are likely to be flooded. Well into the woods you will come to the road to Fishtrap Flowage on the right,

You'll know the cheese curds are fresh if they squeak in your teeth.

which gets you into the river area; the forest and wetlands are abundant with wildlife and wildflowers, and you can get out of the car and step to the water's edge. Continuing past this spur road will loop you back to Kennedy Road. Go left on Lake Road and it's less than a half mile back to WI 133. Go right to continue west.

In **Blue River** at East Street/CH T, you can go right and cross three bridges to get over the river as another cutoff. This puts you near Port Andrew on WI 60 on the north side of the Wisconsin. Blue River offers little more than a couple of taverns serving the standard fare. Boscobel is another 7 miles west on WI 133. You'll see more wetlands along the route through this stretch.

Boscobel is Wisconsin's Wild Turkey Hunting Capital, and hunters flock here in season, which runs from mid-April to late May and mid-September to late November. This little town is also the host of the annual **Muskets and Memories Civil War Reenactment**, one of the largest and most reputable in the Midwest. Contact the Boscobel Chamber of

THE LONG AND WINE-DING ROAD

The river drive is scenic enough and is, in fact, being developed to receive an official designation as a scenic byway. But if you want a little extra, consider a side trip out to **Weggy Winery**. At the juncture of WI 80, go left (north) until CR O. Take this road 3 miles to the right until you come to Oak Ridge Court. Go right here and then follow the first driveway on your right. Situated on the top of a bluff, the winery offers impressive views of the topography and the creases in between the bluffs. Have a tour of the vineyards, get in a little sampling, and then buy a bottle of wine, perhaps, for your picnic before a little Shakespeare at American Players Theatre. You can come back to WI 60 on CH OO. Return to CH O and go right, following it to CH OO and heading right again.

Commerce for more information about this impressive event held the first weekend of August.

Wisconsin Avenue is the main street; go left here into the historic downtown. On your left find **Wisconsin River Outings** in an 1840s feed mill. Let them set you up on the river with a canoe or kayak, or join them for excursions as short as a few hours and as long as a few days. Right across the street from this outfitter is the old **train depot** which is now the **Boscobel Heritage Museum**. It would likely be on the National Register of Historic Places but for some reconstruction to the front room following a tragic accident. A truck full of apples tried to beat a passing train and lost. The vehicle was picked up and plunged into the building killing the driver. Parts of the depot are dedicated to railway history, but the bulk of it is a sort of re-creation of downtown—booth-sized exhibits feature facades that match each building along the main street. The manual telephone switchboard is a remarkable item to see in this age of mobile phones. Attendants are happy to give a free tour of the place.

Certainly the most interesting place to grab a bite to eat is **Unique Café**, an old-fashioned counter-seating diner. Owner and cook Doyle Lewis is a collector of various things from yesteryear, especially signage; the walls and parts of the ceiling are covered with antique tin signs in surprisingly good condition. Ask about the Beatles ring and look for a nice photo of the old covered bridge that once connected Boscobel to the other side of the river. Unique Café serves breakfast and lunch and is open at 6:30 AM for the early birds. Friday they open for dinner as well. **Vale Inn** right across the street from the depot/museum also offers good meals.

Boscobel's depot is full of history—literally. Check out the heritage museum inside.

Over ninety area artists are represented at the **Carriage House**. Local members of the **Amish community** sell produce and crafts right in front, typically on Tuesday and Friday.

Check out the clover-shaped bar across the street at the **Central House**. This building was once the Boscobel Hotel, the first hotel to ever place a **Gideon's Bible** in a room. That room has been restored, and if you are lucky someone at the bar will take you upstairs to see it. Local legend has it that John F. Kennedy stayed in this room during his presidential campaign tour. The rest of the rooms are used around Halloween as part of a local haunted house. Local talk is this place is the real thing.

Not just your ordinary bed and breakfast, **Life O' Riley Farm and Guesthouses** is located on 160 acres approximately 6 miles south of Boscobel. Guests stay in a rebuilt granary, an old schoolhouse, or in a couple rooms at the farmhouse. Mike and Jean Murphy raise their own meat, eggs, and produce, and the granary and schoolhouse kitchens are fully stocked with enough food for breakfast and much more. Look for fossils in the two small rock quarries or explore fifty acres of woods. An Amish

If you explore Eagle Cave, be sure to wear something warm. The temperature never comes over 60 degrees.

community nearby manages a produce auction that is a sight to see. Guests may make dinner arrangements with the innkeepers. Satellite wireless Internet is available. Another option is the **Llaughing Llamas Farm and Country Cabins** about 3 miles south of Boscobel off US 61.

Continuing on the road trip, head west from Wisconsin Avenue on West Prairie Street/WI 133 and turn right (north) on US 61 which will take you across the Wisconsin River for the return path to Spring Green. If you go left on the other side, it will take you to the Great River Road (chapter five).

As you head back east along WI 60, the river comes in close to the right for a few miles, and then the highway passes through bluffs and intermittent farmland. After you pass the juncture with WI 80 and Port Andrew right after that, watch for signs for **Eagle Cave**. This was the first commercial cave in Wisconsin and remains the largest onyx cavern in the state as well. The one-hour tour is chilly but lighted and on an even path. You can also camp here, rent canoes, or arrange river drop-offs/pick-ups. They organize canoe trips with meals included or even camping on the river. This is a great campsite for families.

Continuing along WI 60 you will reach **Gotham**. A minor roadside attraction and perhaps a place to have some bar food is **The Bat Cave**. Inside find plenty of Dark Knight paraphernalia and a shrine to Dale Earnhardt behind the bar. At the stop sign go right on WI 60 where it joins US 14. If you decide to go into **Lone Rock** take a right (south) on WI 130.

Waz Inn, in Lone Rock, serves breakfast, lunch, and dinner in a tavern setting—the burgers come recommended—and also rents canoes. Lone Rock is a nice place to put into the river. The town took its name

If this is Gotham, then there must be a Bat Cave.

from a large piece of sandstone in the water that river travelers used as a landmark. Much of it was eventually cut and worked into foundations in town.

Continue east on WI 60 until you reach WI 23. Head south (right) on WI 23 into **Spring Green** and go west (right) on Jefferson Street to get to downtown. You will pass two eye-catching buildings on your right. One is a local bank, the other is the visitor center where you can get brochures regarding the area. The curving walls of both structures were built with local stone.

The village was settled by Welsh, English, Norwegian, and German immigrants who came generally to farm. But by the end of the twentieth century a sizeable community of artists and craftspeople had appeared. Perhaps it is the same spirit that drew Frank Lloyd Wright to this area.

Whatever the reason, you can now find an assortment of studios and galleries around town. The last full weekend of June the town hosts the **Spring Green Arts and Crafts Fair** with over 200 exhibiting artists and artisans from around the Midwest.

Jura Silverman Gallery showcases Wisconsin artists working in a wide range of media. Housed in a restored cheese warehouse, the 3,000-square-foot gallery exhibits over fifty artists. Colleen Ott operates Gallery Art on 23 were you can see her work with hand-blown glass. Call for a tour and you may get a demonstration. Take a nice drive into the country to visit **Wilson Creek Pottery** located in a former cheese factory just north of town. Potter Peggy Ahlgren creates functional stoneware.

Spring Green's downtown area has that classic yesteryear look to it. An old bank has been converted into a fine dining restaurant appropriately named **The Bank Restaurant and Wine Bar**. The wine list numbers over 200, and the high-end menu places an emphasis on local products. Don't forget that **Riverside Terrace** at the Frank Lloyd Wright Visitor Center back across the river on WI 23 has classy breakfast and lunch fare but also serves fancier dinners.

The Shed, which is north on Lexington, is more of a bar and grill environment for lunch and dinner. It offers house-made pizzas, burgers, and other standard bar fare, but also sit-down meals. In summer watch for "local night," a weekly gathering with live entertainment in the park out back and special meals emphasizing local food and beer. **The General Store** back out on WI 23, if you go south from Jefferson Street, is a small natural/organic market that also serves light meals and good coffee. This is a good place to gather items for a picnic especially if you plan to attend a play in the evening.

There is only one place to have lunch right on the river and that's **Wisconsin Riverside Resort** (formerly, but often still referred to by locals as, **Bob's Riverside**). In addition to some campsites, cabin rentals, and canoeing, kayaking, and tubing, the property has a bar and grill that serves arguably the best hamburger in the area.

A great place to bed down for the night is **Hill Street Bed and Breakfast**, a 1904 Queen Anne Victorian home adorned with beautifully carved antique woodwork, located just a short walk from downtown. Two upstairs rooms share a bath; the rest have private baths. The breakfast is delicious. The **Usonian Inn** gives a nod to Wright's idea for affordable and harmonious design for the middle-class American or U.S.-onian (you-SO-nian). It is a basic but nice motel along WI 60.

As stated earlier, Spring Green can be a midpoint on a weekend trip or a place to stop for the night as you return east along the loop. The drive along the river is lovely, especially in fall, but to really appreciate the beauty that so inspired Frank Lloyd Wright, give yourself plenty of time to linger.

IN THE AREA

Accommodations

Hill Street Bed and Breakfast, 353 West Hill Street, Spring Green. Call 608-588-7751. Kelly and Jay Phelps, and their family of cats host guests in their 1904 Queen Anne Victorian home. Five of the seven rooms have private baths, and Wi-Fi Internet is available. Web site: www.hillstreet bb.com.

The House on the Rock Resort, 400 Springs Drive, Spring Green. Call 1-800-822-7774. Not far from the attraction from which it takes its name, the hotel offers rooms overlooking the Robert Trent Jones, Sr.–designed eighteen-hole golf course. Web site: www.thehouseonthe rock.com.

The Life O'Riley Farm and Guesthouses, 15706 Riley Road, Boscobel. Call 608-375-5798. You'll find kitchens fully stocked with food produced right on the property. The converted turn-of-the-century schoolhouse is best for families or groups, while the rebuilt granary offers a better bet for couples. Two rooms in the farmhouse are also available. Rates go down the longer you stay. Web site: www.lifeorileyfarm.com.

Llaughing Llama Farm and Country Cabins, 15859 Dry Hollow Road, Boscobel. Call 608-375-5798. Four modernized cabins all include whirlpools, full kitchens, and fireplaces. Go about 3 miles south of town on US 61 and go left (east) on Dry Hollow Road. Web site: www .llaughingllama.com.

Tower Hill State Park, 5808 County Road C, Spring Green. Call 608-588-2116. Hike to an old lead-shot tower for a bit of history and an impressive view of the river valley. Camping is available on a first-come, first-serve basis. Web site: www.dnr.state.wi.us.

The Usonian Inn, E 5116 Highway 14, Spring Green. Call 608-588-2323. A nice roadside motel, its design and name are inspired by Frank Lloyd Wright. Web site: www.usonianinn.com.

Walking Iron Bed and Breakfast, 21 State Street, Mazomanie. Call 1-877-572-9877. Spend the night in one of four guest rooms in an 1865 brick Victorian Italianate home. Rooms come with iron beds, private baths, and whirlpools. Web site: www.walkingiron.com.

Attractions/Recreation

American Players Theatre, 5950 Golf Course Road, Spring Green. Call 608-588-2361. See professionally produced Shakespearean or other classic plays at an outdoor theater under the stars. Book in advance. Web site: www.playinthewoods.org.

Arena Cheese, 300 US 14, Arena. Call 608-753-2501. Pick up some fresh cheese for the road or as a gift, and see cheese being made through a viewing window. Web site: www.arenacheese.com.

Boscobel Heritage Museum, Open 10–3 Mon., Tues., Fri. On weekends call for an appointment. Donations welcome. Stop in at this restored railroad depot for tourism information and a look at some exhibits of yesteryear.

Carriage House, 1509 Elm Street, Boscobel. Call 608-375-5005. This gift shop displays the arts and crafts of over ninety area artists and artisans.

Eagle Cave Resort, 16320 Cavern Lane, Blue River. Call 608-537-2988. Fee. Explore Wisconsin's first commercial onyx cavern. Camping and canoe rentals are also on site. Web site: www.eaglecave.net.

Gallery Art on 23, 355 South Winsted Street (Highway 23), Spring Green. Call 608-588-7718. Open daily 11–5, May–Dec., weekends and by appointment Jan.–Apr. Check out hand-blown glass art. You might be able to make an appointment to see a demonstration. Web site: www.galleryarton23.com.

Global View, 6593 Clyde Road, Spring Green. Call 608-583-5311. Shop for some truly impressive Far Eastern treasures in this barn-cum-gallery. Web site: www.globalviewintl.com.

Halle's Vintage Shoppe, 15 Brodhead Street, Mazomanie. Call 608-795-0150. The shop sells retro clothing and decorations. Web site: www.old feedmill.com.

Hembrough Gallery, 33 Brodhead Street, Mazomanie. Call 608-575-7750. See and purchase the captivating abstract photography of Doris Hembrough. Web site: www.hembroughgallery.com.

The House on the Rock, 5754 WI 23, Spring Green. Call 1-800-334-5275. Fee. Explore the unusual house and its infinity room, and the labyrinth of odd, yet strangely compelling collections. Hours are erratic from season to season. Call first. Web site: www.thehouseon therock.com.

Jura Silverman Gallery, 143 South Washington Street, Spring Green. Call 608-588-7049. Check out over fifty artists in this 3,000-square-foot gallery housed in an old cheese warehouse. Web site: www.springgreen .com/jsgallery.

Mazomanie Historical Society Museum, 118 Brodhead Street, Mazomanie. Call 608-795-2992. Open Memorial Day–Labor Day on Wed. and Sun. afternoons or by appointment.

Meister Cheese, 1160 Industrial Drive, Muscoda. Call 608-739-3134. Stop in and see cheese being made and shop for various specialty cheeses. Web site: www.meistercheese.com.

Peck's Farm Market East, 6445 US 14, Spring Green. Call 608-588-7177. Open daily Apr.–Dec. Find a variety of fresh produce, Amish candy, specialty goods, country gifts, and more. Come see a corn maze in the fall and a petting zoo. Web site: www.pecksfarmmarketeast.com.

Taliesin—Frank Lloyd Wright Visitor Center, 5607 County Road C, Spring Green. Call 1-877-588-7900. Fee. Open May–Oct. Tour the fascinating estate of the famous architect Frank Lloyd Wright. Advanced reservations are strongly recommended. Web site: www.taliesin preservation.org.

Walter's General Store, 34 Brodhead Street, Mazomanie. Call 608-795-4455. A former hotel and saloon now offering a wide variety of Wisconsin-produced specialty goods. Web site: www.waltersgeneral store.com.

Wilson Creek Pottery, E6101 County Road WC, Spring Green. Call 608-588-2195. This gallery, set in an old cheese factory, showcases functional stoneware. Open "most days" so call before you make the trip. Web site: www.wilsoncreekpottery.com.

Wisconsin River Outings, 715 Wisconsin Avenue, Boscobel. Call 1-866-412-2663. Rent canoes or kayaks or join guided tours or camping trips up to four days in length. Web site: www.86641canoe.com.

Dining/Drinks

The Bank Restaurant & Wine Bar, 134 West Jefferson Street, Spring Green. Call 608-588-7600. Open Tues.–Sun. for lunch and dinner. Inside a restored 1915 bank building, the restaurant offers fine dining and a wine list with over 200 selections. Web site: www.the bankrestaurantandwinebar.com.

The Bat Cave, 28789 WI 60, Gotham. Call 608-583-5208. Open daily 11 to close. Have a drink or a snack at a rural tavern dedicated to the Dark Knight and Dale Earnhardt.

Central House, 1005 Wisconsin Avenue, Boscobel. Call 608-375-4714. Have a drink at a clover-leaf shaped bar. Upstairs in the no defunct hotel is a room restored as the 1898 birthplace of the Gideon Bible. Fine dining on Thurs.–Sat.

Gordon's Drive-In Restaurant, 122 West Commercial Street, Mazomanie. Call 608-795-2330.

The Old Feed Mill, 114 Cramer Street, Mazomanie. Call 608-795-4909. Open seven days a week for lunch and dinner, this restaurant set in an old millhouse serves soups and salads, sandwiches, and reasonably priced dinners. Web site: www.oldfeedmill.com.

The Shed, 123 North Lexington Street, Spring Green. Call 608-588-9049. This bar and grill offers pizza, burgers, and sit-down dinners. Local beers are on tap. In summer watch for "Local Night," a gathering out back for a special local food meal and live entertainment. Web site: www.shed springgreen.com.

Unique Café, Boscobel. Open at 6:30 for breakfast and lunch. Open for dinner on Fri. Closed Mon. and Tues. This counter and booth diner serves great food, and the owner/chef has an impressive collection of antique signs and other interesting odds and ends set about the place.

Vale Inn, 813 Wisconsin Avenue, Boscobel. Call 608-375-4456. This tavern/café has a varied menu, including Mexican and some vegetarian options.

Vicki's Cozy Café, 132 Iowa Street, Muscoda. Call 608-739-9004. Grab breakfast or a sandwich at this simple eatery located behind Pierce's IGA.

Waz Inn, 234 South Oak Street, Lone Rock. Call 608-583-2086. This is a great tavern setting for some good simple bar food, plus a popular local Friday fish fry. They also rent canoes and help you get to and from the river.

Whistle Stop Café, 18 Brodhead Street, Mazomanie. Call 608 795-2414. Stop in here for breakfast or lunch, or just some ice cream or coffee. Web site: www.oldfeedmill.com.

Wisconsin Riverside Resort, S13220 Shifflet Road, Spring Green. Call 608-588-2826. The only bar and grill on the river, it serves the best burgers around. But the resort offers much more including camping, canoeing, kayaking, tubing, and cabin rentals. Web site: www.wi riverside.com.

Other

Boscobel Chamber of Commerce, 800 Wisconsin Avenue, Boscobel. Call 608-375-2672. Web site: www.boscobelwisconsin.com.

Greater Mazomanie Area Chamber of Commerce. Call 608-795-9824. Web site: www.mazomaniechamber.com

Spring Green Chamber of Commerce, 259 East Jefferson Street, Spring Green. Call 608-588-2054. Web site: www.springgreen.com.

The drive south from La Crosse is characterized by majestic bluffs overlooking the Mississippi.

CHAPTER

5

The Great River Road

Estimated length: 60 miles
Estimated time: 1.5 hours minimum

Getting There: Take I-90/I-94 to La Crosse and start south on WI 35.

Highlights: Tour the Mississippi River by riverboat; visit historic mansions from the days of lumber; have a look at the world's largest six-pack at one of the oldest breweries in the state; spot wildlife along the Mississippi River National Wildlife Refuge. This is also good route for fall colors and spotting bald eagles.

At 2,340 miles, the Mississippi is mighty indeed. The Native Americans thought the same and gave it the name Great River or *Misi-ziibi* in Ojibwe. It forms part of the border between Wisconsin and Minnesota, and the highways that run along its muddy length have been designated a national scenic byway. Wisconsin's portion of the Great River Road offers views of towering bluffs within the Driftless Area, the lands untouched by the last advances of glacial ice.

History has long set up camp beside its banks, from the native Oneota and Sioux to the pioneers and the lumber industry. The river as a mode of transportation gave rise to communities and industry. For nature lovers, the river is also a birder's delight: more than 325 species have been

identified here, and a third of all North American species use the river valley during spring and fall migration. One frequent resident that excites even
non-birders is the bald eagle.

La Crosse and Prairie du Chien offer tourist delights throughout the
year, but many of the tourist-oriented businesses in the smaller communities in between either cut back on hours or shut down completely during winter. Be sure to call ahead of time.

This route begins in **La Crosse**. In 1805 Zebulon Pike set out on a
mission to discover the source of the Mississippi River. His travels took
him to the sandy alluvial plain where the Black, La Crosse, and Mississippi
Rivers all came together. From the top of a bluff, he admired the beauty
of the land dramatically carved by erosion after the melting of the last
glaciers. This was the Prairie of La Crosse, a name given to the area when
the explorers witnessed the Sioux playing a game with a ball and long
sticks with netted scoops at the end of them. These implements reminded
the Europeans of crosses, and the name stuck for both the sport and the
site itself.

In 1841 Nathan Myrick, a New Yorker, traveled up the river to build a
trading post in La Crosse and become the first settler. He traded with the
Ho-Chunk, but it wasn't until more than a decade later that the great pine
forests of northern Wisconsin created a lumbering rush, and La Crosse suddenly became a boomtown. In the 1870s there were thirty-three sawmills
along the Mississippi and Black rivers, and the waterways were used to
float lumber on to its next destination.

Today, La Crosse is a pleasant university community and still one of
the best places to experience the Mississippi. You can book a ride on its
back aboard the **La Crosse Queen**, a replica of a nineteenth-century pad-
dlewheel boat. Ninety-minute to three-hour tours show the highlights of
the river valley, or you can join brunch or dinner cruises as well. Head
down to the west end of State Street in downtown La Crosse to find the
dock at the north end of Riverside Park. Here you will also find the
Riverside Museum, which features artifacts brought up from the 1870
wreck of the steamboat War Eagle, as well as exhibits about the history of
the three rivers and many finds from native cultures from the Mississippi
Valley Archaeological Center.

For a more eco-friendly sail, climb aboard one of the smaller
Mississippi Explorers for pontoon boat cruises to hard-to-reach places
that often include naturalists or local musicians. These cruises depart from

Best Western Midway Hotel at 1835 Rose Street. They can also be found in Prairie du Chien at the other end of this road trip.

To get an idea just how much wealth came out of the lumber business, visit the **Hixon House**, the former home of lumber baron Gideon Hixon. The woodwork in this Italianate house is exquisite, and most of the original furnishings have been preserved. The tour takes about forty-five minutes, and you should purchase your tickets in the yellow building behind the mansion itself. The **Swarthout Museum** brings to life the history of La Crosse County and has some hands-on displays for children.

You can also eat in an historical setting. Housed in an historic red-brick railroad building from the 1880s, **Freight House Restaurant** enjoys national recognition for its naturally aged, hand-cut steaks and succulent seafood. Its wine list received a Wine Spectator Award of Excellence, and the selection of cognacs and single-malt scotches will impress any connoisseur. On the weekends you can enjoy live entertainment. If barbeque is more your style, head over to **Piggy's Restaurant,** set in a restored 1871 foundry building. Hickory and apple wood put the smoke into the town's most popular baby back ribs and duck breasts. Other items include fresh seafood and homemade soups.

For some fancy fare, and the prices to go with it, consider **The Waterfront Restaurant and Tavern**. The food is as good as the view. You can dine outdoors in the warmer seasons. The menu is contemporary American and includes a very nice list of seafood for both lunch and dinner. Not far from there is **Three Rivers Lodge Restaurant**, which also looks out over the water, serves all meals, and emphasizes a menu based on local products.

There is a wide range of chain hotels as well as a number of bed and breakfasts for a more personal stay in La Crosse. One recommended property downtown, **Bentley-Wheeler Bed and Breakfast**, consists of two wonderfully restored historic houses. Another fine choice has more of a rural appeal. **Four Gables Bed and Breakfast** is just south of the city and east of WI 35 on US 14/61. More options are easy to find by contacting the La Crosse Convention and Visitors Bureau.

A TRI-STATE VIEW

The 600-foot **Grandad Bluff** is considered one of the best views in the state. Along with the city of La Crosse you can take in views of Minnesota and Iowa as well. Pack a picnic or have a look through some coin-op binoculars. Head east on Main Street, and it will turn to Bliss Road to take you up the bluff. Then turn right on Grandad Bluff Road.

OKTOBERFEST

Think of this as Germany on the Mississippi. This fall celebration—considered one of the top ten Oktoberfests in the world—actually begins in late September when the city rolls out the barrels of beer and hosts parades, carnival rides, boat rides, and authentic German food and entertainment. Pack your lederhosen for this is all-ages event located in the Southside Fest Grounds at Second Street North and La Crosse Street. Northside Fest Grounds are located in Copeland Park. There's a map on the Web site and brochure.

Gottlieb Heileman began brewing beer at **City Brewery** in 1858. The company soon adopted his name, **G. Heileman Brewing**, and until its closing in 1996, produced a variety of beers, the most famous being Old Style and Special Export. The brewery once rivaled Miller and Anheuser-Busch, and the roadside storage tanks were painted to be the **World's Largest Six-Pack.** Today, independent brewers own and operate the brewery and have taken up its original moniker, City Brewery. The six-pack remains with the labels of the new brewery's flagship beer La Crosse Lager. You will pass this in town on your way south along WI 35. Call for tour information. If a microbrew is more your style, stick around in town and head over to **Pearl Street Brewery.** They have a tasting room.

La Crosse is the home of the world's largest six-pack.

As you head south along the river, south of La Crosse, watch for **Goose Island Park** on the right. Campers will find plenty of sites here, and day-trippers can hike or rent canoes and boats within the park. Hiking trails get you closer to the natural beauty of the river valley and will likely offer views of wildlife, especially birds.

As you continue south along WI 35, passing through the village of Stoddard, watch for a scenic overlook just before the power plant. A steep road leads left up to the top of the bluffs.

It may not be a surprise that **Genoa** was settled by Italians. In 1848 workers from the lead mines in Galena, Illinois moved up the river to settle here. Though joined by English and Germans as well, the town kept an Italian character. Fishing became the prime industry.

There's not a lot to see here, but if roadside attractions interest you, stop at **Old Tool Shed Antiques** on Main Street, which is some kind of cross between a store and a museum. If you are interested in a wine side trip, **Vernon Vineyards** is 20 miles east of Genoa (about a thirty-minute drive) down several country lanes near Viroqua. The winery hosts free wine tours and tastings Friday through Sunday.

About a quarter mile south of Genoa you will see **Lock and Dam #8**. The dam extends to the Minnesota shore and the locks allow over 2,000 river craft through each year. You can have a look from a viewing platform to see the locks in action from sunrise to sunset. An historical marker just south of here recalls the warrior **Red Bird** and thirty-seven Ho-Chunk (Winnebago) warriors attacking a boat that had run up on a sandbar—a scene from the Winnebago War of 1827.

A LONGER RIDE ALONG THE RIVER

If you want to extend this trip, start from Prescott, another 140 miles north of La Crosse. If you continue south past Prairie du Chien another 30 miles you will connect into the route of the mining towns in chapter two.

THE UPPER MISSISSIPPI RIVER NATIONAL WILDLIFE REFUGE

Beginning near Wabasha, Minnesota, and stretching 261 miles to Rock Island, Illinois, this refuge is the longest river refuge in the continental United States. Until a series of locks and dams were constructed in the 1930s by the U.S. Army Corps of Engineers, the free flowing river was not always cooperative for navigation. Wing dams sticking straight into the river attempted to increase the flow down a narrower channel.

Today, the refuge is made up of almost 240,000 acres of islands, marshes, and backwaters. This protected area draws a wide variety of migratory birds each year.

Before the locks, the river claimed a lot of boats with its many sandbars.

WINNEBAGO WAR

Much of the nineteenth century saw various land treaties being signed between the U.S. government and Native Americans, treaties which essentially kept moving the natives farther and farther from their ancestral lands. Tensions between settlers and native tribes, and even among the varied tribes themselves, sometimes erupted in violence. Six members of the Ho-Chunk (Winnebago) tribe were arrested for alleged murder and were imprisoned at Fort Crawford in Prairie du Chien. Four were released, and when federal troops abandoned the fort on orders to relocate, the remaining two were taken along. Rumors spread that the two had been executed.

In retaliation the Ho-Chunk attacked settlers in Prairie du Chien. Days later the Ho-Chunk attacked a passing boat, believing it was the same crew that had abducted and raped several native women. Troops were moved to the area and bloodshed escalated until the Ho-Chunk, believing the federal troops and local militia would destroy their people surrendered Red Bird and five other warriors. This "Winnebago War" was a precursor to the Black Hawk War just five years later.

Great River Resort, just 4 miles south of Genoa, offers simple cabins or an entire house for larger groups. All come with kitchens and modest furnishings. Across the road is the **Genoa National Fish Hatchery** where you can take a self-guided tour of seventeen open-air ponds and six raceways. The hatchery raises twenty-three different species of fish including trout, sturgeon, and northern pike, and also some endangered mussels species. The Bad Axe River meets the Mississippi here, and birdwatchers may have good luck in this area. which is highly regarded by the Audubon Society.

The next village on the road is **Victory** where you can get your fix of English pub fare at **Red Lion Pub and Eatery**. Along with an import-leaning list of over forty beers, you'll find bangers and mash and the expected fish and chips complete with malt vinegar.

Just 1 mile south of Victory is **Black Hawk Recreation Area** with riverside camping, picnic areas, a fishing dock, a sandy beach, and boat launching facilities. Inside the park is **P&M Concessions** selling bait and renting boats and canoes if you want to explore the river. If you are passing through on Friday evening, the **Great River Roadhouse**, just north of De Soto, has a popular Friday-night fish fry. The Chicago-style pizza gets raves and surely will satisfy the heartiest appetite. Stop at **Lisa's This-N-That** toward fall when you can expect pumpkins, preserves, cornstalks, cider, apples, and much more.

Just south of De Soto is Rush Creek Road, an unpaved gravel road to **Rush Creek State Natural Area**. Though not officially a rustic road, this should be. The lane winds into bluffs off the highway eventually passing

THE BLACK HAWK WAR OF 1832

The Sauk warrior **Black Hawk** tried to flee with his people from pursuing federal troops and militia at the end of the war that was given his name. On August 1, 1832, the surviving Sauk finally reached the Mississippi near the mouth of the Bad Axe River where they were caught between troops on the bluffs and a gunboat on the water. Though a white flag of truce was offered by Black Hawk, the so-called **Battle of Bad Axe** ensued as troops and militia indiscriminately massacred hundreds of men, women, and children. Swimmers either drowned or were shot in the water as they attempted to retreat. Only about seventy made it across to be killed by Sioux warriors, the longtime enemies of the Sauk and now allies of the troops. Some managed to find refuge in local Ho-Chunk camps. Black Hawk fled to Fort Crawford to surrender and put an end to the bloodshed. Of his original 1,200 followers only about 150 survived.

SIDETRIP:
APPLE CAPITAL OF WISCONSIN

Gays Mills is just to the east of this route along the banks of a smaller Kickapoo River. The valley is perfectly suited for apples and at least seven orchards are open. Apples start to come in at about mid-August, and the Gays Mills Apple Festival is the last full weekend of September. Take WI 171 east for 13 miles from its juncture with WI 35 less than 3 miles south of Ferryville.

through farmland. Anyone interested in quilting might stop by **Olde Tyme Quilt Shoppe** just up the road from here.

Back on WI 35, Ferryville is the next riverside village. The mini-mart/gas station on the right is also home to **Ferryville Cheese** that has over a hundred varieties of primarily Wisconsin cheeses to choose from. You can also get sandwiches from the deli if you want to take a picnic down the road. Housed in an old bank is **Kay's Potiques**, the gallery of a local stoneware/porcelain artist. The artist sometimes gets kids involved with a little hands-on fun. Places to stay are few along the river, and are mostly of the cabin variety or campgrounds. In Ferryville you might consider **Grandview Motel** that offers clean rooms and a view out toward the river.

Amish crafts are for sale at the roadside market in Ferryville.

Dr. William Beaumont was an army surgeon who during his illustrious career spent five years, beginning in 1828, at Fort Crawford fighting malaria. He became known as the Father of Gastric Physiology thanks to his studies of a peculiar wound on one of his patients. While stationed on Mackinac Island, Michigan, Beaumont treated Alexis St. Martin for a gunshot wound that punctured his stomach. St. Martin survived, much to Beaumont's surprise, but a hole remained open in his stomach. Through this opening Beaumont was able to study the workings of digestion and even conduct experiments by inserting pieces of food and extracting them for observation. St. Martin accompanied Beaumont on several of his postings and ended up outliving the good doctor.

Sugar Creek Park at the southern edge of town hosts a 9–5 **Saturday market** from the second weekend in May to the last weekend in October. Items range from garden plants and flea market items to homemade preserves and crafts. **Amish vendors** bring crafts and baked goods as well.

As you continue south on WI 35, you will pass **Lock and Dam #9** at just under halfway to Prairie du Chien. This is one of twenty-nine such locks between Minneapolis and Cairo, Illinois. The lock chambers are 110-feet wide and 600-feet long.

As you come into **Prairie du Chien** heading south you will see the Cannery on your left. Built in 1912 to can the abundance of local produce, this home of Prairie du Chien City Canning Company specialized in tomatoes and sauerkraut. Today it houses **The Cannery Antiques and Gifts**. Besides a two-floor collection of country art, themed home décor, bath products, and candles, The Cannery also offers a wonderful variety of edibles to satisfy your sweet tooth. You can watch taffy being made, and the handmade fudge is varied and sinful. Jams and jellies, candies, sauces, and ice cream are on offer, and the soup isn't bad either if you're avoiding a sugar rush.

Marquette and Joliet were the first French explorers to see the Mississippi River after traveling down the Wisconsin River. Soon after, the fur trade came to the area. Near where the Wisconsin and Mississippi Rivers meet was a village of the Fox tribe lead by a chief named Alim or the Big Prairie Dog. The French fur traders took to referring to the village as La Prairie du Chien (prairie of the dog).

Gradually the British took over the trade, and soon after, the U.S. government built Fort Shelby here. The Americans and Brits battled for the

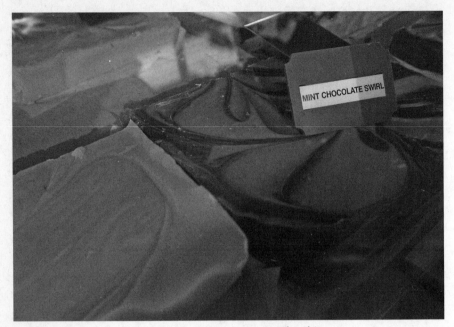

At the end of the byway, fudge awaits in Prairie du Chien.

THE DOUSMANS AND VILLA LOUIS

Hercules Dousman made his fortune in a variety of businesses from fur trading to land speculation. He built his home in Georgian-style in the 1840s on an estate right on the river. After his death his son Louis took it down and built a more modern home, an Italianate mansion of Cream City brick in 1870. As it grew and changed it became known as **Villa Louis** or the House on the Mound, as it was believed to have been built on a prehistoric effigy mound. The house is now open for tours and is managed by the Wisconsin Historical Society.

area during the War of 1812, and the fort was burned to the ground. The first Fort Crawford, its replacement, was built where Villa Louis is today until it was destroyed by flood damage. A second fort of the same name was erected where Wyalusing Academy is now. The fort is remembered along with a lot of local history at the **Fort Crawford Museum**. An exhibit is dedicated to Dr. William Beaumont.

The railroad brought prosperity to Prairie du Chien in 1857 but shifted the success of the town when the depot moved out to **St. Feriole Island**, a 240-acre isle in the Mississippi. Cross onto it via Blackhawk Avenue or Washington Street. Today the island is mostly park land and host to a wide variety of birds, resident and migratory. You will find **Villa Louis** here as well as the **Mississippi River Sculpture Park**. Over two dozen bronze statues representing over 12,000 years of history are planned for the park. The first three are completed, and more will be added each year.

If you want to get away from shore, rent a canoe, paddleboat, pontoon, or boat at **Willy & Nellie's Place** on St. Feriole Island or stay for a round of mini-golf. Another great option for some time

The **Prairie Rendezvous** is an annual **festival** generally held the second week in June. A special camp of tents and teepees is set up on St. Feroile Island near Villa Louis, and the calendar is turned back to the 1840s. Visitors participate in a variety of activities from the days of fur trading, and a flea market is on hand.

on the river is the Mississippi Explorer. These pontoon boats offer great river tours, often with on-board live folk, blues, and bluegrass. Tours depart in the early evening.

Once August rolls around, the apples start to come out. Head up to **Shihata's Orchard and Apple House** in the bluffs above Prairie du Chien. You'll find cider, nineteen varieties of apples, and a wide assortment of

The railroad still runs along the river; the advent of the rails put an end to the era of riverboats.

KICKAPOO INDIAN CAVERNS

Around 450 million years ago during the Ordovician Period, Wisconsin was covered by a warm sea. It was also located south of the equator! The result is an abundance of sedimentary rock, including limestone. The **Kickapoo Indian Caverns** were formed by the sea and later an ancient river. Over the millennia, water exposed fossils and mineral deposits, and rainwater percolating down into the chambers created stalactites and stalagmites. Native Americans once occupied these caverns, and part of the collection of the small museum adjacent to the caverns shows some of the artifacts drawn from within. Go left (north) on Dutch Ridge Road just before Wauzeka if you're heading east on WI 60.

local products (including wines and preserves) at the Apple House. The first weekend of October is the family-style **Orchard Festival**.

The river in the Prairie du Chien area is perfect for **spotting bald eagles** in any season, and a large population of them actually winter here. **Bald Eagle Appreciation Day** is typically in February and celebrated at the Wisconsin Welcome Center/Prairie du Chien Chamber at 211 South Main Street, Prairie du Chien. The event includes viewings, children's activities, presentations by birding experts, live bald eagle programs put on in conjunction with the National Eagle Center in Wabasha, Minnesota, and much more. Call the Prairie du Chien Chamber of Commerce/Tourism Council at 1-800-732-1673.

If you are looking for a bed and breakfast, you have two options right in town. One is **Neumann House**, a Civil War-era home and **Victorian Rose Bed and Breakfast**, the former residence of a nineteenth-century banker.

For the area's best supper club experience, head over to **Kaber's Restaurant.** With over eighty years of experience, Kaber's is your best bet for steak, seafood, and an impressive salad bar. Another great establishment is **Spring Lake Restaurant,** which serves local Angus beef and a general menu in a bar/restaurant setting. On an even more casual note, try **Pete's Hamburgers.** This local legend started as a pushcart in 1909, and over the years, evolved into a burger mecca. It is only open Friday through Sunday and in season.

Wyalusing State Park marks the end of this road trip. The park, which sits at the confluence of the Wisconsin and Mississippi Rivers, offers camping and some excellent wildlife viewing, including over a hundred species of birds. A state park fee applies.

IN THE AREA

Accommodations

Bentley-Wheeler Bed and Breakfast, 938 and 950 Cass Street, La Crosse. Call 608-784-9360. This property actually consists of two restored historic homes within walking distance of the historic downtown. Web site: www.bentley-wheeler.com.

Four Gables Bed and Breakfast, W5648 US 14/61, La Crosse. Call 608-788-7958. Lodgings consist of three rooms in the upstairs of a restored 1906 brick Queen Anne home. Located a quarter mile east of WI 35 on US 14/61 just south of La Crosse.

Goose Island Park, W6488 County Road GI, Stoddard. Call 608-788-7018. This park offers more than 400 camp sites plus boat and canoe rentals. Find it 3 miles south of La Crosse off WI 35. Camping season runs from Apr. to Nov. Reservations are accepted. Web site: www.co.la-crosse.wi.us.

Grandview Motel, 14812 WI 35, Ferryville. Call 608-734-3235. This is a pull-up-to-your-door property with nine rooms decorated with varnished wood and looking out across the parking lot toward the river. Some offer kitchenettes. Web site: www.grandview-motel.com.

Neumann House Bed and Breakfast, 121 North Michigan Street, Prairie du Chien. Call 608-326-8104. This well preserved Civil War-era house puts you within walking distance of downtown attractions. Guests with cat allergies might look elsewhere. Web site: www.prairie-du-chien.com.

Victorian Rose Bed and Breakfast, 225 South Wacouta Street, Prairie du Chien. Call 608-326-2065. Three upstairs bedrooms share a bathroom in this late nineteenth-century home right in historic downtown. Web site: www.victorianrosebedandbreakfast.com.

Wyalusing State Park, 13081 State Park Lane, Bagley. Call 608-996-2261. Fee. Spend a few hours or camp overnight where the Mississippi and Wisconsin River Valleys meet. Hike hardwood forests and spy up to a hundred different species of migrating birds. Turn west on CR C just south of the Wisconsin River bridge. Then turn right on CR X. Web site: dnr.wi.gov/org/land/parks/specific/wyalusing.

Attractions and Recreation

Black Hawk Recreation Area, E590 County Road BI, De Soto. Call 608-648-3314. Just 1 mile south of Victory is Black Hawk Recreation Area with riverside camping, picnic areas, a fishing dock, a sandy beach, and boat launching facilities. The park is open year-round. Also located in the park is P&M Concessions, which offers bait and boat rental, as well as cold drinks, snacks, and various camping supplies. You can reach them at 608-648-3488.

The Cannery, 300 North Marquette Road, Prairie du Chien. Call 608-326-6518. Open seven days a week, this is a gift shopping distraction including country arts and collectibles as well as bath products and candles. They have taffy, made right in front of you, and the handmade fudge is a guilty pleasure. Web site: www.thecannerygifts.com.

City Brewery, 1111 Third Street South, La Crosse. Call 608-785-4283. Check out the world's largest six-pack and take a brewery tour. Web site: www.citybrewery.com.

Ferryville Cheese and More. Call 608-734-3121. Open daily, year round. This mini-mart/gas station offers a deli and an impressive selection of Wisconsin cheeses. Web site: www.ferryville.com.

Fort Crawford Museum, 717 South Beaumont Road, Prairie du Chien. Call 608-326-6960. Open May–Oct., 9–4 pm. Fee. The collection housed in three buildings recalls the historic fort as well as the area's history. Cannons and Redcoats is a reenactment of life here during the War of 1812 and is held in mid-Sept. Web site: www.fortcrawfordmuseum.com.

Gays Mills Apple Festival. Call 608-735-4341. The fest includes an arts and crafts fair, food, music, and a parade. Web site: www.gaysmills.org.

Genoa National Fish Hatchery, S5689 WI 35, Genoa. Call 608-689-2605. Mon.–Fri. 8–3:30. Stop in and learn about how the hatchery is protecting endangered species and stocking lakes and rivers. Special events are hosted in the summer. Web site: www.fws.gov/midwest/genoa.

Hixon House, 429 North Seventh Street, La Crosse. Call 608-782-1980. Fee. Open daily from Memorial Day to Labor Day and limited hours into Nov. See how the lumber barons lived in this well-preserved mansion. Expect the tour to last at least forty-five minutes. Purchase your tickets in the small yellow outbuilding in back. Web site: www .lchsweb.org.

Kay's Potiques, 150 Main Street, Ferryville. Call 608-734-3423. Open weekends, 12–6, from May–Oct. Check out the gallery of hand-thrown pottery by local artist Kay Campbell. Web site: www.kpotiques.com.

Kickapoo Indian Caverns and Native American Museum, 54850 Rhein Hollow Road, Wauzeka. Call 608-875-7723. Fee. Open from Memorial Day Weekend through Oct. 31, but closed Tues. and Wed. and only open on weekends after Labor Day. Go 15 miles east of Prairie du Chien on Highway 60. The caverns offer three one-hour tours a day, with a two-person minimum. No credit cards. You must make a reservation for a tour. Web site: www.kickapooindiancaverns.com.

La Crosse Oktoberfest, 1 Oktoberfest Strasse, La Crosse. Call 608-784-3378. The largest fall festival in Wisconsin is also one of the top ten Oktoberfests in the world. Yes, there is beer, but the German food and entertainment, along with carnival rides, parades and boat tours make this a great family event as well. Web site: www.oktoberfest usa.com.

Lisa's This-N-That, 9903 WI 35, De Soto. Call 608-648-2778. Open seasonally until Oct. 31, the roadside shop offers fall pumpkins and cornstalks, cider, apples, and preserves.

Mississippi Explorer Cruises in La Crosse and Prairie du Chien. Call 1-877-647-7397. Get to places the larger cruises would miss on two-hour eco-tours and musical cruises. In La Crosse they depart early evenings Fri.–Sun. from the Best Western Midway Hotel & Riverfront Resort at 1835 Rose Street. In Prairie du Chien cruises typically depart on Sat. afternoon from Lawler Park on St. Feriole Island. Web site: www .mississippiexplorer.com.

Mississippi River Sculpture Park, St. Feriole Island, Prairie du Chien. See 12,000 years of history as interpreted by a series of bronze sculptures destined to number over two dozen when they all are completed. Web site: www.prairieduchiensculpturepark.com.

Old Tool Shed Antiques, 612 Main Street, Genoa. Call 608-689-2066. Open 10–5 Thurs.–Mon. This shop is a cross between an antiques vendor and a museum of farm implements.

Olde Tyme Quilt Shoppe, 62682 Rush Creek Road, Ferryville. Call 608-648-2081. Virginia Johnson has a showroom in her home quilting studio. It is best to call ahead if you're stopping.

Pearl Street Brewery, 1401 St. Andrew Street, La Crosse. Call 608-784-4832. Sample some of the handcrafted microbrews at La Crosse's other brewery. Web site: pearlstreetbrewery.com.

Riverside Museum, Veterans Memorial Drive, La Crosse. Call 608-782-1980. Fee. Open daily from Memorial Day to Labor Day. Weekends only in Sept. and Oct. See artifacts of native populations and a sunken riverboat, and learn more about how the rivers shaped the community. Web site: www.lchsweb.org.

Shihata's Apple Orchard, 61543 Limery Road, Praire du Chien. Call 608-326-2785. Open from about mid-Aug. to the last weekend in Oct. You'll find cider, nineteen varieties of apples, and a wide assortment of local products (including wines and preserves) at the Apple House. There's also a pumpkin patch. From Prairie du Chien follow WI 27 7 miles north to Limery Road. Web site: www.shihataorchard.com.

Swarthout Museum and Office, 112 South Ninth Street, La Crosse. Call 608-782-1980. Suggested donation. Closed on Mon. This collection brings to life the history of La Crosse County and has some hands-on displays for children. Web site: www.lchsweb.org.

Vernon Vineyards & Winery, S3457A Dahl Road, Viroqua. Call 608-634-6734. Free tours and tastings Fri.–Sun. From Genoa, go northeast on Main St/WI-56 to turn left on CR O. Turn right on Upper Newton Road and then Irish Ridge Road. Turn left at Cahl Lane/Dahl Road. Web site: www.vernonvineyards.com.

Villa Louis, 521 Villa Louis Road, Prairie du Chien. Call 608-326-2721. Fee. Open from May to Nov. Tour the nineteenth-century Italianate mansion of Louis Dousman out on St. Feriole Island. Web site: www.villalouis.wisconsinhistory.org.

Willy & Nellie's, 400 West Blackhawk Avenue, Prairie Du Chien. Call 608-326-8602. Rent canoes or boats to explore the river, or play a round of mini-golf.

Dining/Drinks

Freight House Restaurant, 107 Vine Street, La Crosse. Call 608-784-6211. Open daily for dinner. Set in an historical building, this is one of the city's finest steak and seafood restaurants. Web site: www.freighthouserestaurant.com.

Great River Roadhouse, 1006 Highway 35, De Soto. Call 608-648-2045. Just north of De Soto, this eatery has a popular Fri.-night fish fry and some highly reputable Chicago-style pizza.

Kaber's Restaurant, 225 West Blackhawk Avenue, Prairie du Chien. Call 608-326-6216. This supper club has been doing great steaks and seafood for over eighty years.

Pete's Hamburgers, 118 West Blackhawk Avenue, Prairie du Chien. Call 608-326-6653. Open seasonally Fri.–Sun. This local legend started as a pushcart in 1909, and over the years, evolved into a burger mecca.

Piggy's Restaurant, 501 Front Street South, La Crosse. Call 608-784-4877. Dine on some excellent smoked barbeque fare at this popular La Crosse institution. Web site: www.piggys.com.

Red Lion Pub and Eatery, S6844 Terhune Street, De Soto. Call 608-608-3100. A misplaced English pub set on the Great River, Red Lion offers bangers and mash, over forty different beers (many imports), and of course fish and chips.

Spring Lake Restaurant, 64040 County Road N, Prairie du Chien. Call 608-326-6907. Open for lunch and dinner all days but Mon., the restaurant serves steaks, seafood, chicken, and burgers in a bar/restaurant environment. Beef is acquired locally. Does not accept credit cards.

Three Rivers Lodge Restaurant, 111 Front Street South, La Crosse. Call 608-793-5018. This restaurant serves breakfast, lunch, and dinner with a scenic view of the Mississippi River. The menu emphasizes locally

sourced foods such as wild rice soup and walleye pike. Web site:
www.threeriverslodge.com.

The Waterfront Restaurant and Tavern, 328 Front Street South, La
Crosse. Call 608-782-5400. Located in an office building just south of
Riverside Park. Take in great river views along with fine-dining menus
for both lunch and dinner. Seafood and steak is the focus. Web site:
www.thewaterfrontlacrosse.com.

Other

Great River Road. Web site: www.wigreatriverroad.org.

La Crosse Convention and Visitors Bureau, 410 Veterans Memorial
Drive, La Crosse. Call 1-800-658-9424. Web site: www.explore
lacrosse.com.

Prairie du Chien Chamber of Commerce/Tourism Center, 211 South
Main Street, Prairie du Chien. Call 1-800-732-1673. Web site:
www.prairieduchien.org.

CHAPTER

6

The Kettle Moraine Scenic Drive

Estimated length: 120 miles
Estimated time: 2.5 hours minimum

Getting There: Take I-43 to WI 23 west. Then take WI 67 north to Elkhart Lake.

Highlights: Elkhart Lake, the delightful tourist town and home of **Road America**; the impressive topography of the deposits the last glaciers left behind; a trip into the past at **Old World Wisconsin**; the picturesque **church at Holy Hill**; a variety of great hiking.

What do you get when two massive glaciers collide? Kettle Moraine shows you the answer. During the most recent phase of the Ice Age, ice sheets extended far enough south to cover a goodly portion of present-day Wisconsin. So many of the land features resulting from glaciation are exhibited here that the state gave its name to the most recent period of activity. The Wisconsin Glaciation Period showed three major advances and retreats of ice from between 100,000 and 10,000 years ago. Road tripping here is like driving through one big outdoor geology classroom.

The Kettle Moraine, as the region is called, is a series of these curious glacial deposits that were formed when the Lake Michigan and Green Bay lobes of the most recent ice sheet came together. Much of this terrain is

KAMES, KETTLES, AND ESKERS

Sounds like the brothers down the road with the whiskey still out back, but these are actually features created by glaciers. The ice sheet reached depths of over 1 mile, and as it moved across the land it performed some major grinding of the land. Sand, rocks, and boulders made up glacial debris known as "drift," which was then deposited when the ice melted or "retreated" as they say. The deposits along the edge of the glacier formed hills and ridges called **moraines**. The peculiar indentations characteristic of this region of the state are known as **kettle moraines**; large masses of ice were trapped within the moraines, and when that ice melted, a depression was formed in the middle of the hill.

But there were other formations as well. Streams flowing down through cracks in the glacier carried debris with them, which was then deposited at the bottom in conical shapes called **kames**. In other cases streams flowed through tunnels at the base of the glacier, and the sand and gravel they deposited formed long ridges or **eskers**. **Drumlins** on the other hand, are not formed by deposits. Rather they are elongated hills, shaped something like a half of an egg, with the axis of the hill laid out along the direction of the glacier that formed it as it pushed over the land.

---

protected within the Kettle Moraine State Forest, which has Northern and Southern Units; the backbone for this byway is the Kettle Moraine Scenic Drive, which follows its length. In nearly all places the drive is clearly marked with green signs and arrows, so you won't necessarily have to be carefully measuring distances between the frequent turns. For a condensed chart of the mileage, pick up a brochure or go to the state forest's Web site for a printable file. Since this is a state forest, most of the parks and trails require a vehicle sticker, which can be found at self-pay stations or any park office. A single-day sticker is good on the day of purchase for all sections of the park from Elkhart Lake to Whitewater.

The drive begins in a lovely town that may make you want to linger an extra day. **Elkhart Lake** has a pleasant balance between small town charm and tourism development. The community has had practice; since the early part of the last century this has been a retreat for the well heeled from Chicago who once arrived by train. Part of the attraction is recreation on Elkhart Lake, the deepest lake in Wisconsin, but the town is probably most famous to racing fans.

Rhine Street is the main street that leads you from WI 67 to a central intersection bisected by railroad tracks. At the center of town you will find the **Elkhart Lake Chamber of Commerce Visitor Information** office right across from the Elkhart Lake Historical Society, which has a small free museum in the century-old train depot. The Feed Mill is a collection of shops also at this intersection; it is the former mill painted bright red. As you drive around Elkhart Lake, you will see signs for the names of certain sections of the historical road race circuits; the start and finish line is right behind the feed mill.

For eats, there are options aplenty. **Lake Street Café** has wood-fired pizzas, which are wonderful. The dinner menu goes a bit pricier and fancier with steaks, lamb, and seafood. The wine list has often won awards.

You don't have to stay at **Osthoff Lake Resort** to eat at its restaurants. This AAA Four Diamond property has two great eateries: **Lola's On the Lake,** which offers fine regional cuisine with an impressive wine list and Sunday brunch, and **Otto's,** which does all three meals with seasonal outdoor, lakeside seating. The resort is also home to an **Aspira Spa**, which might not be a bad place to start your weekend even if you aren't staying the night. There is a spa suite available.

Back Porch Bistro is another resort supper club, overlooking the lake and offering more supper club fare, steaks, and seafood. **Siebkin's Resort** has been around as a family-owned inn since 1916. Choose from new

---

ROAD AMERICA

When the local economy was going through a slump at the advent of the 1950s, Jim Johnson, a local bank president, decided the solution to their woes was the latest trend in America: road racing. The community and Governor William Kohler (who kept a summer home here) came together to bring the Chicago Region Sports Car Club of America (SCCA) in to set up a course and organize races. CR P, where this byway will pass just south of town, held the starting and finishing line. The 3.5-mile course followed CR J north, then passed through town and returned west along what is now CR JP. Several races of distances up to 60 miles were divided by car engine power, driver skill level, and even gender. The route was soon nearly doubled in length, and by 1952 attendance figures were estimated to be more than 100,000. Though the open-road racing ended that same year, 1955 saw the completion of a premier closed-circuit raceway, Road America.

Road America now sees a variety of professional events from NASCAR and American Le Mans Series to vintage car races and motorcycle races. Nine major weekends are open to the public from May to October.

Smile: you're in Eagle, Wisconsin.

condos or historic, Victorian-decorated rooms. The resort's Stop Inn Tavern is familiar to the international racing crowd, and the ice cream shop offers Wisconsin-made Cedar Crest ice cream. For a fabulous steak, try the supper club **Sal's Elkhart Inn**. It's a casual environment with a varied menu, as well as a sports bar downstairs.

To get your first taste of the natural beauty of this byway, consider **Broughton Sheboygan Marsh,** a 13,000-acre park just northwest of town with thirty acres developed for park visitors to explore and view wildlife. The park offers camping as well. Good food is right inside the park at **Three Guys and a Grill at the Marsh Lodge**. Sip a hand-muddled Old Fashioned at the bar and order something from the lunch or dinner menu grilled over hardwood charcoal.

Starting out on the byway from Elkhart Lake, head south on WI 67, and just before you leave town you'll come to CH J and A. Go right following the green scenic road signs.

You'll come to a stop sign at Lake Street. **Jay Lee Inn Bed and Breakfast,** a 1902 Victorian Federal home, is just a few hundred feet to the right from here, and beyond that the street goes into downtown. The inn enjoys a nice quiet location in a neighborhood that is well shaded with old trees. The breakfast here is fantastic, and the owners are also quite helpful for local recommendations.

Continuing on the byway, cross Lake Street and follow the curve on CH A and J out of Elkhart Lake. South of town CH A goes right (west), and you follow it through some hills. As with most stretches along this route, take time to notice both the tiny wonders (wildflowers along the roadside) and the grander sights (the oddly shaped hills and bluffs, the moraines left behind by the glaciers).

You'll pass along "Schoolhouse Straight," and then you'll come to CH P at a stop sign. This marks "Kimberley's Korner." Continue on CH A and P heading south. The first couple miles are farmland, but you can see the hills in the distance. You will cross CH C, which would take you to Crystal Lake to the east, but you stay straight. Just past CH C the road dips before you and curves right to go around the bluffs. This is still CH A.

The next village is Glen Beulah. Look for a sign to the Barta Dam mill pond on the left. It was common to dam creeks to create a water supply for a local mill. The view is pleasant, but there is nothing here but a picnic table. On the other side of town, go left (south) on CH A. You'll cross WI 23 and come to the village of Greenbush. At the central intersection, take Plank Road to the right one block to find the indoor/outdoor museum at **Wade House**.

Sylvanus and Betsy Wade were the first pioneers to settle in Greenbush in 1844. Halfway along a stagecoach line between Fond du Lac and Sheboygan, this was a perfect place for an inn. As the tiny village grew, the Wades kept a tavern and housed guests in their expanding cabin until 1850 when they were able to build a proper inn. It was an instant success, and remained successful for the next ten years. But when the railroad bypassed Greenbush, business began to decline, and by around 1910, the inn had closed. The family stayed on until 1941. Thereafter several people tried to restore it. The Kohler family—of plumbing fixture fame—took on the project and eventually saved the house and donated it to the Wisconsin

The Wade house once had a steady business of stagecoach travelers.

State Historical Society. In 1968 the Wesley Jung Carriage Museum was opened on-site, and in 2001, the Kohler Trust for Preservation rebuilt and opened the Herrling Sawmill here as well. Visitors can visit all these places as well as see a blacksmith shop, watch a vintage game of baseball, or have a horse-drawn wagon ride. A café is on-site.

Return to CH T and go right (south) to continue along the byway. You will pass a trailhead for the Ice Age Trail about 1.6 miles from here.

ICE AGE NATIONAL SCENIC TRAIL

This 1,000-mile hiking trail roughly follows the edge of the farthest reaches of the most recent glaciers around 15,000 years ago. And I do mean roughly: most of the trail follows rustic paths created in a fashion that lessens ecological impact and avoids erosion issues. The result is a hike that really feels like you've left civilization a bit, and odds are you won't see another soul on the trail. Don't be discouraged by the length—plenty of segments are perfect for a short out-and-back trek. The trail meanders down from Door County along Kettle Moraine deep into southern Wisconsin as far south as Janesville and then works its way back north up the center of the state before heading west to end at Interstate State Park on the St. Croix River. There is no fee for hiking the trail, though those parking lots that are within state parks do require a park sticker.

In less than a mile watch for the left turn leaving CH T to take Kettle Moraine Drive. The road has no shoulders and gets narrower. Trees, brush, and wildflowers stand right up next to the road, and you will see stands of cedar, pine, maple, and sumac, as well as aspen colonies. Watch for critters; none of them are very diligent about looking both ways before crossing.

The road follows curves up and down small hills giving the byway a nice roller-coaster effect. You'll pass the Greenbush Group Camp on the right, and then the canopy really closes in over the lane, making it a tunnel of greenery. At State Forest C area there is a picnic spot, shelter, pit toilets, and parking alongside the road. This is a state park fee area only if you choose to stop.

The road continues past this,

ASPEN OR POPPLE?

The silver-white barked trees you see in thick stands are aspens. Unlike oaks or maples, which drop hundreds of acorns or seeds, aspen send out root suckers that send up shoots as far as 120 feet from the parent tree. These develop into full trees. Each tree can live as long as 150 years, but the root system survives much longer. In northern Wisconsin they are often referred to as "popple," a variant on poplar, which, though a different tree, shares the genus *Populus* with the aspen. The "quaking aspen" takes its name from its leaves that constantly quiver in the slightest of breezes. Watch for colonies of these trees, especially in fall when they produce some blazing yellows and reds.

downhill through the forest's tunnel, and you will begin to see the kettles. When you pass a metal guard rail, you will see a crushed gravel wayside where a sign reads Kettle Parking. Stop here, and it's a short walk along a trail to a viewing platform to your right that overlooks a proper kettle. This one is almost perfectly circular. Thousands of these remain along the line of Kettle Moraine. When they actually have water in them, they are referred to as kettle ponds or kettle lakes.

Another hundred feet past here, the road turns right at a T intersection. On your left see farmland as you continue straight. The next stop sign is at WI 67. The byway continues left from this T intersection about 0.4 mile to CH A where you'll go right (south). After passing through some farmland toward forest, straight ahead, you will come to CH U. Go right, following the Kettle Moraine Scenic Drive sign, and you will find Parnell Tower on the right. This is another fee area. A short drive takes you to a parking area where you can find water, picnic tables and grills, and pit toilets. The park's Parnell Loop is a 3.5-mile trail. Those not interested in hiking still might want to see the view. The first section of the trail ascends some railway-tie steps to the top of the bluff where you can climb a sixty-foot observation tower overlooking the glacial landscape. Look to the west and the moraines there are conspicuous. Leaving the parking lot go right (west) on CH U to continue past some pine plantation on your left.

The shortest distance between two points may be a straight line, but the makers of the Kettle Moraine Scenic Drive believed it wasn't the most scenic. Stay alert for some frequent turns. Generally they are well marked with the drive's green sign. Look for Woodside Road on the left at 1.4 miles. Go left. Pass wetlands on your left, and after 0.5 mile you'll come to Shamrock Road and go left, cutting through that wetlands area.

Come to a stop sign, and go left on Scenic Drive. This really starts to feel like you are going in a circle, but you're not as you head south on a serpentine road through the woods under a closed canopy. Watch to either side for kettle depressions and the willow trees fond of the water-filled depressions. You will come to a small country churchyard and the 1861 St. Michael's Catholic Chapel. Remodeling over the years makes it seem a lot newer than its building date suggests.

Kettle moraines are sometimes filled with water or supporting bogs.

Come out to farmland again, and at the next stop sign, go right on CH V. Follow this to Butler Lake Road and go left. This will take you past Butler Lake Trail and Parnell Esker on your left. The esker was formed when the last glacier began to melt. The meltwater rushed down through an ice tunnel, and glacial deposits began to fill it. When the glacier disappeared completely, the sediments remained, and now you can see the esker, a sort of snake-like ridge nearly 2 miles long. The park road to the lake cuts right through it. You can climb the short distance to the top on a trail that starts at the parking lot.

Go left when leaving the parking lot, continuing on Butler Lake Road. At the next stop sign, you are at Division Road. **Long Lake Recreation Area** is straight ahead. The state park offers camping, picnic areas, restrooms, and drinking water. The byway goes left (south) on Division Road. The next stop sign is CH F; go right to Dundee. Cross the creek in Dundee, and to your right you'll see the mill park right behind the 1855 millhouse. Go right

THE FATHER OF THE ICE AGE TRAIL

In 1926 the Milwaukee Chapter of the Izaak Walton League, one of the nation's oldest conservation organizations, purchased some land near Campbellsport to be set aside for hikers. A trend of land protection started, and in 1937, the Kettle Moraine State Forest was established. In the 1950s Milwaukee attorney Ray Zillmer, a chapter leader, proposed an 800-mile national park that would preserve the finest features of the last advance of glaciers in Wisconsin and offer a contiguous path. Thus the vision of the Ice Age Trail was born. In 1958 he founded the Ice Age Park and Trail Foundation. The idea gained momentum in Congress, but Zillmer died in 1961 before ever seeing his dream realized. Each year the trail is closer and closer to completion.

at the first intersection—this is WI 67—and just on your right is the **Hamburger Haus,** a popular place to pick up some char-grilled hamburgers, brats, fries, or ice cream. Restrooms are in back as is a small sandbox full of toys for the kids. The Haus is a fun, walk-up-window sort of place with picnic tables, which also means it closes for the winter. You can park behind here if you want to have a look at the **Dundee Mill**. A small **museum** is in the works there. Go back to where you turned into town on WI 67 and go right. You are now heading west on WI 67 and in about 0.3 mile you will break left from WI 67 taking CH G to stay on the byway. But you really should go straight up the hill on WI 67 to visit the Ice Age Trail visitor center and then backtrack to this point.

The **Harry S. Reuss Ice Age Visitor Center** will school you on the geological history of Wisconsin. Learn about the flora and fauna, see a ten-minute video in the theater, and have a chat with a naturalist. A viewing deck looks out over some land features with clear signage to show you what you're looking at. The parking lot has access to an overlook trail as well.

Return to the byway, heading back to CH G and going right (south, away from Dundee). Go left on CH SS to New Prospect. Just past town come to CH GGG and go right, and you'll head into the forest again briefly. To the left is Forest Lake, and you will also see **Parkside General Store**, which sells **gourmet popcorn and fudge** in season. Just past here on the right is Mauthe's Lake Recreation Area with picnic and swimming areas, a fishing pier, pit toilets, and a designated pet picnic area.

When you arrive at CH S, take a right toward New Fane. In New Fane at the stop sign, go left on Kettle Moraine Drive once again. You will cross WI 28 and continue straight through the town of Kewaskum. Thereafter, cross CH H. At the next stop sign go right on Ridge Road, which curves around Smith Lake and wetlands but mostly passes through farmland. You'll start seeing residences, but at the next stop sign go right on Newark Drive and over a creek before crossing Sleepy Hollow Road onto Lighthouse Lane. The lighthouse is actually part of the bowling alley on your left here.

This is the end of the northern section of the drive. You are now at CH D. To the left less than 0.4 mile is the city of West Bend. To your right you will see US 45. Go right on CH D, passing under the highway. Scenic Drive signage is lacking here. Go west on CH D about 2 miles and look for Kettle View Road on your left and follow that.

You will cross Beaver Dam Road and then go right on Schuster Drive, getting some nice views as you go down a long hill and over another. The Scenic Drive arrow will send you left at the next stop sign at Glacier Drive. As you pass through some residential areas, the view ahead is blue hills on the horizon. The road goes downhill to cross WI 33, and you are now on South WI 144. Slinger is another 7 miles from here.

WI 144 will take you past the long Big Cedar Lake on the left and soon after that you'll pass over US 41; this is the end of WI 144 and as you start to see Slinger, the green Scenic Drive signs start to reappear. Go straight across WI 175 in town, and when you come to WI 60, a four-lane highway, go right (west) and this will take you to Hartford.

Just before you enter Hartford, watch for the Pike Lake Unit of Kettle Moraine State Forest. Go left on Kettle Moraine Drive (not Powder Hill Road) just past the park office. The state park offers camping, swimming, picnicking, a viewing tower on top of Powder Hill (a kame), and an astronomy trail. The Ice Age Trail also passes through here.

Continue south on Kettle Moraine Drive, cross CH E and then come to the bottom of a hill to a stop sign. Go right here on Waterford Road, a narrow lane through brush and forest. At CH K go left at the stop sign. Be careful as you pull out, the traffic from the left comes fast, and you don't have much time to see it. As you come to the top of the hill, look off to the left to see Holy Hill church in the distance. You should go left on WI 167 to visit the scenic church. Otherwise, at WI 167 go straight across on CH K.

The Holy Hill Basilica is a shrine to the Virgin Mary and attracts over 300,000 visitors each year. In 1842 the Irish founded Erin Township and dedicated the hill to Mary. They were the first to call it "Holy Hill." The Irish were replaced by Germans a few decades later. Two shrines were constructed at the hilltop before the present-day Neo-Romanesque construction was proposed and then completed in 1931. The holy site overlooks the surrounding 400-acres of preserved woodland, and there is an observation deck with a phenomenal view. Mass is given daily, and a gift shop and café are on site. To get here go east on WI 167 and take Stationway Road south up to the site.

Continuing south on CH K, cross CH Q and then you are on CH E in Waukesha County. This will take you into the town of Monches. Krauski Glass is the studio of Bob and Mary Krauski who create etched and stained glass artwork. Hours are erratic, but they are likely open on the weekends.

Turn right on CH E at the south end of town. At CH VV, go right at the stop sign and head into North Lake where CH VV ends. Go left at the stop sign on WI 83 and continue south. Come to CH K and take a right and enter Stone Bank and go left on CH C. You will find yourself on a bit of a land bridge, with water on both sides, as you head south out of town.

Cross WI 16, and the next city is **Delafield**. Settlers began constructing cabins here in 1839. (You can see the remains of a pioneer's site inside of the Lapham Peak Unit of the Kettle Moraine State Forest just south of town.) Delafield itself was established in 1843. Nelson Hawks, a settler from New York, moved his family here, and in 1846 he built a three-story inn to serve stagecoaches. **Hawk's Inn** is still standing and is now on the National Register of Historic Places. Guided tours are available but limited

INCREASE LAPHAM

Born in 1811, Increase Allen
Lapham is considered Wisconsin's
first great scientist and the Father
of the U.S. Weather Service. He
grew up out east but moved to
Milwaukee (then Kilbourntown) in
1836. He had a knack for scientific
observation and went on to pub-
lish works about plants and animals in Wisconsin, archeology,
history, geology, and a book about
the geography of the Wisconsin
Territory. He lobbied for the creation of the national weather service, noting the value of forecasting
foul weather along the Great
Lakes. He died in 1875, but his
name outlives him in several places
throughout the state; the highest
point in Waukesha County, in fact,
is Lapham Peak.

to Wednesday mornings year-round or Saturday afternoons from May to October.

Cross I-94 on the overpass. From here you can go west to Madison or east to Milwaukee. The byway continues straight south on CH C. Just about a mile after the overpass you will see the entrance to the **Lapham Peak Unit of the Kettle Moraine State Forest**. This state park has the highest point in Waukesha County at 1,233 feet above sea level. You can add another 45 feet to that with the observation tower, which affords a spectacular view on to the horizon in all directions. The park contains picnic and grilling areas and over 20 miles of hiking trails, most of which are groomed for ski-ing in winter. Some of those trails are lighted at night during ski season. The Ice Age Trail passes through the park and offers a backpack campsite. A nature trail and a second observation platform are wheelchair accessible. Examples of kettle moraines, Native American marker trees, and the ruins of an old home-stead can be seen along the trails.

Where CH C meets and joins US 18, go right following them west. Less than a mile later, CH C and your byway break south (to the left). At the next stop sign, CH C goes right and you follow it. When you come to the intersection of CH C and CH D, you go straight on CH C. The signage here is confusing. Look for Waterville Road on your left just 200 feet after the stop sign. This is Rustic Road 86. Take it left, and the paved backroad will wander a few miles through the state forest. (Continuing on CH C will take you to WI 67 where you go left to continue on the byway.)

On the Rustic Road you will pass the entrance to Pine Woods Campground and come to the end of Waterville Road. The Rustic Road goes left, but you should go right on CH ZZ. You will pass the Donald J. Mackie picnic area on the right and then the parking area for Scuppernong

NATIVE AMERICAN MARKER TREES

You may see a strange tree in the forest, one with a bend that resembles an elbow in its thick trunk. It is believed that these bends were made when the tree was but a sapling. The formation was used by Native Americans, and perhaps subsequently by pioneers copying the practice, to mark trails or even water sources. Travelers lost in the woods or passing near dark would align their route by the angle of the tree. The state park at Lapham Peak has marker trees that can be seen along the park's trails.

The Native Americans once used marker trees to find their way through the forest.

Trail, which offers some very nice hiking through varied forests and a couple scenic overlooks on a cedar-chip trail. This is a fee area, and there is a map of the trails at a kiosk. The parking area has restrooms. Continuing past the park to WI 67, go left to continue on the byway.

You will pass some wetlands to the right and see a parking area for the Ice Age Trail. Hiking this is free, but the trail is not a loop and would be hiked as an out-and-back. The byway continues through the forest and then passes into open meadows and farmland.

You will know you have arrived at the town of Eagle when you see the bright yellow smiley-faced water tower to the right. If you've arrived in the morning, **Hen House Café** offers a great home-cooking-style breakfast. Otherwise, **Coyote Canyon Grille** has big hamburgers, a bit of Tex-Mex, and pizza in a tavern setting.

Go to the right on WI 59 to continue on this byway. But to take a side trip to **Old World Wisconsin**, take a quick, soft left after you've gotten on WI 59 and go south on WI 67. The historical park is 1.5 miles south of Eagle, and *not* where the actual address might send you on a GPS device.

If you've ever tried to imagine life as a pioneer in nineteenth-century Wisconsin, you must visit this open-air museum. Actors play shopkeepers, farmers, blacksmiths, and various other characters in a park comprised of more than sixty historic structures that were moved here from around the state. Farmers work the fields with oxen and plows, farm women prepare meals over wood-fire stoves, and blacksmiths pound out horseshoes and candle holders. Activities are interactive making this a great learning experience for all ages. Settlements throughout the rolling prairie park are dedicated to Norwegians, Finns, Germans, Danes, and African-Americans. You can attend class in a one-room schoolhouse. It's all walkable, but there is also a shuttle that makes a regular route through the property. A gift shop is onsite as is a limited-menu snack restaurant.

Just south of Eagle on the way to Old World Wisconsin is **Eagle Centre House Bed and Breakfast**, a replica of an 1846 stagecoach inn built in the Greek revival style. The five guest rooms have period furniture and private baths. Two of the larger rooms have double whirlpools and fireplaces.

Continuing on the byway, west on WI 59 from Eagle, you have another 5 miles to Palmyra. As you come over hill outside of Eagle, the view stretches to a faraway blue-tinted horizon. The **Kettle Moraine State Forest—Southern Unit office** is just under 3 miles west of Eagle, and you can pick up park information, visit a small museum and gift shop, or buy a state park sticker here.

As you approach **Palmyra**, you will see Miller Spring Lake to your left. Palmyra's downtown is small but has that century-old look to it. The byway passes right through it, going straight on CH H/Main Street. If you're looking for food, **Mary's Café** is a recommended local hangout that will provide some home-style fare including good soups and pie.

As you follow CH/Main Street out of town, you may see some green Jefferson County Bike Route signs; don't confuse those with the Kettle Moraine Scenic Drive signage.

If you're thinking about going fishing with the kids and you want to make it easy, **Rushing Waters Fisheries** just outside of town might be your

A blacksmith makes a candleholder at Old World Wisconsin

thing. You don't pay an entrance fee, and you don't need a fishing license. Just pay for what you catch. This eighty-acre farm has clear ponds and raceways full of rainbow trout. You can buy bait here and rent equipment if you didn't bring your own.

You are entering a great area for biking of all sorts. The rolling hills of the country highways are great challenges for road bikes, but two state trails are dedicated to mountain bikers. The **John Muir Trails**, which can be biked or hiked, take you through a wide range of terrain: wetlands, prairie, hardwood forest, and pine plantation, and right along the upper edges of some fantastic kettles, some of which hold bogs. The five loops vary in length from 1.5 to 10 miles. The **Emma Carlin Trails** are consistently in the hills and mostly through forest, and an impressive scenic overlook is the highlight. The **Nordic Trails** across the highway from John Muir offer hiking until the snow falls. After that point the trails are groomed for cross-country skiing. You will find a parking lot, water and pit toilets at each trail, and a warming house at the Nordic Trail. All three are part of the Kettle Moraine State Forest land, and as such require users to purchase a trail pass. There are self-pay stations at each of them, or you can purchase them at nearby La Grange General Store.

Located at the corner of CH H and US 12, not far from the John Muir and Nordic Trails, **La Grange General Store** offers great deli food and coffee shop items. As a convenience store, it places an emphasis on organic foods and energy-packed foods for the frequent bikers, as well as a good selection of wines and beers. You can rent or purchase bikes—road and off-road models—in the connecting shop **Backyard Bikes and Ski**. When the snow arrives, you can also get cross-country ski rental equipment here.

Cross US 12 and continue south on CH H to stay on the byway. Going right on US 12 will take you into the city of Whitewater, but not far from this intersection hikers will find the **Whitewater Lake Segment** of the **Ice Age Trail**. You will see the trailhead parking lot at Sherwood Forest Road on the north (right) side of US 12. The trail heads south from there on the other side of the highway and ends where this byway ends in the Whitewater Lake Recreation Area, still inside the Kettle Moraine State Forest.

But continuing on the byway, cross US 12 and stay on CH H until you come to Kettle Moraine Drive. Follow this to the right and it will take you all the way to the end of this byway through farmland before crossing CH O and into more interesting terrain.

At CH P, go straight across into the **Whitewater Lake Recreation Area**. The road will make a loop around the lake and come back to this point. The park has camping, picnic areas, pit toilets, swimming beaches, and boat launches.

The lake will be on your left. Go left on Lakeshore Road, keeping the lake on your left. At Parkside Marina you can find boat rentals in the summer. Continuing around the lake past the boat landing, you will find the water on both sides of you. A picnic area lies out on a point to the left here. The lake is small and soon you will be back at Kettle Moraine Drive where you can go right to get back to CH P. Take this left (north) and it joins WI 59 as it heads into Whitewater, which makes a nice place to stop for the night. Consider the 1861 mansion **Hamilton House Bed and Breakfast**. This was once a stop on the Underground Railroad. If you were thinking of hiking the Ice Age Trail, the inn does a drop off/pick up for inn guests so that they can hike the segment one way.

IN THE AREA

Accommodations

Broughton Sheboygan Marsh Park, W7039 County Road SR, Elkhart Lake. Call 920-876-2535. This 13,000-acre park has 64 campsites and facilities include showers and boat/canoe rental. Follow CH J northwest out of Elkhart Lake.

Eagle Centre House Bed and Breakfast, W370 S9590 WI 67, Eagle. Call 262-363-4700. Web site: www.eagle-house.com.

Hamilton House Bed and Breakfast, Whitewater. Call 262-473-1900. This 1861 mansion offers rooms with private baths and will do drop offs/pick ups for the Ice Age Trail segments near Whitewater. Web site: www.bandbhamiltonhouse.com.

Jay Lee Inn Bed and Breakfast, 444 South Lake Street, Elkhart Lake. Call 920-876-2910. This 1902, Victorian Federal home offers seven rooms (five with private baths) and a gourmet breakfast. This is close to downtown and on the historic road race circuit. Web site: www.jayleeinn.com.

Osthoff Lake Resort, 101 Osthoff Avenue, Elkhart Lake. Call 920-876-3366. This AAA Four Diamond resort has a variety of rooms and suites, and the property sits right on the lake. This is home to two recommended restaurants and the Aspira Spa. Web site: www.osthoff.com.

Whitewater Lake Visitor Center, W7508 Kettle Moraine Drive, Whitewater. Call 262-473-6427. Camping is allowed mid-May–mid-Oct., but the office is only open from Memorial Day to Labor Day.

Attractions/Recreation

Aspira Spa at the Osthoff Resort, 101 Osthoff Avenue, Elkhart Lake. Call 1-877-772-2070. A full service spa with a spa suite available as well. Web site: www.aspiraspa.com.

Backyard Bikes, LaGrange General Store, W6098 US 12, Whitewater. Call 262-495-8600. Stop here to rent a bike (or repair your own) before getting on one of the nearby mountain-bike trails or riding the country roads. They also rent cross-country skis for the nearby Nordic Trail. Web site: www.backyardbikes.com.

Dundee Mill and Park, Dundee. This 1855 mill is being developed as a small museum. Intentions are to open it to visitors on the weekends. Web site: www.dundeemillandpark.com.

Emma Carlin Trail, located on CR Z just south of WI 59. Call 262-594-6200. Trails are 2 to 4 miles in length and good for hiking and mountain biking. State trail fee applies. Web site: www.dnr.state.wi.us/Org/land/parks/specific/kms/trails.html.

Hawks Inn Historical Museum, 426 Wells Street, Delafield. Call 262-646-4794. Fee. Nelson Hawks built this stagecoach inn in 1846. The inn is open for tours Sat. 1–4 from May to the end of Oct., and Wed. mornings year-round. Donations accepted. Take CR DR/Main Street east to Wells Street. Web site: www.hawksinn.org.

Henry S. Reuss Ice Age Visitor Center. Call 920-533-8322. Winter hours change from Nov.–Mar. A mile west of Dundee on WI 67. Speak with a naturalist, watch a ten-minute video, and check out some interactive exhibits on Ice Age history. Web site: www.dnr.wi.gov/org/land/parks/specific/kmn/iac.html.

Holy Hill Basilica, 1525 Carmel Road, Hubertus. Call 262-628-1838. Visit a shrine to Mary with a spectacular view. A café and a gift shop are on site. Web site: www.holyhill.com.

John Muir Trails, located on CR H just north of US 12 in La Grange. Call 262-594-6200. Trails up to 10 miles in length are challenging for mountain bikers and hikers alike. State trail fee applies. Web site: www.dnr.state.wi.us/Org/land/parks/specific/kms/trails.html.

Kettle Moraine State Forest Headquarters—Southern Unit, S91 W39091 WI 59, Eagle. Call 262-594-6200. The park office has brochures and park information, state park stickers, and a small museum and gift shop. Web site: www.dnr.state.wi.us/org/LAND/parks/specific/kms.

Krauski Glass, W302 N9493 County Road E, Hartland (Monches). Call 262-966-7500. This husband and wife team is nationally recognized for their etched and stained glass artwork. Open most weekends with erratic hours or by appointment. Web site: www.krauskiartglass.com.

Lapham Peak Unit of Kettle Moraine State Forest, W329 N846 County Road C, Delafield. Call 262-646-3025. Open 7 AM–9 PM (until 10 PM in winter). Fee. Climb a forty-five-foot observation tower, have a picnic, or enjoy miles of hiking, mountain biking, or cross-country skiing. Web site: www.dnr.wi.gov/org/land/parks/specific/lapham.

Old World Wisconsin, S103 W37890 Highway 67, Eagle. Call 262-594-6300. Open daily, May 1–Oct. 31. Fee. Experience nineteenth-century Wisconsin history in this open-air museum with guides dressed in character. Located just 1.5 miles south of Eagle. Web site: www.oldword wisconsin.org.

Parkview General Store, N 1527 Hwy GGG, Campbellsport. Call 262-626-8287. Closed Mon. Closed for the season from Nov. to Apr. 15. Gourmet popcorn and fudge. Need I say more? Web site: www .parkview-store.com.

Road America, N7390 WI 67, Elkhart Lake. Call 1-800-365-7223. This is an internationally acclaimed, closed-circuit racetrack. People will actually come here and camp. Web site: www.roadamerica.com.

Rushing Waters Fisheries, N301 County Road H, Palmyra. Call 262-495-2089. Go trout fishing at this eighty-acre farm. You only pay for what you catch. No license or fee required and equipment is available for rent. Web site: www.rushingwaters.net.

Wade House, W7824 Center Street, Greenbush. Call 920-526-3271. Open daily May–Oct. Fee. Guides in period dress teach visitors about the life and times surrounding this 1860 stagecoach inn. Visit a sawmill, blacksmith shop, carriage museum, and the inn itself. Web site: www.wadehouse.wisconsinhistory.org.

Dining/Drinks

Back Porch Bistro, 283 Victorian Village Drive, Elkhart Lake. Call 920-876-3645. Open for lunch and dinner. The back porch of the Victorian Village Resort is a supper club that overlooks the lake.

Coyote Canyon Grille, 105 West Main Street, Eagle. Stop here for some bar-and-grill food with some Tex-Mex options and pizza. Web site: www.ccgrille.com.

Hamburger Haus, N3059 Highway 67, Campbellsport (Dundee). Call 920-533-5046. A seasonal drive-up joint with picnic tables, this is a classic way to have a char-grilled burger, brat, or some ice cream.

Hen House Café, 110 East Waukesha Road, Eagle. Call 262-594-5552. This small café offers good home-style cooking and terrific breakfasts.

La Grange General Store, Cafe & Deli, W6098 US 12, Whitewater. Call 262-495-8600. You can get fair trade coffee or a great deli sandwich here. The store also offers conveniences such as sunscreen, wine and beer, and an assortment of organic and energy foods. Web site: www.backyard bikes.com.

Lake Street Café, 21 South Lake Street, Elkhart Lake. Call 920-876-2142. Expect sandwiches and wood-fired pizzas for lunch and more upscale steak and seafood entrées for dinner. The wine list has consistently won awards. Web site: www.lakestreetcafe.com.

Lola's on the Lake Restaurant, at Osthoff Lake Resort, Elkhart Lake. Regional cuisine for dinner with a view of the lake. Web site: www.osthoff.com.

Mary's Café, W1242 WI 59, Palmyra. Call 262-495-4447. Small town, homestyle cooking at its finest, Mary's does great pies and soups.

Otto's Restaurant, at Osthoff Lake Resort, Elkhart Lake. Serves all three meals and has screened-in seating in seasonable weather. Web site: www.osthoff.com.

Sal's Elkhart Inn, 91 South Lincoln Street, Elkhart Lake. Call 920-876-3133. A great place for steaks and whole lot more, this supper club is casual and has a sports bar downstairs.

Siebkens Resort, 284 South Lake Street, Elkhart Lake. Call 920-876-2600. Choose from a modern condo or a Victorian-themed room in one of two historic buildings at this lakeside resort founded in 1916. The Main Dining Room offers dinner, while the Stop-Inn Tavern does a more casual lunch and dinner. Both eateries have screened-in porches. Web site: www.siebkens.com.

Three Guys and a Grill at the Marsh Lodge, W7039 County Road SR, Elkhart Lake. Call 920-876-2535. Web site: www.threeguysandagrill .com. Closed Mon. This supper club specializes in meals grilled over hardwood charcoal, but offers a varied lunch and dinner menu.

Other

Elkhart Lake Chamber of Commerce, 41 East Rhine Street, Elkhart Lake. Call 920-876-2922. Web site: www.elkhartlake.com.

A real taste of Italy awaits at Il Ritrovo in Sheboygan.

CHAPTER

7

The Lake Michigan Shoreline

Estimated length: 70 miles
Estimated time: 2 hours

Getting There: Take I-43 north to CR V just south of Sheboygan.

Highlights: See the sunrise and explore the dunes of Kohler-Andrae State Park; have a real Italian pizza in Sheboygan; shop for art at a most unusual gallery in Algoma; tour a World War II submarine at the Wisconsin Maritime Museum; see Native American effigy mounds; sample Wisconsin wines.

Lake Michigan wasn't just affected by one Ice Age, but four over the last two million years. The basin of the lake, however, was put in its present form by glaciers from the latest, the Wisconsin Period. Meltwater gave it its start forming glacial lakes that grew beyond the current shorelines but then shrank when the retreating glaciers unblocked the passage between Lakes Michigan and Huron. This allowed waters to drain east around 6000 B.C. The lake's name comes from the Ojibwe *mishigami*, which means "great water." French explorer Jean Nicolet is believed to have been the first European to see the lake in the 1630s.

Lake Michigan is the only Great Lake that is wholly within U.S. borders. Its 1,640 miles of shoreline show sandy beaches and dunes in many

The fragile dunes at Kohler-Andrae State Park are protected from hikers' feet by a plank walk.

places, and once you get north of the Milwaukee area, the towns along its shores are small and slow-paced yet offer a great variety of things to see and do.

The perfect place to start a trip along this lake is **Kohler-Andrae State Park.** When the sun rises up over the deep blue waters and strikes the tops of the dunes and the miles of sandy shoreline, you get the full effect of the natural beauty of this park. On this byway you will find many lovely views along the shores, but this is arguably the best and the most pristine. The park's Sanderling Nature Center provides a fascinating educational element, and with 105 campsites, you can make much more than a day trip out of a visit here.

Heading north on I-43, take CR V to the right (east). You will take another immediate right to stay on CR V toward the park. The entrance to the park is right at a bend in the road; just go straight in. Pets are allowed only in a designated area. The Black River runs through the western side of the park, and its marsh has a boardwalk, which is good for birders.

The byway continues from the park entrance heading north 1 mile to where CR V becomes CR KK. Almost 2 miles from the park, turn right on Panther Avenue and take the next right on Ninth Avenue to get to Sheboygan Indian Mound Park. This fifteen-acre forest includes a winding stream and eighteen effigy mounds created in about AD 500–750 by ancestors of the Wisconsin Woodland Indians. The shapes are of deer and panthers, and one of the mounds shows a reproduction of a burial that was excavated here by archaeologists. Many other mounds existed throughout the state but were destroyed by farming and development. The hiking trail has interpretive signage for the native plants.

Return to CR KK (also Twelfth Street) and go right, continuing north to Washington Avenue where you will take another right. Green road signs will indicate that you are on the Lake Michigan Circle Tour route. You'll see the power plant in front of you. Go left on Lakeshore Drive, which will put Lakeview Park on your right.

After a couple blocks the view opens to the lake. The road makes a little S and becomes Seventh Street passing General King Park, which offers a playground, a small beach, and picnic tables and grills. Take a left on Indiana Avenue and go half a block to a traffic circle. Harbor Center is on your right. You can get there on South Pier Drive, which is the first right turn out of the traffic circle.

Harbor Center is a lovely new development along the banks of the Sheboygan River to where it meets the lake behind break walls. If you're hungry, don't miss **Islander Café**. The breakfasts here are top-notch, and the French toast stuffed with fruit and cream cheese is excellent. Lunch is just as good with sandwiches, wraps, pasta dishes, and soups.

If you are more inclined to take something on the road, get a gourmet sandwich at **Pier 57 Deli and Lounge**. They often do box lunches for those heading out to fish.

Part of the Wisconsin appeal is the endless assortment of outdoor activities. The outfitter **EOS,** also on South Pier Drive, can get you into whatever you like: biking, kayaking, camping, and more. Surfing Lake Michigan is a surprising local sport, but Sheboygan claims to be the Freshwater Surfing Capital of the World. EOS rents surf boards and can tell you where the nearby hot spots are.

A trip on the lake is recommended. Stop in at **Sheboygan Shoreline Cruises** also along the pier. Seasonal trips on the *Spirit of the Lake* run just under two hours, or you can join a sunset cruise with a dinner buffet. A

Sunrise on Lake Michigan is not to be missed.

full bar is on board, and when the wind off the water is chilly or the sun is too strong, there is indoor seating.

At the end of the pier area to the right is the **Blue Harbor Resort**, a rather big production hotel with an indoor water park and a spa. Suites and villas can accommodate families and large groups. If you are not staying here, the wine and tapas bar is a nice stop along the trip. Breakfast is arguably better at Pier 57 Deli though.

Something not to miss is the **John Michael Kohler Arts Center**, a collection of galleries, a theater and performance spaces. Since 1967 the center has been an advocate for art and artists through their residency program and public events, shows, and exhibits. A stop at the **Sheboygan County Historical Museum** can put more backstory to your time here. Set in an historical 1850 home, each room is dedicated to another theme. Exhibits cover local baseball, medicine, maritime, farming, and circus histories as well as the story of the local Native Americans. An original log cabin from a nineteenth-century homestead is on the property as well.

Downtown is off the lakeshore route, but if you are lingering for a day or weekend, you won't be disappointed with the food here. For the Italian fans, you have two places that should top the list. If it's pizza you want, go to **Il Ritrovo**. This is Italian-style, thin, crisp crust with a bit of chew to it and all-natural moderately applied ingredients, not the massive topping, bread crust variety some may be used to. They have approval from Napoli's Verace Pizza Napoletana Association, which certifies that their margherita pizza is truly Napoletana, using ingredients from very specific regions of Italy. Right across the street is a more formal dining venue with the same ownership and with the same commitment to authenticity. **Trattoria Stefano** is as good as it gets. Chef and owner Stefano Viglietti makes annual pilgrimages to Italia to discover more ideas and perfect his art. The connecting **gourmet Italian grocery** next door to Il Ritrovo features the very same products that chef Stefano uses at the restaurants. Also in the neighborhood is **Victorian Chocolate Shoppe,** which will satisfy your sweet tooth and make some good treats for the road or friends back home. Choose from over sixty varieties including some sugar-free selections.

OFFICIALLY ITALIAN PIZZA

For most people good pizza is a matter of personal taste. For the Italians it is sometimes a matter of precise specifications. Just as champagne is actually just "sparkling wine" outside of the specific French region, so now is Traditional Pizza Neapolitan a controlled label. Now you see what Italian lawmakers spend their time on. For the pizza to be legit it must be baked in a wood-fired oven at 800 degrees (F) and use all-natural, fresh ingredients, including type 00 flour, San Marzano tomatoes, all natural *fior di latte* (a mozzarella cheese made from cow milk) or *mozzarella di bufala* (which is made from buffalo milk), fresh basil, salt, and yeast. The dough must be hand-worked or low-speed mixed, and the resulting crust has to conform to the measured thickness. Who said Italians were picky about food? Only three places in Wisconsin currently have this certification, and one is Il Ritrovo in Sheboygan.

For something with a local neighborhood feel and great Sheboygan beer, stop in at **Hops Haven**. Hops lovers will find some good selections, and the black-cherry porter is legendary. The brewpub serves food now.

Sheboygan is surely a great distraction, but continuing on the byway, starting from that traffic circle near the harbor, take Eighth Street across the Sheboygan River and follow the arrow right on Riverfront Drive to stay on the Lake Michigan Circle Tour. Go right on Pennsylvania Avenue and then left on Broughton Drive to continue along the lakeshore.

DELAND PARK REMEMBERS

The *Lottie Cooper* was a lumber schooner. In April of 1896 the temper of a Lake Michigan gale wrecked the ship, and it was lost for many years. During the construction of the Harbor Centre Marina, the forgotten schooner was found buried in the muck. It finally found safe harbor here at the park.

During the Vietnam War, the United States solicited the help of the Lao and Hmong but on the sly. Because many of these soldiers and their operations were secret, they did not receive the same acknowledgement that other veterans have. The memorial in Deland Park brings a dark page of history to light and pays tribute to the service of non-American and American veterans alike.

On your right you will see Deland Park and the marina. This is one of the best places to surf on Lake Michigan. There is a bar and restaurant at the marina and a local beach at the park. On the street side of the park are the remains of a lumber schooner.

Continue north on Broughton Drive past the great expanse of sand at Deland Park's beach and then North Point Park. Five miles off shore here is the site of one of the most tragic Great Lakes shipwrecks. On November 21, 1847, the steamship *Phoenix* had over 225 passengers on board. Fire broke out and burned the vessel to the water line. There were fewer than forty-five survivors. The shoal out here has caused other tragedies. Another schooner, the *Ahnapee*, was also lost when it ran up on the shoal on June 9, 1884. The crew survived, but before the vessel could be saved a gale rose up and obliterated it.

Broughton Drive turns west and inland and comes to a tricky intersection. Take the hard right down past the water treatment facility, and it will curve west again on Park Avenue keeping Vollrath Park on your right. The first right past the partly forested park is Third Street.

Go right on Third Street, and it will pass the park and through a bit of residential neighborhood before you see the lake again. Third Street soon curves west and inland, becoming North Avenue. Follow this to Fifteenth Street/CR LS where you go right (north). You are now leaving the designated Lake Michigan Circle Tour route, and it is now called Lakeshore Road. (Notice the County Road label is LS for Lakeshore.) The byway heads through mixed forest and meadows often full of wildflowers. Blue-flowered chicory is common along the roadside in summer. The root of this wildflower was often used as a coffee substitute.

Wisconsin is also a **great golf** destination. Evidence is coming up on your right at **Whistling Straits,** which is the site of two world-class courses

Lose yourself in some art at The Flying Pig a gallery, garden, and coffee shop.

designed by Pete Dye. Something akin to Ireland, these links have hosted the PGA Championship and the Palmer Cup. The **Whistling Straits Restaurant** has won the AAA Three Diamond Award, and the wine list received a nod from *Wine Spectator*. The view of the lake is as impressive as the food.

As you pass the Whistling Straits property, your view will be of the grass-covered dunes. Just after the dunes, the road joins the lake again for some nice views before heading back into the woods again.

The next village on the byway is Cleveland. At the stop sign, follow CR LS/Washington Avenue to the right into "downtown." Note the abundance of brick houses. At the stop sign you will see the local boat landing. Go left continuing on Lake Shore Drive/CR LS.

Watch for the sign for Heuel Studio and Gallery on the north end of Cleveland. Robert Heuel was once an illustrator for *Esquire* magazine, but he has a long career as an accomplished oil painter specializing in portraits and landscapes. His home studio is an informal setting for seeing some of

USS *COBIA*

During World War II, Manitowoc built twenty-eight Gato-class submarines very similar to the USS *Cobia*. From November 1943 to the end of the war, the *Cobia* was deployed to the South Pacific where it was quite successful in the war against Japan. Notably it sank supply ships bound for Iwo Jima, including a shipment of twenty-eight tanks. The crew only suffered one casualty during its wartime service, but the closest call was an eight-hour pummeling by Japanese depth charges in the Gulf of Siam that left the sub buried in the muddy seabed. Skillful maneuvers unstuck the *Cobia* before air ran out. After being decommissioned in 1970, the *Cobia* was moved to Manitowoc where it now is part of the Maritime Museum. A tour of the cramped quarters, control room, and torpedo rooms give an impression of what life underwater must have been like.

his work and having a delightful chat with the artist and his wife. They set no formal hours, and it is advised to call first for an appointment.

The next 2 miles of CR LS are designated a deer crossing. They don't always read the signs, so just be on your guard at all times. Watch for **Truettner's Berry Farm** at CR C on the left a few miles north of Cleveland. Strawberries and raspberries are for sale here.

Manitowoc is your next town, and CR LS becomes Tenth Street. The name Manitowoc originates with the Potawotami tribe, which allegedly found here a large wooden cross put up by a Jesuit priest and took to calling it the Great Spirit tree, from the word *manitou*, the Great Spirit of their own culture.

Throughout the state you may find ice cream parlors scooping up **Cedar Crest Ice Cream**. This is its factory home, and you can stop at the parlor to get a cone. (There are no factory tours.) Right across the street is **Zutz's Cheese House** where you can shop for gift boxes or get some deli slices. The hours are erratic as the owner also sells real estate and may step out from time to time.

Continue on Tenth Street until Washington Street/US 151. If you go left here and stay on US 151 until I-43, you will come to the impressively large and clean **Manitowoc Area Visitor Center** where you can find a boatload of brochures and maps. The byway, however, goes right (east) on Washington Street. Ahead is a giant grain tower that shows the logo of a non-Wisconsin beer; at one time it was part of the area's Rahr Brewery. For local beer (and some pretty good grub as well) stop in at **Courthouse Pub** directly across from the courthouse, which is on your right when you get to Eighth Street.

Go left past the 1927 neoclassical-style Manitowoc Savings Bank and see some other great old buildings just before you cross the bridge over the Manitowoc River. This is a one-way street—to go back you must go west to Tenth Street. On the other side of the river, take the first right to get to the **Wisconsin Maritime Museum**. The collection gives a comprehensive look at the life aquatic in the Great Lakes and an interactive waterways exhibit is a fun way for kids to learn about locks and water flow. Don't worry, there are waterproof aprons provided. Entrance to the museum includes a tour of the USS *Cobia*, the submarine docked outside.

If you are coming from or going to Michigan, Manitowoc is one end of the SS *Badger's* run across the lake. This **car ferry** connects Manitowoc to Ludington, Michigan. The trip takes four hours and is run twice a day in summer and once a day in spring and fall. Fares are per person in addition to a vehicle fee.

Manitowoc offers a couple nice bed and breakfast inns. Not far from downtown is **WestPort Bed and Breakfast**, an 1879 Italianate Victorian

Tour a real World War II sub at the Wisconsin Maritime Museum.

Explore the torpedo room on the U.S.S. Cole.

home with four guest rooms and a very nice breakfast. For something lean-
ing more toward the country, consider **Bedell Hill Bed and Breakfast**. This
Greek-revival farmhouse is set on two acres; the original silo is still there.

To continue on the byway, keep following Maritime Drive past the
maritime museum and head north on WI 42. The paved bike trail along
the lakeshore is the 5.5-mile **Mariner's Trail** that follows the lake from the
marina in Manitowoc to the Lighthouse Inn in Two Rivers. The **Fitness
Center** has **bike rental** stations at both locations or their main office in
Manitowoc.

Just on your way out of Manitowoc lies **West of the Lake Gardens,** a
six-acre collection of flower gardens near the lake. The bike path passes in
front of it as well. Entry is free.

As you make the short trip from Manitowoc to Two Rivers, the byway
passes along the lakeshore again with a pullout along the way. The water
looks almost Caribbean in bright summer sun, but make no mistake, the
temperature is chilly at its best.

As you enter Two Rivers, you will see the **Lighthouse Inn**, a standard motel right on the lake. The restaurant serves a good Friday-night fish fry. If you choose to stay here, be sure to get a lakeside room.

The byway curves left into downtown on Washington Street and crosses West Twin River. Go left at the traffic lights at Sixteenth Street to Hawthorne Avenue and go right (all this is WI 310) to get to **Woodland Dunes Nature Center**. The park offers some easy short hikes including some handicap accessible boardwalks through woods, meadows, and marshlands on this 1,200-acre preserve. This is great for birding.

On the East Twin River, you will find the **Rogers Street Fishing Village and Great Lakes Coast Guard Museum**. The complex includes an 1886 lighthouse and exhibits on commercial fishing (which continues today) and shipwrecks. Five sheds make up the village, and a 1936 fishing tug can be boarded.

HOME OF THE ICE CREAM SUNDAE

Two Rivers, known to locals as "T'Rivers," also holds the nickname Cool City for a delicious reason. A simple if unusual request led to an ice cream institution. In 1881 George Hallauer approached Edward C. Berner, the owner of a soda fountain and asked him for some ice cream with chocolate sauce. It doesn't sound so odd, but in those days the syrup was only used for sodas. Berner complied and sold it for a nickel. It became a Sunday special. One day when a little girl asked for one on the wrong day, it was decided they could pretend it was Sunday. Thus a legend was born.

Phil Rohrer's Restaurant is a great little greasy spoon with minimal seating at the counter and booths. Phil opened this place in 1962, and you can still find him behind the counter. The fresh pie and homemade soups are a big draw, but you can't go wrong with any of the standard diner fare.

The **visitor center** is rolled into the **Historic Washington House**, an 1850s inn with an ice cream parlor. Have a sundae, grab some brochures, and check out the murals in the old ballroom upstairs. Right across the street see the **Hamilton Wood Type and Printing Museum**. In our digital age it is fascinated to see the original machinery used to prepare and cut wood type. The guides make the exhibits come to life.

The byway continues on WI 42, following Twenty Second Street over the East Twin River. Where WI 42 turns left (north) just after the bridge, stay straight on CR O to get to Point Beach State Park. Going straight here also takes you to Nashotah Beach, which offers a concession stand and some beachside parking and facilities for a picnic and a swim. If you want to bypass these parks, just stay on WI 42 north to Kewaunee.

CR O becomes Sandy Bay Road and **State Rustic Road 16,** a 5-mile ride through the state forest. Along this path is the three-bedroom **Point Beach Guesthouse.** According to the owners, its construction was funded by Al Capone as a favor to the original land owner who once allowed the Chicago bootlegger to operate a still and speakeasy in his woods.

A mile farther down the road, **Point Beach State Park** has 6 miles of beach and dunes (though these dunes are not quite as extensive as Kohler-Andrae). The forest shows pine plantation and hardwoods, and the campsites are not far from the water. Come here for a hike or a walk along the sands. The sunrise is a mystical experience over Lake Michigan. The Rawley Point lighthouse, operated by the U.S. Coast Guard, is not open to the public but makes for great photos at the property's edge. The lighthouse is a 1994 reconstruction and enlargement of an old Chicago River lighthouse and the only one of its kind. At 113 feet, this is the tallest octagonal skeletal light tower on the Great Lakes, and it can be seen 28 miles away.

The Rustic Road weaves right through the park forest until it ends at the junction of CR Z and CR O. The road then curves left inland back to

Before the lighthouse at Point Beach was built, 26 ships had run ashore or foundered off the point.

WI 42. Back on WI 42 go right (north) and you are another 17 miles from Kewaunee. The byway now passes through farmland with the lake typically not visible to the east. You will pass the nuclear-driven Kewaunee Power Station, a giant concrete tower with a white dome.

Many French explorers, priests, and traders, including Jean Nicolet, René-Robert Cavelier de la Salle, and Father Jacques Marquette, stopped where Kewaunee is today, and in the 1790s, fur trader Jacque Vieau made a trading post here. In the 1830s a find near the mouth of the river caused a "gold rush," and land speculators bought up the land and

Buy a flying pig at The Flying Pig, a funky cool art gallery.

sold it at outrageous prices. The "gold" turned out to be iron pyrite—fool's gold. Landowners turned those lemons into lemonade when they discovered how much lumber was worth.

Spend the night in the 1881 Italianate-style **Duvall House Bed and Breakfast**. This is just walking distance from the lake and downtown. The inn has four guest rooms and a nice sunroom. A bigger scale inn is part of the town's revitalization efforts and is **Kewaunee Inn at Hamachek Village**. Since 1858 there has been a hotel on this site. The current three-story brick building was constructed in 1912 and changed hands and names over the years. Not all of the guests have checked out, however; locals will swear there are three ghosts still hanging about.

Check out **Kunkel's Korner** for breakfast, lunch, and pastries downtown or **Annie's Emporium**, which has thirty-two flavors of ice cream, great coffee and tea, sweets, and a light lunch/snack menu. Where the Kewaunee River meets the lake just to the right of downtown, you can see the **lighthouse,** and at the riverside is **an old tugboat** that can be toured in summer.

About 8 miles west of Kewaunee is **Parallel 44 Vineyards and Winery**. The 44th parallel connects this region with Bordeaux, France, and Tuscany,

Italy, and owners Steve Johnson and Maria Milano are bringing a deeper connection with wine. The nine-acre vineyard produced its first harvest in 2007, and the wines were ready for sale in 2008. Stop in for a tasting. Tours are only on Saturday afternoons. Sleepy Hollow Road is part of **State Rustic Road 7**, a 3.5-mile drive past picturesque barns, an old lime kiln, a flour mill, and glacial deposits.

The byway continues north on WI 42 crossing over the Kewaunee River. On the other side of the river, watch for Duvall Street on the right. This will take you a short distance to **Barnsite Gallery**, a barn that has been beautifully redone to hold some outstanding collections from regional and national artists.

As you continue north on WI 42 on the byway, you will pass through Alaska and then run closer to the lake again. Coming up on your left, look for a corrugated tin building surrounded by various plants and garden art. From the front of the building on the second floor, you will see a pig with wings. If ever an art gallery was a destination, this is it. **The Flying Pig** represents works from as many as 200 artists, local, national, and even international. You can find large pieces or small, serious or whimsical, and in a wide variety of media. In the gardens outside are a children's play area and a bench for the non-shopper who can also get food, tea, coffee, or even beer from inside. Saturdays in the summer bring live music. This place is fun; don't miss it.

Why would a couple of Brits come all the way to Algoma, Wisconsin? Why, to open a bed and breakfast, of course. Get a taste of the UK at **Britannia Bed and Breakfast**. The seven luxurious suites look right out to the waves from private decks, and three of them offer Jacuzzis. Breakfast is British style, complete with baked beans. You'll pass the inn on your way into town.

Algoma is the end point of this byway. The small town is a big destination for sport fishing. The number of salmon coming out of here is unmatched elsewhere, and record-breaking trout have been caught as well. If fishing is your thing, get in touch with **Kinn's Sport Fishing**, which has over forty years of experience and has as many as nine large full-time boats for full- and half-day charters. Algoma maintains a **fishing hotline** so you can know what fish are running.

Algoma had some old-school ad murals repainted on the buildings in town adding to its small town atmosphere. The town's **little red lighthouse** at the end of the pier is often photographed. A catwalk connects it to the breakwater, but you cannot walk out to the lighthouse itself.

Algoma's bright red lighthouse is a frequent subject for shutterbugs.

The sunrise over the lake is predictably excellent, especially with the lighthouse in your camera lens. If you are here for breakfast, **Dairy Dean's Restaurant** is your best bet. For a steak and seafood supper club dinner, consider the **Hotel Stebbens.** It has a small town tavern feel to it, and it is

CHRISTMAS TREE SHIPS

The *Rouse Simmons*, a 123-foot, three-masted schooner, used to be a sign of Christmas season to the people of Chicago. Each year ships hauled Christmas trees down from Michigan. In November of 1912 the lake was a furious beast; a severe snowstorm took down ten freighters in just four days, and four hundred sailors were lost. Captain Herman Schuenemann, a native of Algoma (then the German town of Ahnapee) set sail with a full load of trees on November 25. A storm was on the boil, and other ships sought shelter. Schuenemann didn't get far before the ship was being battered by 60-mile-an-hour winds and gradually taking on water and ice. The *Rouse Simmons* was last spotted by the Coast Guard at Kewaunee. Though the captain's wallet was brought up by fisherman twelve years later, there was no sign of the wreck until a scuba diver found it in 1971 off the shore near Two Rivers.

a short walk to the pier. It is also an actual hotel with a small handful of affordable rooms. Grab a beer at the bar or feast on some upscale pub fare at the **Steelhead Saloon.**

For something a bit more contemporary, find **Caffé Tlazo** right on the highway in town. The menu leans toward Mediterranean, and you can get great sandwiches, soups, and salads. The coffee is fairly traded and organic, and the smoothies are excellent. **Bearcat Fish House** is a must stop if you enjoy fresh smoked fish. The shop is open year round and also has cheese for sale.

And where there's cheese, there's wine. Well, ideally of course. **Von Steihl Winery** is right downtown in the former Ahnapee Brewing Company building. Stop and sample the various wine, including an award-winning Riesling and a brandy-fortified cherry wine. A tour of the old building costs a nominal fee and is worth checking out.

From Algoma you can backtrack to Manitowoc to connect with I-43, or continue up WI 42 for the Door County chapter's byway.

IN THE AREA

Accommodations

Bedell Hill Bed and Breakfast, 4825 Broadway Street, Manitowoc. Call 920-683-3842. Set on two acres, this Greek-revival farmhouse offers one suite with a kitchenette. There is a dog onsite. Follow WI 42 west to Whitewater Drive. Take that south, and it becomes Michigan Avenue. A short distance later Broadway splits to the right.

Blue Harbor Resort, 725 Blue Harbor Drive, Sheboygan. Call 1-866-865-5080. Choose from a variety of 182 family-sized suites and sixty-four villas at this lakeside resort. An indoor water park is the center of activity, and there is also a full-service spa. Web site: www.blueharborre sort.com.

Britannia Bed and Breakfast, N7136 WI 42, Algoma. Call 920-255-3471. Three of these seven waterfront suites have Jacuzzis, and all have private bath and entrance and French doors to lakefront decks. The British owners serve a full authentic British breakfast complete with baked beans. Rates drop a bit in winter. Web site: www.britanniabb.com.

Duvall House Bed and Breakfast, 815 Milwaukee Street, Kewaunee. Call 920-388-2141. This 1881 Italianate Victorian home offers four rooms with private baths. Located right on WI 42 as it comes into town, the inn is also a short walk from downtown, the river and the lake. Enjoy the sunroom. Web site: www.duvallhouse.net.

Kewaunee Inn at Hamachek Village, 122 Ellis Street, Kewaunee. Call 920-388-0800. Choose from water view, city view and standards in this 1912 three-story brick hotel. Three ghosts are said to make periodic appearances. The hotel is newly remodeled and has a restaurant and tavern. Web site: www.kewauneeinn.com.

Lighthouse Inn, 1515 Memorial Drive, Two Rivers. Call 920-793-4524. The accommodations are somewhat dated but the location is supreme looking out to the lake. Be sure to get a lakeside room, however. The hotel restaurant serves decent food. Web site: lhinn.com.

Point Beach State Forest, 9400 County Road O, Two Rivers. Call 920-794-7480. The state park vehicle fee applies. With over 6 miles of sandy beach and a forest rich with pine and hardwoods, this park is a natural wonder. Camp at one of the 127 sites, hike or bike the trails, or get a photo of the nearby lighthouse. Web site: www.dnr.wi.gov/org/land/parks/specific/pointbeach.

Point Beach Guest House, 7609 County Road O, Two Rivers. Call 206-905-4648. This is a complete three-bedroom house along a rustic road outside Point Beach State Park. The house has a full kitchen, laundry facilities, a screened porch, and a fireplace. Weekly rates available. Web site: www.pointbeachguesthouse.com.

Red Forest Bed and Breakfast, 1421 25th Street, Two Rivers. Call 920-793-1794. This charming home has four guest rooms with private baths. Three blocks north of WI 42. Web site: www.redforestbb.com.

WestPort Bed and Breakfast, 635 North Eighth Street, Manitowoc. Call 1-888-686-0465. Stay on North Eighth Street after crossing the Manitowoc River until St. Clair Street. This 1879 Italianate Victorian-style Cream City brick home features four guest rooms—two with whirlpool tubs, three with gas fireplaces, and all with private bath. Special touches are the lavender-scented bed linens and a four-course candlelit breakfast. Web site: www.thewestport.com.

Attractions/Recreation

Barnsite Gallery, 109 Duvall Street, Kewaunee. Call 920-388-4391. Set in a remodeled barn, this gallery is another great stop for art fans. Regional and national artists are represented and the gallery hosts two- to five-day workshops. Web site: www.barnsiteartstudio.com.

Bearcat Fish House, 295 Fourth Street, Algoma. Call 920-487-2372. Bearcat specializes in fresh smoked fish; stop by and try some or take a pack home with you. His shop also sells cheese and other gifts. Web site: www.bearcatsfish.com.

Cedar Crest Specialties, 2000 South 10th Street, Manitowoc. Call 920-682-5577. Open daily Apr.–Nov. Stop in at the factory's ice cream parlor and get a cone of some fine Wisconsin product. Web site: www.cedar cresticecream.com.

EOS—Expedition Outdoor Supply, 668 South Pier Drive, Sheboygan. Call 920-208-7873. This outdoors outfitter can hook you up with what-ever you need: bikes, camping gear, kayaks, and—believe it or not—surfboards. Web site: www.eosoutdoor.com.

The Fitness Store, 1410 Dewey Street, Manitowoc. Call 920-684-8088. Rent bikes for the Mariner's Trail and others at the main location or at rental points at the Manitowoc marina and the Lighthouse Inn. Web site: thefitnessstore.com.

Hamilton Wood Type & Printing Museum, 1619 Jefferson Street, Two Rivers. Call 920-794-6272. This free museum showcases the old printing method and is the only museum in the world dedicated to this topic. The guides make it worth the stop.

Robert Heuel Studio and Gallery, 1461 Lakeshore Drive, Cleveland. Call 920-693-3328. A master oil painter, Heuel paints portraits and land-scapes in his lakeside home. Call for an appointment to have a chat with the artist and his wife and see his work.

John Michael Kohler Arts Center, 608 New York Avenue, Sheboygan. Call 920-458-6144. This 100,000 square-foot art complex brings art and artists together into the Sheboygan community. Ten galleries, a theater and performance spaces, and so many interactive opportunities, such as the ARTery for those with children and workshops for all ages, make this an impressive community center. Open daily except for major public holidays. Web site: www.jmkac.org.

Kinn's Sport Fishing, Sunrise Cove Marina, 70 Church Street, Algoma. Call 1-800-446-8605. The company has over forty years of experience and a fleet of at least nine large full-time boats. Full- and half-day charters set out for trophy salmon and trout from mid-Apr. to mid-Oct. Web site: www.kinnskatch.com.

Kohler-Andrae State Park, 1020 Beach Park Lane, Sheboygan. Call 920-451-4080. Open 6 AM–11 PM. State park fee applies. Stroll through the preserved dunes on a boardwalk or take a walk along the sandy beach. This is an excellent place to watch a sunrise or have a picnic. A nature center, open in the afternoon, offers information about the unique nature of the area. The park's 105 campsites are available year round and should be reserved in summer. Web site: www.dnr.state.wi.us.

Mariner's Trail. This 5.5-mile paved bicycle and walking path passes along the Lake Michigan shoreline and connects Manitowoc and Two Rivers. One end begins at the marina in Manitowoc; the other is at the Lighthouse Inn in Two Rivers. Web site: www.marinerstrail.net.

Parallel 44 Vineyard and Winery, N2185 Sleepy Hollow Road, Kewaunee. Call 920-388-4400. Head west from Kewaunee 8 miles on WI 29 and take Sleepy Hollow Road left (south). The vineyard had its first harvest in fall of 2007. These are not fruit wines; this is the real deal made from cold-resistant grapes. Stop in for tastings daily from May–Dec. and on weekends Jan.–Apr. Tours are on Sat. afternoons. Web site: www.parallel44.com.

Rogers Street Fishing Village & Great Lakes Coast Guard Museum, 2102 Jackson Street, Two Rivers. Call 920-793-5905. Open daily, May–Oct. Fee. This historic complex includes an 1886 lighthouse, five fishing sheds, and a 1936 fishing tug. Learn the history of commercial fishing, shipwrecks, and the rescue operations. Web site: www.rogersstreet.com.

Sheboygan County Historical Museum, 3110 Erie Avenue, Sheboygan. Call 920-458-1103. Originally an 1850's home, the museum covers medical, maritime, local baseball, farming, circus, and Native American history. A nineteenth-century log cabin is on site as well.

Sheboygan Shoreline Cruises, 644 South Pier Drive, Sheboygan. Call 920-451-0201. Spirit on the Lake has room for up to thirty-five passengers and includes indoor/outdoor seating and a full bar while cruising the beauty of Lake Michigan. Tours depend on demand and run from June to mid-Oct. Web site: www.sheboyganshorelinecruises.com.

Truettner's Berry Farm, 3904 County Road C, Manitowoc. Call 920-726-4766. Strawberries and raspberries are grown here, and you can pick your own.

Victorian Chocolate Shoppe, 519 South Eighth Street, Sheboygan. Call 920-208-3511. Choose from over sixty kinds of handmade chocolates including some sugar-free varieties.

Von Stiehl Winery, 115 Navarino Street, Algoma. Call 1-800-955-5208. Stop in for free tastings of these grape and fruit wines anytime. The tours of the building, the former Ahnapee Brewing Company, are more frequent in the spring, summer, and fall. Call for exact times, especially in winter. Web site: www.vonstiehl.com.

West of the Lake Gardens, 915 Memorial Drive, Manitowoc. Call 920-684-6110. Web site: www.westofthelake.com. Located just north of town on WI 42 (Memorial Drive and WI 42 are one and the same). The gardens are open daily from Mother's Day to mid-Oct. Created in 1934, this six-acre estate of the late Ruth and John West features a Rose Garden, Japanese Garden, Sunken Garden, and Formal Garden.

Whistling Straits, N8501 County LS, Kohler. Call 1-800-344-2838 for advance reservations or 1-866-847-4856 for same-day reservations. Play the same links as the pros. Here are two first-class rounds of eighteen along the shore of Lake Michigan. Web site: www.destinationkohler.com.

Wisconsin Maritime Museum, 75 Maritime Drive, Manitowoc. Call 920-684-0218. Open daily 9–6, Memorial Day–Labor Day. Fee. Find out more about shipbuilding and commercial fishing. Then tour the USS *Cobia,* a World War II submarine permanently docked behind the museum. Children will love the hands-on waterways room. Waterproof aprons are provided. Web site: www.wisconsinmaritime.org.

Woodland Dunes Nature Center, Call 920-793-4007. Take some short nature hikes and see some wildlife at this 1,200-acre preserve between

Manitowoc and Two Rivers. Two trails are handicap accessible. No pets or smoking allowed. Trails are open during daylight hours and trail guides are at the Nature Center or in a metal box outside when the office is closed. Web site: www.woodlanddunes.com.

Zutz Cheese House, 1921 South 10th Street, Manitowoc. Call 920-684-4873. This cheese showroom does a strong mail-order business around the holidays. You can stop here and get some cheese to go.

Dining/Drinks

Annie's Emporium, 406 Milwaukee Street, Kewaunee. Call 920-388-2112. Web site: www.anniesicecreamemporium.com. In one of the oldest buildings downtown, this ice cream shop has thirty-two flavors and also serves locally roasted coffee, regional chocolate and candy, and light lunch/snack items.

Caffé Tlazo, 607 Fourth Street/Highway 42, Algoma. Call 920-487-7240. Set in a renovated 1891 Italianate house, the café serves sandwiches, salads and soups with a Mediterranean bent, as well as fair-trade, organic coffee, tea, and smoothies.

Dairy Dean's Restaurant, 824 Fourth Street, Algoma. Call 920-487-5668. This standard diner serves a traditional breakfast for a reasonable price. Popular with the fishing crowd.

Hotel Stebbins Supper Club, 201 Steele Street, Algoma. Call 920-487-5521. A tavern and supper club, this hotel restaurant serves steak and seafood dinners daily, but is closed on Mon. in the off season. This is also a small hotel with a handful of affordable rooms. Web site: www.thehotelstebbins.com.

Il Ritrovo, 515 South Eighth Street, Sheboygan. Call 920-803-7516. This is arguably one of the top authentic Italian pizzas in the state. They use a wood-fired oven to make thin-crust traditional pie, and they have even gotten the official approval from Napoli's Verace Pizza Napoletana Association to be able to legally call their margherita pizza traditional Napoletana.

Islander Café, 528 South Pier Drive, Sheboygan. Call 920-458-2233. The breakfasts here are excellent, especially the eggs Benedict and the fruit and cream-cheese stuffed French toast. Get good coffee and a variety of sandwiches and pasta dishes for lunch. Web site: www.theislander cafe.com.

Kunkel's Korner Restaurant, 301 Ellis Street, Kewaunee. Call 920-388-0834.

Pier 57 Deli and Lounge, 644 South Pier Drive, Sheboygan. Call 920-457-7437. Stop in here for a gourmet sandwich, which can also be made to go.

Phil Rohrer's Restaurant, 1303 22nd Street, Two Rivers. Call 920-794-8500. A classic little diner, Phil's serves homemade soups and pies and good, hearty diner fare with counter and booth seating. It's really a local institution. Where WI 42 goes right (east) on 22nd Street, go left (west) instead.

Steelhead Saloon, 530 Fourth Street, Algoma. Call 920-487-3899. Grab a beer or a brandy old-fashioned at the bar or enjoy a meal of upscale pub fare including gourmet burgers.

Trattoria Stefano, 522 South Eighth Street, Sheboygan. Call 920-452-8455. From the same owner of Il Ritrovo, this fine Italian restaurant provides authentic recipes from a chef who makes an annual pilgrimage to Italia to keep honing his skills.

Whistling Straits Restaurant, N8501 County LS, Kohler. Call 1-800-344-2838. With a perfect lake view, this AAA Three Diamond restaurant offers British Isle influenced cuisine for lunch and dinner and an extensive wine list.

Other

Algoma Chamber of Commerce, 1226 Lake Street, Algoma. Call 920-487-2041. Web site: www.algoma.org.

Algoma Fishing Hotline. Call 1-800-626-3090.

Kewaunee Chamber of Commerce, 308 North Main Street, Kewaunee. Call 920-388-4822. Web site: www.kewaunee.org.

Manitowoc Area Visitor Information Center, 4221 Calumet Avenue, Manitowoc. Call 920-683-4388. Located just east of the interchange of

I-43 and US 151, the large complex has clean restrooms and a wealth of area information and maps. Web site: www.manitowoc.org.

Sheboygan Chamber of Commerce, 712 Riverfront Drive # 101, Sheboygan. Call 920-457-9491. Web site: www.sheboygan.org.

SS *Badger,* Manitowoc Dock, 900 South Lakeview Drive, Manitowoc. Call 920-684-0888. The car and passenger ferry connects Manitowoc and Ludington, Michigan, with once-a-day runs in spring and fall and twice-a-day journeys in summer. Web site: www.ssbadger.com.

See how glass is blown at Oulu Glass.

CHAPTER

8

Lake Superior Country

Estimated length: 180 miles
Estimated time: One day at least, but recommended extra day to visit the Apostle Islands

Getting there: From Duluth, Minnesota, take US 53 across the St. Louis River into Superior, WI. At Exit 1 follow the loop into US 53 South and 1.8 miles later it will join US 2. If you are coming from the south, you can pick up this byway in Ashland. Take US 51 north to Hurley and go west on US 2 or come up WI 13 directly into Ashland.

Highlights: A trip to **Aminicon Falls** will take you back one billion years in geological history, while the **Washburn Historical Museum** will show you more recent occurrences in this corner of the state. The Lake Superior shoreline is as gorgeous as it is long and communities such as Iron River and Bayfield cater to tourists looking for local delicacies, quaint shops, or a cozy place to bed down for the night. The **Apostle Islands National Lakeshore** encompasses twenty-one islands known as the "Jewels of Lake Superior," and a car ferry will take you across to the largest of them.

The natives called the lake "Kitchi-Gami," a name which poet Henry Wadsworth Longfellow fashioned to "Gitche Gumee" in a poem. But sixteenth-century French explorers dubbed it *le lac superieur*, which merely means "the upper lake" as it is north of Lake Huron, and so we are left with today's anglicized version. As the largest freshwater lake in the world, it truly is Superior, and its history of storms and shipwrecks makes it seem more like a temperamental sea. Weather changes suddenly up here, and with such a cold body of water, a shift in wind can make even a sunny July day raise goose flesh.

As you cross into Wisconsin on the US 53 bridge, you can see the towering ore docks along the lakeside, reminders of the days of iron when massive ships hauled taconite from the region to steel mills in the East. About 12 miles east of Superior, US 2 and US 53 part ways. Stay on US 2 and just past the juncture look for CR U on the left. 0.3 mile down the road on the left is the **Amnicon Falls State Park** entrance. The park office is not always open, in which case you need to self-register and pay the daily vehicle fee. At the office, pick up a copy of a free booklet narrating the landscape and the walking trails. Follow the road to the right, and it will take you to a parking area near two waterfalls and a covered bridge.

This park is a mini-course in geology. The Amnicon River tumbles along its way to Lake Superior to the north. If you are sure-footed, you can walk along the jagged rock at the water's edge all the way to where it tumbles fifteen feet at Upper Falls. Prior to this point the rock is basalt, remnants of volcanic activity that occurred one billion years ago. There is a staircase from the parking lot down to the bottom of the falls where you can get a good picture. The water passes from there under a covered bridge before slipping down over the Lower Falls. At that point, however, you will find sandstone that was formed by sediments from streams that once flowed into an ocean that covered most of the state half a billion years ago. You can see the varied colored horizontal layers in the rock, and to the northeast you can see a smooth cliff where fractured rock fell away long ago.

Most people don't think of Wisconsin at the mention of a fault line, but around 500 million years ago, the Douglas Fault was created by a massive shift in the basalt bedrock. The fault runs from Ashland almost to the Twin Cities. As the bedrock on the southern side of the fault rose slowly at a 55-degree angle, it created the gateways for the Upper Falls and two other waterfalls in the park: Snake Pit Falls and Now and Then Falls. Look for potholes in the basalt that were made by swirling debris from rapidly flowing glacial meltwater during the Ice Age.

As you continue east on US 2, look for signs for **Oulu Glass** as you approach Iron River. The Jim and Sue Vojacek family loves glass. Everyone

Amnicon Falls is a pleasant stop for a picnic or a walk in the woods.

seems to have a hand in it. Jim's been blowing glass since the late 60s. Sue uses stained pieces to create her own artwork. Their studio and gallery are as much a part of the attraction as the colorful creations inside and might strike visitors as something out of *The Hobbit*. Oulu Glass is closed from January to May 1. Workshops are offered from time to time, and you can see demonstrations in November and December. The short drive from the highway is partly on unpaved roads and colorful in the fall.

Continuing east on US 2 you'll arrive in **Iron River**. Immediately on your left as you enter town is **White Winter Winery** separated from the road by a parking lot. Jon Hamilton comes from a long line of beekeepers and has had a lifelong fascination with mead, an alcoholic drink made from fermented honey and water. He and his wife Kim founded the winery in 1996 and have created several different flavored meads and developed a line of fruit spritzes as well. Stop in for some free samples and a chat with the friendly staff. Come in July when Iron River hosts a blueberry festival or on summer Sunday afternoons for free live music at the winery.

If you leave hungry, I recommend a side trip for a meal experience before heading into Ashland. Take CR H south from Iron River 12 miles where you will come to a gleaming aluminum building on the right side of the road. This was once the site of the 1923 Delta Store, a whistle stop on the Duluth Atlantic and South Shore Railroad and the heart of a community dispersed among the pines and lakes around here. What stands here now is the **Delta Diner**, a restored 1940s Silk City diner brought in all the way from upstate New York. Sit at the counter or grab a booth, and enjoy some hearty and creative food. The typical diner burgers and breakfasts are superb, but the real attractions are dishes like the puffy oven-baked omelets with spicy shrimp or portabella mushrooms, the Mexican Benny (a sort of eggs Benedict with chipotle sauce over hash browns), or the barbeque pork sandwiches. Owner and master chef Todd Bucher spends a lot of time

Travelers have driven all the way from the southern half of the state just to have a meal at the Delta Diner and then go home

The Northern Great Lakes Visitor Center offers a variety of exhibits interpreting the Lake Superior natural history.

developing new and unusual menu items. His wife Nina runs a coffee shop and ice cream parlor next door with outdoor seating.

Continue east from here on CR H until you come to CR E. Go left (north) and rejoin US 2 heading east into Ashland. Just before you arrive at the Ashland city limits you will come to CR G and the site of the **Northern Great Lakes Visitor Center** on your left. A nice interactive museum brings Native American culture, local history, and science together in a way that is engaging for children and adults alike. Wheelchair-accessible walking paths and boardwalks venture out into the woods behind the building and a five-story observation tower—reachable by elevator—allows you to see for miles in all directions. Admission is free, and short documentaries are shown in the theater throughout the day. There is a coffee shop serving eco-friendly coffee, a gift shop, and an excellent collection of free maps, brochures, and booklets about area attractions.

As you approach Ashland you'll see Chequamegon (sheh-WAH-meh-gun) Bay on the left. Across the waters are Washburn and Bayfield. The first wayside on the left is **Maslowski Park** where you can stop and fill up your water bottle at an artesian well that flows continuously. Lake Superior can be bone-chilling; the shallow and sheltered bay is one of your best bets for warmer waters.

Ashland saw the boom of the iron ore industry, and at one time there were five towering ore docks along its shore, including a massive cathedral-like, concrete-and-steel structure that is only recently being dismantled. When those days passed, it looked as if Ashland was in its death throes. However, an influx of progressive-minded individuals, attracted by the area's natural beauty, and the survivor mentality of the locals, have kept this city alive. Now you can drive down Main Street and it still looks like 1950s America, but you can also find a couple hip shops, such as the **Black Cat Coffeehouse,** which serves organic meals and espresso on Chapple Avenue, and a wonderful all-natural bakery right across the street called **Daily Bread**. A **farmers' market** is hosted nearby from July through October. Several historically themed **murals** have been painted on downtown buildings, most notably one honoring war veterans on the side of the Bay Theatre across the street from the Vaughn Public Library.

For some fancier fare, such as steaks or marlin, stop by the **Deep Water Grille. South Shore Brewery**, a fantastic microbrewery, serves the suds for the restaurant, and their beers are available for carryout in bottles or refillable half-gallon jars called growlers. Brewmaster Bo Belanger swears business could survive on his nut brown ale alone. If you plan on spending the night in Ashland, consider the **Hotel Chequamegon**, a Victorian-themed inn overlooking the lake and a marina.

Backtrack on US 2 west to WI 13 and go right (north) 7.5 miles. As you follow WI 13 into Washburn, you will find a large brownstone building on your left in the heart of town. Once a bank in 1890—you can still see the safe inside—it is now home to a craft store and art exhibit on the first floor, and the small but fascinating **Washburn Historical Museum** on the second. There's a model of the DuPont explosives factory that once operated just outside of Washburn. Stories of two fatal explosions are preserved here in newspaper clippings and signage, and a photo of one of the crews includes my grandfather, Lawrence Girga.

Located on the left as you come into Washburn, **North Coast Coffee** has Wi-Fi for the Internet addicted; this is your best bet for a cup of Joe and some fresh-baked goods in the morning, as the breakfast options in town are rather limited. Shoppers will be interested in **Woven Earth** fair-trade arts, and **Backyard Birding and Gift Shop** will appeal to those interested in our fine feathered friends. **Chequamegon Books and Coffee** is a nice place to browse for something to read. **Stage North**, one block down Second Avenue West toward the lake, is a 145-seat theater putting on local productions.

As you head out of town you will see **Memorial Park** on the right, which offers some camping and lake access. Those looking for something cozier might try the **Nordic Bay Bed and Breakfast,** a Scandinavian-style inn set lakeside. Three guest rooms share two communal baths, and there is a playroom for children. An air-conditioned two-bedroom cabin can sleeps up to eight in summer when using the sun porch.

Bayfield is another 12 miles from Washburn. Along the wooded route watch for a pair of silos on the right. This marks a deli and restaurant known as **Racheli's at Twin Silos**. Ugo Racheli (from Italy) and his wife Marcia began producing their own line of Italian products, and soon opened the deli. The restaurant spun off from there, and they are already expanding it. Hours have been limited, but that may change in the near future.

Just 3 miles before Bayfield is Ski Hill Road; a left here will take you 2 miles to the **Lake Superior Big Top Chautauqua**, a canvas-covered summer entertainment venue that shouldn't be missed. Closer to Bayfield you'll find **Bodin's Resort Beachside Cottages**, which offers one- and two-bedroom cabins overlooking the lake, with views of the Apostle Islands.

Bayfield has become the centerpiece of the area's tourism industry. The town of just about 900 offers a collection of galleries, shops, inns, and restaurants, and is considered the gateway to the Apostle Islands. Bayfield's

THE CHAUTAUQUA

The Chautauqua was a rural adult-education movement in the late nineteenth century to the mid-1920s. The institution provided culture and entertainment for rural communities in the form of speakers, preachers, and teachers, as well as musicians and other entertainers. The first Chautauqua was formed at a campsite on a New York lake of the same name by a Methodist minister, John Heyl Vincent. Touring tent Chautauquas soon evolved. Bayfield hosted several before World War I. Then in 1986, the **Lake Superior Big Top Chautauqua** was founded. Over the years big names such as Johnny Cash and Willie Nelson have performed here. The 900-seat tent theater hosts seventy-plus nights of summer entertainment and has a weekly radio show on Wisconsin Public Radio.

An entire summer line up of entertainment awaits at the Lake Superior Big Top Chautauqua.

annual Apple Fest, held the first weekend in October, sees around 40,000 people.

You will pass the Bayfield Fish Hatchery on your left and see **Weber's Orchards**, where you can buy or pick your own apples, pears, and other produce. Right across the highway from the orchard, you'll find a collection of arts and crafts stores including **Klein's Hitching Post**, which offers fine wood carving, the **Bayfield Quilt Co.**, and **Eckels Pottery**. The **Gourmet Garage** is a knock-your-socks-off bakery, and during Apple Fest you can expect an abundance of apple pies here.

Take a right down Manypenny Avenue to get to the marina area. The first restaurant on your left will be the pink-painted, flamingo-themed bar and restaurant, **Maggie's**. The décor consists of flamingo trinkets, lights and a train running along a shelf near the ceiling. You can expect fresh local fish, pastas, pizza, burgers, and salads, as well as a full bar. Your best bet for breakfast might be **The Egg Toss Café** on Second Street and Manypenny Avenue. This cozy café does omelets and eggs Benedict as well as waffles and donuts.

Just across the street at the corner of the brick-paved Second Street you'll find **Stone's Throw**, an old mill converted into a gallery. Pottery is made on-site, but the collection also includes work from over a hundred artists of varying media.

For such a small town, Bayfield has quite a variety of bed and breakfasts and inns and the Chamber of Commerce web site has a comprehensive list of them. One downtown option is **Silver Nail Guesthouse**, with rooms with Jacuzzis. Lodging doesn't get much classier than the **Old Rittenhouse Inn**. Just blocks from the lake, the twenty guest rooms and suites are located in three historic homes. The Rittenhouse is an impressive 1890 summer cottage, which has been written up in many publications, and the Chateau, a 1908 Queen Anne Victorian is equally charming. The **gourmet restaurant** at the inn is also highly regarded, and reservations are recommended. A bit more casual is **Ethel's at 250** just down the road. It has a varied menu, but the pizza is perhaps the most popular item.

Right down by the marina at the end of Manypenny Avenue, **Bayfield Maritime Museum** is a small warehouse to the right, full of photos and exhibits about boats and commercial fishing. Out front you'll see an old pilothouse. Going left on First Street (if you're facing the lake) will take you to the **car ferry** to Madeline Island. **Pier Plaza Restaurant and the Pickled Herring Lounge** has outdoor seating along here and is a decent place for a casual meal or drinks on First Street.

The **Apostle Islands National Lakeshore**, located along the Bayfield Peninsula, includes 12 miles of shoreline and twenty-one of the twenty-two islands also known as the Jewels of Lake Superior. Since 2004, 80 percent of the land area of the islands is protected as the Gaylord Nelson Wilderness Area, named for the late former governor and U.S. senator. Nelson was the principal founder of Earth Day and instrumental in the creation of this national park. Visitors come to the islands for their natural beauty—including some original growth forest, sandstone formations, and caves—abundant wildlife, and its collection of nine historical lighthouses.

The only Apostle Island you can get to with your car, and the only one outside the national lakeshore, is Madeline Island. A few of the rest of the islands can either be seen with serious kayak expeditions or boat rentals, or else with a boat tour offered by **Apostle Islands Cruise Service** based in Bayfield. Daily shuttles run to specific islands allowing you to visit lighthouses, hike, or picnic, or you can join narrated cruises throughout the day. Departures and destinations are very dependent on weather conditions and a minimum number of passengers, which means you won't know until the day of the trip the precise details or availability. Always have a back-up

The Apostle Islands National Lakeshore offers stunning beauty such as these caves along the shore of Sand Island.

plan. Camping on the islands comes with a fee. You can either get there on your own if you have paddling experience, or hook up with an outfitter such as **Trek and Trail**, which offers day and overnight trips to the islands as well as sea kayak instruction. You can also get to the mainland lake caves from Meyers Beach. They also offer two **cabins for rent** at the north end of Bayfield. For an alternative look at the lake, don your dry suit and go under with **Superior Adventure Diving**. The abundant shipwrecks in Lake Superior are well preserved on account of the cold water.

The Bayfield Peninsula has been a great place for growing berries. In places only a local might know, there are actually wild blueberries around here. Spare yourself the search; head to one of several berry farms for **pick-your-own strawberries, raspberries, and blueberries**. From Bayfield head west on Washington Avenue up the hill to CR J. Go right through fields of wildflowers in summer to get to **Hauser's Superior View Farm.** The bright red central building is a 1920s mail-order barn from Sears-Roebuck. The name of the farm comes from the panorama you can see if you climb the steps to the hayloft. Labels on the windowsill identify what you can see. Downstairs is Bayfield Winery featuring a variety of hard ciders, meads,

MADELINE ISLAND

The largest of the Apostle Islands, **Madeline Island** was known to the Ojibwe as Moningwunakauning, "the home of the golden-breasted woodpecker." In 1693 French soldier Pierre l'Sueur built a trading post, and by 1718 a fort was erected. This was the center of France's fur trade on Lake Superior until the English took over New France. The current island name comes from the wife of Michel Cadotte who established a permanent settlement on the island. He married Equaysayway, the daughter of Ojibwe Chief White Crane and her Christian name became Madeline. Today, the 2.6-mile crossing to the island is made by car ferry from March to about mid-January. An ice road connects the community to the mainland in winter and an air-powered sled operates the intervening freeze/thaw periods.

The ferry arrives in La Pointe. An island walking tour map is available at the Madeline Island Chamber of Commerce. Mopeds and bicycles from **Motion-to-Go** are a nice alternative to bringing your car over. The mopeds have park passes for Big Bay State Park. Go right at the post office on Main Street and then left on Middle Road to find their big blue building. Alternatively, tour the shoreline with a rented kayak from Apostle Islands Kayaks. The outfitter offers guided tours or simple rentals to see the caves at Big Bay State Park or even visit nearby islands.

Just a one block north of the ferry landing is **Madeline Island Historical Museum**, a complex of historical buildings. The museum store sells a variety of gifts from books to Ojibwe crafts.

Tom's Burned Down Café has been "redefining classic elegance since 1992" when its original manifestation fell victim to a fire. In trying to preserve a bit of local history, Tom Nelson had bought Leona's, a beer bar and dance hall originally from the 1950s, and moved it to its present site in town. Just as he was re-opening it, the disaster struck, and he was left with nothing more than the deck he had set it on. Today it is an open-air bar with the occasional live music and a quirky collection of metal art.

Resembling a lighthouse, **The Inn on Madeline Island** offers an assortment of rooms, condos, houses, and cottages on the island, including many lakeside accommodations. The inn's restaurant, the **Pub Restaurant and Wine Bar,** sits poolside and serves local fish, steaks, and stone hearth pizzas.

If you're coming with a tent, **Big Bay State Park** offers sixty campsites and shower facilities. The park has a nice 1.5-mile beach perfect for rock hunting or sunbathing (and swimming, but don't expect Caribbean water temperatures!) as well as 9 miles of hiking trails and a variety of birds (over 230 species recorded).

and fruit wines, plus jams and salsas. A major part of the farm's business is perennial plants, but you can also pick raspberries and apples.

Just a bit farther down the road is **Rocky Acres** where you not only pick your own, you also pay and make change on your own. Pre-picked berries are set in a roadside stand, and you just leave your money in the box. You can save about half the price by going out into the fields and picking your own raspberries, blueberries, and strawberries. This family farm and ode to honesty has been around for over thirty years. Jack Erickson, once a commercial fisherman, retired and put all his efforts into the berry farm. His daughter Brenda helps out. Another 4 miles takes you back to WI 13 just north of Bayfield. On the way you'll see signs for **Rabideaux's**, another rec-

Pick your own berries near Bayfield: strawberries, raspberries, and blueberries.

In addition to apples and berries, another fine product of the Bayfield Peninsula is wine.

ommended berry farm, and **Bayfield Apple Company**, which doesn't just sell its namesake but also one of the largest crops of raspberries in the state.

Go left (north) on WI 13 and the town of Red Cliff is just 3.6 miles from Bayfield. You'll find a small casino here. On the right side of WI 13 just north of town look for **Native Spirit Gifts**, which sits across a

The **Red Cliff Reservation** is part of the Lake Superior Ojibwe (Chippewa) people, which is just part of a larger nation known as the Anishinabeg. Chief Buffalo lead a community on Madeline Island known as the La Pointe Band. After a U.S. government-forced move to Sandy Lake, Minnesota, during which almost 400 tribal members died of exposure, starvation, and disease, the tribe returned to their spiritual center at La Pointe and petitioned President Millard Fillmore with the support of Wisconsin citizens appalled by the tragedy. The result was the creation of reservations in Wisconsin including the one at Red Cliff where much of the La Pointe Band settled.

parking lot from a geodesic-roofed gas station. The store sells local wild rice and offers a nice collection of Ojibwe items including walking sticks, dream catchers, CDs, jewelry, and flutes.

You are now approaching the mainland portion of the Apostle Islands National Lakeshore. At CR K go right and follow it to Park Road. This will take you to the **Town of Russell Recreation Area**, which offers some camping, and past that, the park office of the National Park. The **Little Sand Bay Visitor Center** used to be a local dance hall with rooms to rent upstairs. Inside now is a small display of local history, a viewable video "On the Edge of Gichi Gami," and an assortment of books and guides for purchase and free brochures. You will also find restrooms. This office is open from mid-June to Labor Day only, but the park is open year round. The beach here looks out to Sand Island nearby, and one can launch a boat or canoe here.

From the park return to CR K and go right, following it all the way back out to WI 13. Go right (west) and it will take you to the end of the park where you will find the parking area for **Meyers Beach**. There is a self-pay station here for the fee to launch a boat or picnic along the beach. Paddlers and boaters leave from here to see the **sandstone cliffs and the Mawikwe Bay Caves** along the national lakeshore. In winter visitors can actually walk out on the ice to arrive at the caves. The **Lakeshore Trail** follows the edge of the sandstone cliffs as well. Exercise extreme caution and stay away from the edge: the erosion that formed the caves continues! The parking area has pit toilets but no water. The closest kayak rental is back in Bayfield.

Continuing west you will leave the path most traveled by tourists, but one that still possesses natural beauty and a humble small town appeal. The next town, **Cornucopia**, has the look of an old fishing village, and, in fact,

Though much of the commercial fishing industry is now history like these old boats in Cornucopia, you can still find the daily catch along this byway.

you'll see some old vessels propped on shore at the wayside as you arrive. A collection of shops is here offering an assortment of gifts. Across the small marina behind them is **Halvorson Fisheries**. This family business still does commercial fishing and owns four of the ten commercial fishing licenses on the lake. Primarily, they catch whitefish and herring, and you can pick up fresh, smoked, or pickled fish at the shop.

Continuing west through town past the marina area, go left on Superior Avenue to find **Siskiwit Bay Coffee and Curiosities** for a cup of coffee or an espresso. **Ehlers Store** right across the street sells everything you might need from coffee beans and groceries to wine, fresh meat, and wild rice. For a very short side trip, go left (east) at the stop sign on CR C and drive a short distance to Siskiwit Falls Road. Go left and continue to a bridge where you can see the modest falls below.

Back on WI 13, **Herbster** is another 8 miles west. You will cross creeks and pass through more second growth forest with occasional views to the lake on your right. In Herbster you will find **Northern Lights Gifts and Crafts** on the left, which has sketchy hours outside of June and July. The artwork comes from artists who live within a 100-mile radius of Herbster. Go right (north) on any village street and it will take you down to the lakeshore. The sandy beach has grassy patches and scattered driftwood. There is a very basic local campground toward the east end of town offering unsheltered tent sites right on the shore. You can see the north shore of the lake across the water here, but odds are you won't find another soul. On WI 13, **South Shore Convenience Store** sells gas, including diesel. At the time of writing, this was the only gas station along this northern shore road.

As you come into Port Wing, you'll find **Garden House Bed and Breakfast** on the left. This is another sleepy village. Port Wing, founded in 1901, was the home of the state's first school bus—a canvas-covered, horse-drawn wagon or sleigh—in 1903. Take the first right on Washington Avenue and it'll lead you to **Trout Run Art Gallery and Ice Cream**. Inside this 1895 former saloon is a nice collection of pottery and oil and water-color paintings. On summer weekends you can participate in ninety-minute art workshops for about $20. Back on WI 13 continuing west, **Ruxy's Cottage Café** is right on the highway and offers good breakfasts and lunches. Soups and baked goods are made in–house, and the burgers use hand patties. On the west end of town, Twin Falls has a picnic area, trail, and a half-mile stroll to an overlook of the two-level falls. In dry periods, however, it's more of a trickle.

From Port Wing you can take CR A south to Iron River and US 2. Otherwise, it's another 45 miles back to Superior following WI 13 to where it connects to US 2 just east of the city. You will follow along the lakeshore until WI 13 starts south and passes through Brule River State Forest. Though you leave the lake behind you, there is a part of it that always seems to stay with you, and this feeling, for many travelers, beckons them back.

IN THE AREA

Accommodations

Bodin's Bayfield Resort, 78800 Bodin Road, Washburn. Call 715-373-2359. These beachside cottages offer one and two bedrooms overlooking panoramic Lake Superior and five of the Apostle Islands. The facilities include a large lawn area, sandy beach, and access to onsite watercraft.

Garden House Bed and Breakfast, 9255 Sunnyside Lane, Port Wing. Call 715-774-3705. This private home on a five-acre lot in a quiet village offers a two-bedroom suite or single room, each with private bath and air-conditioning. Web site: www.garden-house.com.

Hotel Chequamegon, 101 Lake Shore Drive West, Ashland, 54806. Call 715-682-9095. This hotel overlooks the marina and Chequamegon Bay. Web site: www.hotelc.com.

The Inn on Madeline Island, La Pointe. Call 1-800-822-6315. Choose from a variety of homes, cottages, and condos as well as rooms in a lakeside complex. Web site: www.madisland.com.

Nordic Bay Bed and Breakfast, 900 Superior Avenue, Washburn. Call 715-373-5891. The inn overlooks the lake with a staircase to the shore. Three rooms share two communal baths. A separate cabin can accommodate groups of up to eight people. Web site: www.nordicbaybb.com.

The Old Rittenhouse Inn, 301 Rittenhouse Avenue, Bayfield. Call 715-779-5111. The 1890 Rittenhouse and 1908 Queen Anne Victorian Chateau are the best of these three bed and breakfast properties offering a total of twenty rooms/suites. The gourmet restaurant is highly regarded and open for breakfast and dinner year-round, and lunch during high season. Call for reservations. Web site: www.rittenhouseinn.com.

Silver Nail Guesthouse, 249 Rittenhouse Avenue, Bayfield. Call 715-779-3383. Located right downtown, this inn has five rooms including a two-room suite. All offer Jacuzzis, air-conditioning and wireless Internet. Web site: www.silvernailguesthouse.com.

Attractions/Recreation

Amnicon Falls State Park, County Road U, Superior. Call 715-398-3000. Open 6 AM–11 PM. Fee. See dramatic cuts of whitewater through ancient basalt. Web site: www.dnr.state.wi.us/org/land/parks/specific/amnicon.

Apostle Islands Cruise Service (Authorized NPS Concessioner), City Dock, Bayfield. Call 715-779-3925. This is the only authorized company to run boat tours of the national lakeshore. Destinations and running times are dependent on the weather and the number of passengers. Web site: www.apostleisland.com.

Apostle Islands Kayaks, 690 Main Street, La Pointe. Call 715 747-3636. Choose from a variety of single or double kayaks to follow the shore, see the caves at Big Bay State Park, or even visit other nearby islands. Web site: www.apostleislandskayaks.com.

Apostle Islands National Lakeshore, 415 Washington Avenue, Bayfield. Call 715-779-3397. The park is open year-round but the hours of the Bayfield Visitor Center vary with the seasons. For Little Sand Bay Visitor Center call 715-779-7007. Web site: www.nps.gov/apis.

Bayfield Apple Company, 87540 County Road J, Bayfield. Call 715-779-5700. Stop here for apples, raspberries, and an assortment of jams, fruit butters, and ciders. Web site: www.bayfieldapple.com.

Bayfield Maritime Museum, First Street, Bayfield. Call 715-779-9919. Open 10–4 mid-June–Sept., closed Mon. Fee. See 150 years of history at this museum located between the Coast Guard Station and City Hall. Web site: www.apostleisland.com/BMM.htm.

Bayfield Quilt Co., 84460 WI 13, Bayfield. Call 715-779-3095. Open Mon.–Sat., 10–6. Shop for homemade quilts or stop in for classes. Web site: www.bayfieldquilt.com.

Big Bay State Park, 2402 Hagen Road, La Pointe. Call 715-747-6425. Seven miles from the ferry, this park offers camping with shower facilities, hiking, and 1.5 miles of shoreline, which include picturesque sandstone bluffs. Reservations are recommended and can be made by calling 1-888-947-2757. Web site: www.dnr.state.wi.us/org/land/parks/specific/bigbay.

Eckels Pottery and Fine Craft Gallery, 85205 WI 13, Bayfield. Call 1-866-779-5617. Purchase some beautiful pottery and watch it being made. Web site: www.eckelspotterybayfield.com.

Ehlers Store, 88545 Superior Avenue, Cornucopia. Call 715-742-3232. This general store offers everything from groceries and wine to hardware.

Gourmet Garage, 85130 WI 13, Bayfield. Call 715-779-5365. This bakery gets raves. The apple pie is legendary.

Halvorson Fisheries, Bell Marina, Cornucopia. Call 715-742-3402. This family commercial fishing outfit sells fresh, smoked, and pickled fish including herring, whitefish, and smelt.

Hauser's Superior View Farm, 86565 County Road J, Bayfield. Call 715-779-5404. Open 10–5 daily May–Oct. An historic barn houses Bayfield Winery and sells fresh berries and perennial plants. Web site: www .superiorviewfarm.com.

Klein's Hitching Post, 84420 WI 13, Bayfield. Call 715-779-5707. Open daily (but not consistently) 10–6, May–Oct., and then weekends until Christmas. Check out some fine oak carving and gifts.

Madeline Island Historical Museum, 226 Colonel Woods Avenue, La Pointe. Call 715-747-2415. Web site: madelineislandmuseum .wisconsinhistory.org.

Motion-to-Go Bicycle and Moped Rentals, two blocks from the ferry, La Pointe. Call 715-747-6585. A great way to see the island is on two wheels; the mopeds even have state park stickers for Big Bay. Take a right on Main Street and a left on Middle Road and it's the big blue building. Web site: www.motion-to-go.com.

Native Spirits Gifts, WI 13, Red Cliff. Call 715-779-9550. Closed during lunch and on Sun. The roadside shop sells an assortment of Ojibwe crafts and cultural items.

Northern Great Lakes Visitor Center, 29270 County Road G, Ashland. Call 715-685-9983. Free. Open daily 9–5. Stop in for a nice interactive museum dedicated to Superior Country, a gift shop, an observation tower, and plenty of brochures on the area. Hiking trails explore the grounds. Web site: www.northerngreatlakescenter.org.

Northern Lights Gifts, WI 13, Herbster. Call 715-774-3427. All artwork is produced within a 100-mile radius. Open daily, June and July, otherwise give a call first. Web site: www.norlightsgifts.com.

Oulu Glass, 1695 West Colby Road, Brule. Call 715-372-4160. Open daily 9–5, 12–5 on Sun. Closed Jan.–May 1. Free demonstrations Nov.–Dec. The blown and stained glass work by this husband and wife team is extraordinary. Their studio is a sight in itself. Web site: www.ouluglass.com.

Rabideaux's Bayfield Fruit Company, 35465 County Road J, Bayfield. Call 715-779-5509. Pick your own strawberries and raspberries.

Rocky Acres Berry Farm, 87340 County Road J, Bayfield. Call 715-779-3332. Pick your own raspberries, strawberries, or blueberries.

Stagenorth, 123 West Omaha Street, Washburn. Call 715-373-1194. This 145-seat community theater hosts plays, films, concerts, speakers, and even televised Packers games. Web site: www.stagenorth.com.

Stone's Throw, 40 South Second2n Street, Bayfield. Call 715-779-5200. This gallery offers work from over a hundred artists in media ranging from pottery and glass to prints and fabrics. Web site: www.stones throwbayfield.com.

Superior Adventures Dive Center, WI 13, Pikes Bay Marina, Bayfield. Call 715- 292-3483.

Trek & Trail, 7 Washington Avenue, Bayfield. Call 1-800-354-8735. This outfitter offers day and overnight trips to the Apostle Islands as well as kayaking instruction and trips to the sea caves on the mainland. They also have two cabins for rent at the north end of town. Web site: www.trek-trail.com.

Trout Run Gallery and Ice Cream, 83315 Washington Avenue, Port Wing. Call 715-774-3799. This 1895 saloon turned gallery and ice cream shop also does weekend art workshops throughout the summer. Web site: www.troutrunart.com.

Washburn Historical Museum, 1 East Bayfield Street, Washburn. Call 715-373-0243. Free. Closed Jan.–Mar. Have a look into the history of the area including the former Du Pont explosives plant.

White Winter Winery, 68323 Lea Street, Iron River. Call 715-372-5656. This winery specializes in mead wine, made from fermented honey, and a few fruit spritzes. Stop in for samples or come on a summer Sunday for live music. Web site: www.whitewinter.com.

Dining/Drinks

Black Cat Coffeehouse, 211 Chapple Avenue, Ashland, 54806. Call 715-682-3680. A hip hangout for the java addicted, and an Internet-free zone.

Daily Bread, 212 Chapple Avenue, Ashland, 54806. Call 715-682-6010. This artisan bakery makes excellent bread and also serves deli sandwiches. Web site: www.ashlandbakingcompany.com.

Deep Water Grille and South Shore Brewery, 800 West Main Street, Ashland, 54806. Call 715-682-4200. This is arguably the best food in town, and the handcrafted South Shore beer is not to be missed. Web site: www.southshorebrewery.com.

Delta Diner, 14385 County Road H, Delta, 54856. Hours vary month to month. Call 715-372-6666. This sleek 1940s Silk City Diner serves outstanding classic diner fare with a twist. Travelers have crossed the state just to come here for a meal. Web site: www.deltadiner.com.

The Egg Toss Café, 41 Manypenny Avenue, Bayfield. Call 715-779-5181. This breakfast outlet is one of the best. Omelets, waffles, eggs Benedict, and huevos rancheros. Web site: www.eggtoss-bayfield.com.

Ethel's at 250, 250 Rittenhouse Avenue, Bayfield. Call 715-779-0293. Expect some mighty fine pizza and pasta and much more at this popular eatery in an historic building. Web site: www.ethelsat250.com.

Maggie's, 257 Manypenny Avenue, Bayfield. Call 715-779-5641. This flamingo-themed restaurant offers lunch and dinner with a menu of fresh fish, pizza, pastas, burgers, salads, and more, plus a full bar. Web site: www.maggies-bayfield.com.

North Coast Coffee, 26 West Bayfield Street, Washburn. Call 715-373-0241. This coffee shop also offers a few simple baked goods and free wireless Internet.

Pier Plaza Restaurant and the Pickled Herring Lounge, 1 Rittenhouse Avenue, Bayfield. Call 715-779-3330. The menu offers a standard assortment of burgers, sandwiches, and salads, but the main attraction is the outdoor deck—good for people-watching and a view into the marina. Web site: www.bayfrontinnbayfield.net.

Racheli's at Twin Silos, 77130 WI 13, Washburn. Call 715-373-5008. This deli/restaurant produces its own line of Italian foods. The deli is open Mon.–Sat., and the restaurant serves dinner Thurs.–Sat., but there are plans to expand those hours. Call for reservations.

Ruxy's Cottage Café, 8805 WI 13, Port Wing.Call 715-774-3565. This is a great place for pancakes and homemade pie, but the soups are also quite nice, and the burgers are handmade patties.

Siskiwit Bay Coffee & Curiosities, 88610 Superior Avenue, Cornucopia. Call 715-742-3388. Sip coffee or espresso indoors or out, or shop for gifts and collectibles.

Tom's Burned Down Café, La Pointe. Call 715-747-6100. This unique open-air bar is the result of a devastating fire. The site features live music and an art gallery. Open mid-May–Oct. Web site: www .tomsburneddowncafe.com.

Wild Rice Restaurant, 84860 Old San Road, Bayfield. Call 715-779-9881. This upscale restaurant offers a variety of gourmet choices and gives a nod to local products, especially the wild rice. Web site: www.wildrice restaurant.com.

Other

Bayfield Chamber of Commerce and Visitor Bureau, 42 South Broad Street, Bayfield. Call 715-779-3335. Web site: www.bayfield.org.

Madeline Island Chamber of Commerce, near the ferry dock, La Pointe. Call 715-747-2801. Web site: www.madelineisland.com.

Madeline Island Ferry Line. Call 715-747-2051. Four ferries make the 2.6-mile crossing from Bayfield to La Pointe on the island about two dozen times daily during open water periods from Mar. to mid-Jan. Cars, campers, bikers, and pedestrians are all welcome. Web site: www.madferry.com.

CHAPTER

9

Hayward and the Land of the Lumberjacks

Estimated length: 80 miles
Estimated time: 2 hours minimum

Getting There: If you are coming from Ashland or the Superior/Duluth area, take US 63 south from US 2. From the south, travelers will likely start in Hayward, arriving there by US 63 as well.

Highlights: Natural beauty of the **Chequamegon-Nicolet National Forest**; lumberjack shows; area history at the **Sawyer County Historical Museum**; the **Namekagon River**; the giant musky at the **Fresh Water Fishing Hall of Fame**; three scenic waterfalls at **Copper Falls State Park**; outstanding **fishing, hiking, and outdoor recreation** during all seasons. This may be one of the best chapters to do in winter as this region is popular for **snowmobiling** and **cross-country skiing**.

Chequamegon-Nicolet National Forest covers over 1.5 million acres across northern Wisconsin. Such a rich forestland, with its abundant wildlife and scenery, makes it difficult to imagine that so much of this land was clearcut by the lumber industry in the early twentieth century. Many of the old-growth trees are gone, but what we can see today is testament to nature's

With two brewpubs, little Hayward may have the most breweries per capita in Wisconsin.

ability to bounce back. More than that, however, it is a beneficiary of the efforts of conservation and restoration. Much of the forest was replanted by the Civilian Conservation Corps in the 1930s.

The region around Hayward and Cable is quite popular for outdoor recreation. From fishing and hunting to cross-country skiing, hiking, and mountain biking, outdoor activities are based upon vast forestland, an abundance of lakes and rivers, and a population of wild creatures that includes deer, black bear, porcupine, and beaver, as well as once eliminated animals such as elk and timber wolves.

Some tourist regions of Wisconsin shut down for the winter season; this place just straps on the winter boots (or skis) and keeps plugging along. Fall colors are vibrant here, and both Cable and Hayward offer local color routes through them.

The byway, if driven from Drummond to Mellen, can be done in a couple hours. There is much to do here, however, and many places to linger. The Rustic Route option, fall color tour routes, and side trips can make this into a weekend trip or more.

If you are coming south from the Duluth area, Drummond is your first stop. Once a mill town, this sleepy village lies just off US 63 about 9 miles north of Cable. The public library houses a **history museum**, but other than that the attraction here is the great outdoors. Centrally located to the Eau Claire Lakes, the Pike Lake Chain, Lake Owen, Lake Namekagon, and the Delta Lakes, Drummond offers nice fishing, swimming, and hiking, and in winter, snowmobiling, cross-country skiing, and snowshoeing are popular pastimes. **Bear Country Sporting Goods** can help you with fishing licenses, snowmobile/ATV trail permits, boat rentals, hunting and fishing guides, and any sort of outdoor equipment you might need. Their Web site (www.bearcountrysportinggoods.com) is also home to **North Country Vacation Rentals**, which offers a variety of cabin rentals in the area. **Black Bear Inn** serves lunch and dinner and specializes in Lake Superior fish and Italian.

Drummond is also host to the Sno-Jack Bar Stool Races. Held every year on the Saturday of President's Day weekend, the race offers cash prizes to competitors who ride bar stools mounted on skis. Bear Country Sports has more information about this hilarious event and the accompanying Chili Feed at 715-739-6645. From Drummond continue south on US 63.

Henry Schoolcraft worked for the U.S. government as an Indian agent. In 1831 the Sioux and Ojibwe were at odds, and Schoolcraft paddled from Chequamegon Bay near Ashland southward along the waterways in an effort to prevent war between the two nations. But it wasn't until the

COLOR TOURS

Both the communities of Hayward and Cable have laid out "color tours," surrounding roadways that pass through some of the best portions of deciduous forest around these communities. Pick up maps for these at the local visitor centers if you are here in the fall. The routes are well marked with signs and numbers. The fiery colors of autumn come earlier in northern Wisconsin, sometimes by even a couple of weeks. To watch for the arrival of peak colors, use the Fall Color Watch on TravelWisconsin.com.

lumber boon years later that Cable attracted a significant population. Prior to this, there were no roads in. When the rail line from Hudson on the Mississippi River finally connected in November of 1880, the door was open. The town became a rail hub employing as many as 700 workers. Saloons and hotels sprang up hastily but were soon destroyed by an 1882 fire. Once the railroad was built, the workers who had laid it moved on. As the lumber boom passed its peak, it became clear that the region needed other means of survival. Early on it was clear that the natural beauty and the abundance of lakes and rivers were draws in themselves, and so began the tourism industry.

The **Cable Natural History Museum** can show you more about the Chequamegon-Nicolet National Forest and the plants and creatures that inhabit it. Wildlife displays range from insects to large mammals, and you can attend lectures and field trips in the summer. Just across the street is a fine place to have breakfast, lunch, dinner, or just a good cup of coffee. **The Brick House Café** has some vegetarian options and also a carry-out menu. Grab a sandwich or wrap for the road. Also located in the center of town is **Whispering Pines Gift and Gallery,** a collection of original art that includes pottery, photography, woodworking, and hand-blown glass among other things.

Spend a night or more in the Chequamegon-Nicolet National Forest at **Cable Nature Lodge**, 7 miles east of Cable on CR M. The lodge, surrounded by spruce and overlooking forest and wetlands, offers seven smoke-free rooms with private baths. The twenty-two acres was once part of North Wisconsin Lumber Company, but the trees have made quite a comeback. Open for all meals, **Rookery Pub and Café** is onsite and emphasizes local produce and meats as much as possible. The menu is eclectic and gourmet, ranging from bison carpaccio to a Friday-night fish boil of whitefish. Some exceptional wildlife photography can be seen and purchased here at the **Kristen Westlake Gallery**.

Turkeys enjoying a bit of reprieve before Thanksgiving.

Another hotel option is the 129-room **Telemark Resort**, just over a mile out of town on CR M and south on Telemark Road. The 900-acre property caters to the active crowd of all ages. Three of the Chequamegon Area Mountain Bike Association's trails start right here, and the resort hosts the annual Chequamegon Fat Tire Festival.

Garmisch Resort is set on Lake Namekagon and is both a good place to stay and to eat. The lodge was built in the 1920s as a private retreat. Guests stay either in lodge rooms, complete with fireplaces, or cabins with kitchens and varying numbers of bedrooms.

CHEQUAMEGON FAT TIRE FESTIVAL

With over 2,500 participants, this mountain-biking festival is the largest of its kind in the United States. Hosted by Telemark Resort in Cable, the event presents food and entertainment and product displays. But the central events are the two races: The Chequamegon 40, a 40-mile race with 1,700 riders; and Short and Fat, a 16-mile race. Registration fills up fast, so if you are planning to participate, sign up well in advance (months, not days). The race is typically the second weekend after Labor Day.

MUSKY CAPITAL OF THE WORLD

The muskellunge or musky is sort of the grand kahuna of freshwater fishing in the Midwest. Often sought as a trophy fish, the musky can grow to over five feet in length and can weigh up to almost seventy pounds. The record in fact is listed as sixty-nine pounds, eleven ounces. In 1955 it became the official state fish. A predator, the musky not only eats other fish, it has been known to swallow frogs, muskrats, and ducks. Local stories may include someone's toes dangling over the edge of the dock, but this is merely an urban legend. Maybe.

The restaurant serves all meals and is popular for a Friday-night fish fry. Casual dining is available in the Bierstube.

East of Cable on CR M is Rustic Road 95, which leads you 16 miles down an unpaved road through the Chequamegon-Nicolet National Forest. The other end connects to WI 77 just east of Hayward. In the center of the rustic road is a loop that you could use as a turnaround if you aim to continue down CR M or return to the route herein, down US 63. Several trails for bikes, ATVs, or snowmobiles cross this road, so stay alert. The Lynch Creek Trail, 5 miles down the road, leads to a wildlife viewing area.

Heading south out of Cable on US 63, you will cross the Namekagon River, which will accompany you all the way to Hayward. The name of this river and the lake just east of Cable comes from the Ojibwe for "place of sturgeon." The drive from Cable to Hayward is just over 17 miles. If you're looking for something to read on your vacation, there's a quaint colorful bookstore 1 mile south of town on your right called **Redbery Books**. The staff is knowledgeable, and the selection, while not huge, is high quality and diverse.

A cabana bar, a theater, a pleasant coffee shop with martinis, and a motel in back—this is what you'll find at this quirky roadside complex in **Seeley**. The bar and grill **Sawmill Saloon** has logging tools hanging from the ceiling and a few animals mounted on the walls. The menu is typical pub fare—burgers, wraps, and deep-fried cheese curds. Right next door is **Mooselips Java Joint** where you can get your coffee fix, have the same menu as next door, or even go for a martini night on Fridays. After the martinis you may need a place to stay. Built around a 1930s schoolhouse, **Lenroot Lodge** has ten rooms with heated hardwood floors and two beds. The construction incorporates recycled telephone poles and log columns from blown-down trees. Four of the ten guest rooms are in the old classroom complete with blackboard, and one is handicap accessible.

Sawmill Saloon is decorated with the lumberjack theme.

Back in the nineteenth century, it was still the woods that drew people to Hayward, but for a different reason initially. In 1882 Robert Laird McCormick, A. J. Hayward, and Frederic Weyerheueser established the North Wisconsin Lumber Company in Sawyer County. Lumberjacks came in droves, and the town became a collection of taverns and hotels and had quite a raucous reputation.

The burning of the Hayward sawmill in 1922 didn't mark the end of the lumber industry, but it never ran again at the levels prior to that date. Hayward turned its attention towards tourism, and families from Chicago and Milwaukee came to seek escape from big-city living among the region's 500 lakes.

As you come into town go left at the lights at Highway 27/CR B and it will take you over the Namekagon where you should turn left to see "the giant fish." This is the **National Fresh Water Fishing Hall of Fame and Museum**. You can climb into the mouth of this four-story musky for a photo op and spend some time checking out fishing artifacts at the museum. Educational videos are shown all day in the theater. Alternatively, stop in at **Moccassin Bar** to see Cal Johnson's world record musky and a sort of wildlife museum—and by that I mean various examples of a taxidermist's work with the local animals.

Hayward's **Main Street** shows a couple blocks of gift shops and specialty stores. One such place is **Tremblay's Sweet Shop,** a family business established in 1963 by Denis and Marlene Tremblay that offers a fine collection of in-house-made confections including fudge, turtles, taffy, and truffles.

If you need an ice cream fix, stop over at **West's Dairy** on the corner of Second and Dakota. They've been serving homemade ice cream, malts,

The biggest catch in Hayward is the giant fish at the National Fresh Water Fishing Museum.

and sundaes since the 1920s. You can also get sandwiches here as well as a cup of Joe and Wi-Fi signal.

With two local brewers for a town of just over 2,300, Hayward may have the most brewpubs per capita in Wisconsin. The **Angry Minnow Brewpub's** name is a sort of humorous take on the fact that the giant musky gets all the attention at the expense of the bait. Well, big brewers be damned, this little brewpub and restaurant is doing just fine. Housed in an 1889 office building of the North Wisconsin Lumber Company, the restaurant serves quality sandwiches for lunch and finer dinners including homemade pastas and a Friday-night fish fry.

There's always room for more good local beer, and **Muskie Capital** brews alongside a great regional restaurant, the **Old Hayward Eatery**. The eatery, set in a modern wood lodge, has a wood-fired oven, excellent for pizzas, and offers a variety of specials including slow-roasted Angus prime rib. It's open daily in summer for lunch and dinner. The menu also includes some vegetarian options, Chicago-style beef and sausage, and six house beers.

With such a remarkable national forest and woodlands, it's hard to imagine what the Hayward area must have looked like at the end of the logging boom. A good place to stop and get an idea is the **Sawyer County Historical Museum**. Housed in a 1928 ranger station, the exhibits cover everything from native Ojibwe culture and the lumberjack days to Victorian lifestyle, fishing, and the resort industry. A diorama shows what Main Street once looked like.

Hayward lays claim to being the **golf** capital of Wisconsin and has a list to back it up. Between Hayward and Cable, the area has twelve courses, eight of which offer the full eighteen holes. The Hayward Area Chamber of Commerce has a printable online map.

Two notable courses are **Hayward Golf & Tennis Club** and **Big Fish Golf Club**. Hayward Golf is an eighteen-hole par-seventy-two public

THE LORD OF THE NAMEKAGON

Robert Laird McCormick, one of the lumber barons, built a home in 1887 in Hayward for him and his family. Fitted with the most modern amenities of the time and imported European furnishings, the house garnered the reputation of being a palace.

McCormick and his business partners eventually moved west to the forests of Washington, and from then on, the acting heads of North Wisconsin Lumber Company took up residence here. Now more than a century later, **McCormick House Inn** allows travelers to sleep in a palace fit for a lumber baron.

HAYWARD AREA FESTIVALS

For a town so small, Hayward fills some big britches when it comes to largest festivals.

The Birkebeiner or the "Birkie" occurs in late February and is the largest cross-country ski race in America. International competitors come for this three-day event, which includes several different skill races and a sprint down Main Street. For more information, check out the Web site, www.birkie.org

Honor the Earth Pow-wow is the largest pow-wow in North America. Tribes gather to honor the Creator with plenty of drumming, songs, and dances. Food and crafts are on hand, as well as softball and golf tournaments on this third weekend in July.

The weekend after Father's Day weekend is Hayward's largest summer celebration, the **Musky Festival**. The Musky Festival Queen will be crowned, and there is a large arts and crafts show, children's games, food, a Musky Run, and, of course, a fishing contest. Live music and street dances are hosted on Friday and Saturday nights, and a parade wraps things up on Sunday.

Get ready for some log rolling and the fastest axe work you'll ever see. **The Lumberjack World Championships** are held at the **Lumberjack Bowl** on a three-day weekend in July each year. Crowds and competitors—both male and female—from around the world come to see professional competitors climb poles, wield axes and saws, and roll their competition off of floating logs. There's more information online at www.lumberjackworldchampionships.com

For a good calendar of these and other events, contact the Hayward Area Chamber of Commerce or go to their Web site: haywardareachamber.com.

---

course first opened in 1924. It was redesigned in 1998 by Ken Killian and stands as one of the most popular courses in northern Wisconsin. The 168 acres include four water hazards and is close to the center of Hayward. Coming into town on Highways 63 and 27, take Main Street to Armory, and then go left on Wittmer Street.

Big Fish also has the full eighteen for a par seventy-two. Pete Dye designed this course and *Golf Digest* named it one of the best new golf courses in 2005. A full-service golf shop is onsite, and lessons can be had.

Lodging is varied and spread out throughout the area. **Spider Lake Lodge Bed and Breakfast** is a 1923 log lodge with a bit of elegance to it. The screened-in porch overlooks Big Spider Lake as does the dining room where hearty breakfasts are served.

For something a bit more rustic, check out the log cabins at **Mallards' Landing**. Each has its own kitchen, deck, and dining area. Located on the Namekagon River, it is still just a short walk to downtown. For standard motel rooms, Super 8 and AmericInn are here in Hayward.

If you miss the Lumberjack World Championships, you can still see some displays of their skills at **Fred Scheer's Lumberjack Shows** over at the **Lumberjack Village**. The acts combine actual events that would occur at the lumberjack championships with a bit of comedy and showmanship. During matinees, kids can crosscut saw with a lumberjack during the intermission.

SIDE TRIP:
SCARFACE WAS HERE

Many are the Northwoods places that claim a Chicago mobster once spent a night or had a shootout in their establishment, but this 17-mile side trip near Couderay is the real deal. **The Hideout, Al Capone's Northwoods Retreat and Museum of the Roaring Twenties** is as amazing as it is a mouthful. Set on a wooded hill, the ten building estate is built with eighteen-inch walls, a guard tower, and even a prison cell for rival gangsters. Guided tours last about forty-five minutes. The eight-car garage is now a restaurant and gift shop.

Once these lands were cut completely bare; now second-growth forest makes this the Northwoods again.

BEWARE OF THE ELK!

You may be surprised by a sign that reads ELK CROSSING. This is not a joke. In 1995 after being absent from Wisconsin for over 150 years, twenty-five elk were reintroduced to the Clam Lake area. The population is around 150 now. Many (but not all) have radio collars that activate blinking lights on highway signs that indicate one is nearby.

The elk is the largest species of deer in North America after the moose. Male elk grow antlers, which they shed each year. During mating season, especially the first three weeks of September, the males engage in antler wrestling and bugling, loud cries to establish dominance and call to females. The Rocky Mountain Elk Foundation (www.elkfoundation.org) has worked with the Wisconsin Department of Natural Resources and University of Wisconsin-Stevens Point to bring these magnificent creatures back. Your best chance of seeing or hearing one is along Highway 77 in the immediate area of Clam Lake.

You will also find **mini-golf** here, gift shops, and the **Pancake House**, a breakfast and lunch eatery overlooking the Lumberjack Bowl and Lake Hayward.

Have a wine tasting over at **HookStone Winery.** The winery uses grapes and other fruit juices from California and Washington to make twelve different varieties. Founded in 2005, HookStone has grown quickly in popularity, and several varieties sell out fast each year. If you try some now but want to buy later, they do mail orders to certain states.

Leave Hayward heading east on WI 77. You will pass Rustic Route 95 on your left that comes down from CR M east of Cable. You can use this to head back that way; otherwise follow WI 77 to Clam Lake.

In **Clam Lake** the Elkhart Lodge is a simple tavern eatery though not a destination in itself. Try some Chicago-style stuffed pizza over at the **Chippewa Tavern,** also on the highway. At this intersection, go left (northwest) on CR GG, and to stay on it, you will take an immediate right (northeast). Pine forest and ferns grow right up alongside the road for much of the next 20 miles from here to Mellen. You will see some occasional exposed rock, plus there are some deciduous trees along here, but nothing overwhelming for fall colors. Nevertheless. this is a lovely drive, and the reward will be one of the state's most beautiful parks.

Mellen was once home to the largest tannery in North America. It was originally named Iron City when railways connected it up to the docks in Ashland, but in 1888 the community took its name from the general man-

Copper Falls State Park is arguably the most stunning park in the area thanks to three excellent waterfalls—Copper Falls, Brownstone Falls, and Tyler's Fork Cascades—as well as ancient lava flows, gorges, and good hiking trails. The best time to go is when waters are high in which case the falls are all the more dramatic. In addition to picnicking, fishing, and swimming, guests can enjoy camping at one of the fifty-four regular campsites, a backpack site, or a rustic cabin for people with disabilities. In snowy periods 8 miles of trails are maintained for cross-country skiers. The park is also a stop on the North Country National Scenic Trail. Follow CR GG to Mellen. North of Mellen take WI 169 east to the park entrance.

At 30 feet, Brownstone Falls at Copper Falls State Park is actually taller than the park's namesake itself.

ager of the Wisconsin Central Railroad, William Solon Mellen. A Mellen veneer plant once supplied the birch for Howard Hughes's massive airplane, the *Spruce Goose*. Before heading out to the state park, you can stop for fast food or the fixings for a picnic at **Penokee Mountain Deli**.

Unless you plan to camp at Copper Falls State Park, there is no place to stay here. Your options are to head back to the Hayward-Cable area, or go north to Ashland, which is part of the Lake Superior chapter. In either case the views of the waterfalls and the crisp, pine-scented air are a perfect way to end the day.

IN THE AREA

Accommodations

Cable Nature Lodge, 20100 CR M, Cable. Call 715-794-2060. This woodland country lodge has seven rooms and is set on a hill overlooking forest and wetlands. Continental breakfasts are included except on Fri.–Sat. when guests can dine at a discount at the onsite café and pub. Winter specials are available, but contact the lodge for specifics. Rooms start at $109. Web site: www.cablenaturelodge.com.

Lenroot Lodge, Call 715-634-7007. Rates start at around $70 in slow seasons. Built around a 1930s schoolhouse, the ten-room lodge used some recycled materials for its construction. Situated behind Sawmill Saloon, the location is minutes from Cable or Hayward and right on top of the Namekagon River. The name Namekagon is Ojibwe in origin and means "place of sturgeons." Web site: www.seeleywis.com.

Mallards' Landing, 10427 WI 27, Hayward. Call 715-634-0910. Seven cabins along the banks of the Namekagon River all come with TVs, kitchens, decks, and room enough for families. Downtown is a short walk away. Web site: www.mallardslandinghayward.com.

McCormick House Inn, 10634 Kansas Avenue, Hayward. Call 715-934-3339. This 1887 home once housed a lumber baron. Interiors of the six guest rooms are modern with some original artwork and antiques. Amenities include Egyptian cotton, high-thread count sheets, private baths, Wi-Fi, and DVD players. Web site: www.mccormickhouse inn.com.

North Country Rentals, Black Bear Inn, US 63, Drummond. Call 715-739-6645. Rents a wide variety of cabins in the Cable-Drummond area. Web site: www.bearcountrysportinggoods.com.

Spider Lake Lodge Bed and Breakfast, 10472W Murphy Boulevard, Hayward. Call 715-462-3793. The seven rooms at this 1923 log lodge are rustic-luxurious. A hearty country-style breakfast is served with a view of Big Spider Lake. Web site: www.spiderlakelodge.com.

Telemark Resort, 42225 Telemark Road, Cable. Call 1-877-798-4718. Just east of Cable, this 129-room lodge is popular year-round and offers rooms, suites, and condos. The 900-acre resort is heavy on activity options for all ages. Mountain bikers will delight in the proximity of trails. Rates start at $71 on weekdays out of season. Summer and snowy periods start at around $87. Web site: www.telemarkresort.com.

Attractions and Recreation

Big Fish Golf Club, 14122W True North Lane, Hayward. Call 715-934-4770. An eighteen-hole par-seventy-two public course. Web site: www.bigfishgolf.com.

Cable Natural History Museum, 13470 County Road M, Cable. Call 715-798-3890. Open year round, Tues.–Sat. 10–4. This free museum offers nature exhibits, many related to the nearby national forest, and periodic lectures and field trips during the summer. Web site: www.cablemuseum.org.

Chequamegon Fat Tire Festival, Telemark Resort, 42225 Telemark Road, Cable. Call 1-877-798-4718. The largest mountain-bike racing event in the United States, over 2,500 riders participate in 40- and 16-mile runs. Register months in advance if you care to participate. It typically takes place the second weekend after Labor Day. Web site: www.cheqfattire.com.

Copper Falls State Park, 36764 Copper Falls Road, Mellen. Call 715-274-5123. A day-use or annual fee applies. Three attractive waterfalls pass through dramatic gorges here. Enjoy many miles of hiking trails including a 7-mile portion of the North Country National Scenic Trail. Camping is available. Web site: www.dnr.state.wi.us.

Hayward Golf & Tennis Club, 16005 Wittwer Street, Hayward. Call 1-877-377-4653. An eighteen-hole, par-seventy-two public course. Web site: www.haywardgolf.com.

The Hideout: Al Capone's Northwoods Retreat and Roaring Twenties Museum, 12101 West County Road CC, Couderay. Call 715-945-2746. Fee for tours/museum. From Hayward follow County Road B to NN south to CC east. Tours are forty-five minutes, daily in summer, limited hours until the end of Oct., and then closed for winter. The restaurant may stay open for several weeks after that, "depending on the weather." Web site: www.alcaponehideout.com.

HookStone Winery, 10588 Main Street, Hayward. Call 715-634-9463. The winery offers several grape and fruit wines as well as specialty olive oils, sauces, and candies. Tastings are available daily, though winter hours may be shortened. Web site: www.hookstone.com.

Kristen Westlake Gallery (inside Cable Nature Lodge), 20100 County Road M, Cable. Call 715-794-2060. Westlake's spectacular nature photos are on exhibit at the lodge. Web site: www.wisconsinphotos.com.

National Fresh Water Fishing Hall of Fame and Museum, 10360 Hall of Fame Drive, Hayward. Call 715-634-4440. Closed from Nov. to Apr. 15. Open daily from 9:30–4 or 4:30. Fee. Get a photo of yourself inside the mouth of the giant musky and have a look at the collection of fishing artifacts. Web site: www.freshwater-fishing.org.

Redbery Books, 42785 US 63, Cable. Call 715-798-5014. Just south of Cable, this is a fine, diverse collection for vacation reading. Open Mon.–Sat. plus Sun. during summer. Web site: www.redberybooks.com.

Sawyer County Historical Society & Museum, 15715 County Road B, Hayward. Call 715-634-8053. Open in the afternoons in the summer. Open only on Thurs. Oct.–May. See the site for more detailed hours. Fee. See a collection that covers the native Ojibwe culture as well as the logging boom and Hayward's development as a resort area. Web site: www.sawyercountyhist.org.

Scheer's Lumberjack Shows, Lumberjack Village, Hayward. Call 715-634-6923. Fee. One mile south of Hayward on County Road B. Show times vary from June to Aug. Web site: www.scheerslumberjack show.com.

Tremblay's Sweet Shop, Main Street between Second and Third Streets, Hayward. Call 715-634-2785. A fine collection of in-house made confections including fudge, turtles, taffy, and truffles. Web site: www.tremblay sweetshop.com.

Whispering Pines Gift and Gallery, 13355 County Road M, Cable. Call 715-798-3133. Have a look at a collection of art in varying media from pottery and woodworking to photography and prints.

Dining/Drinks

Angry Minnow Restaurant and Brewery, 10440 Florida Avenue, Hayward. Call 715-934-3055. Serving lunch and full dinners Tues.–Sat., the Minnow also serves six of its own beers on tap. Web site: www.angryminnow.com.

Black Bear Inn, US 63, Drummond. Call 715-739-6313. Stop in for Italian, seafood, burgers, and little bit of everything. Sat. night is prime rib, and there's an all-you-can-eat Friday fish fry. Open daily in season, hours vary, but limited days and hours in winter.

The Brick House Café, 13458 Reynolds Street, Cable. Call 715-798-5432. The café breakfast, lunch and dinner daily from a more refined menu than your typical diner. Carry-out sandwiches and wraps are nice for those on the go. Web site: www.thebrickhousecafe.net.

The Chippewa Tavern, WI 77, Clam Lake. Call 715-794-2450. This roadside eatery serves Chicago-style stuffed pizza plus chicken dinners, steak sandwiches, Friday-night fish fry, and homemade chili and soups.

Garmisch Resort, 23040 Garmisch Road, Cable. Call 1-800-794-2204. This lodge and cabin rental is set on the shores of Lake Namekagon. The restaurant serves great meals and is popular for its Friday-night fish fry. The Bierstube offers more casual lakeside meals. Head east from Cable on CR M. One and a half miles past Cable Nature Lodge, go left another 1.5 miles on Garmisch Road. Restaurant hours vary throughout the year; phone first. Web site: www.garmischresort.com.

Old Hayward Eatery & Muskie Capital Brew Pub, 15546 County Road B, Hayward. Call 715-934-2337. Set in a modern wood lodge environment the food is as good as the on-site brewed beers. Wood-fired pizzas, fish fries, and slow roasted Angus prime rib are just a few of the specialties. Some vegetarian options available.

Penokee Mountain Deli, 128 South Main Street/WI 13, Mellen. Call 715-274-2227. Stop in for some fast food or to pick up some meat, cheese, or sausage for a picnic outing at Copper Falls.

Rookery Pub and Café (inside Cable Nature Lodge), 20100 County Road M, Cable. Call 715-794-2060. The menu highlights regional produce and meats and offers creative dishes ranging from bison and wild rice to steaks and fish. Web site: www.cablenaturelodge.com.

Sawmill Saloon/Mooselips Java Joint, Call 715-634-5660. Dine on good tavern fare and homemade pizzas or savor a cup of great coffee next door. Wi-Fi available. Web site: www.seeleywis.com.

West's Dairy, 15848 West Second Street, Hayward. Call 715-634-2244. Homemade ice cream, sundaes, and malts, plus sandwiches and coffee are on order here at this 1920s establishment. Web site: www.wests haywarddairy.com.

Other

Cable Area Chamber of Commerce, 13380 County Road M, Cable. Call 715-798-3833. Located just one block east of Highway 63 on CR M, the visitor center has a wealth of brochures and maps, including the Fall Color Tour. Web site: www.cable4fun.com.

Clam Lake. Web site: www.clamlakewi.com.

Hayward Area Chamber of Commerce, 15805 US 63, Hayward. Call 715-634-8662. Web site: www.haywardareachamber.com.

CHAPTER

10

Minocqua's Northwoods

Estimated length: 80 miles

Estimated time: 3 hours minimum

Getting There: Take US 51 north to Minocqua.

Highlights: Learn about life in a traditional Ojibwe camp at Waswagoning; hike trails around several of the plethora of lakes; visit a zoo and pet many of the 500 animals; see a lumberjack show.

With over 3,200 lakes in this area, the towns of Minocqua and Woodruff and the plethora of cabins and cottages may seem more like island communities. In fact, Minocqua itself is nicknamed the Island City for its peninsular thrust into the lake of the same name. Some Wisconsinites may think of this as Northwoods Chicago for the numbers of tourists traveling up for summer vacations or winter adventures. But as much as Minocqua gleams with a bit of tourism polish, the surrounding communities and backroads have the old school charm of escaping to the woods. In fact, it will surprise many to know that a vast majority of the land here is in government control and spared from commercial development. Instead there are pristine lakes and forests; trails for biking, hiking, snowmobiling, and cross-country skiing; hideaways for a quiet reprieve in arboreal splendor; and restaurants of the Ma's-in-the-kitchen variety.

The view along Scotchman Lake Road.

CHARLIE'S CHEESE

Of course, Wisconsin is much more than cheese, but no one can blame you for wanting some for your trip. Before you start your byway, consider an extra mile's drive past your starting point on the Rustic Road, to Hazelhurst's Charlie's Fine Cheese. Choose from a collection produced by various Wisconsin cheese factories. Among the options you'll find aged cheddar (as old as eleven years!), fresh cheese curds on Thursdays, and flavored specialty cheeses. Local products such as maple syrup and jams and jellies are also for sale.

Using Minocqua as a hub, this byway traces a curving path through woods and water before returning you to the center of the attraction. The drive itself is nearly three hours but with time to linger at shops and restaurants, as well as natural attractions or cultural heritage sites, this can occupy your whole weekend.

Heading south from Minocqua just about 2 miles you will begin west on State Rustic Road 58, which begins at US 51 on Blue Lake Road. The road is paved but unlined and without shoulders. This will take you along the edge of Blue Lake and through a mixture of pine and hardwood forest.

Expect stunning fall colors here. The bicycle path that you will cross less than a mile down the road was once the railroad bed of the main line to Minocqua. Now it is the Bearskin State Trail. If you want to bike it, check out **BJ's Sportshop** or **Chequamegon Adventure Company** in Minocqua for rentals and a state trail passes. The latter also rents kayaks and canoes.

Just over 2 miles down Blue Lake Road you'll find State Rustic Road 59, Sutton Road, which goes right (north) for 4.5 miles and connects to WI 70 about 3 miles west of Minocqua. You can see some old log cabins from the days of the homesteaders. The surface is gravel and sand with a few paved portions, and there can be a washboard effect if it hasn't been graded recently. This is a short alternative, a teaser if you will, of the larger byway.

Continuing on Blue Lake Road you will pass **Blue Lake Pines and Suites**, which offers lakeside suites with kitchenettes. Blue Lake has no public boat landing, but the resort has canoes and kayaks for guests.

WILD ANIMALS: UP CLOSE AND PERSONAL

Odds are good that you will see plenty of local residents from the animal world along this drive, but there are two wildlife centers nearby that can show you them up close and in an educational setting. **Peck's Wildwood Wildlife Park** on WI 70 is a zoo with over 500 animals. You can expect to see wolf, black bear, elk, bobcat, buffalo, deer, mountain lion, tiger, wallaby, ring-tailed lemur, and eagle. The nursery offers some personal contact with some of the animals. An onsite trout pond lets you fish without a license. Also nearby is **Northwoods Wildlife Center**. You can tour this animal rehabilitation center and learn about the residents from onsite naturalists. The center is particularly involved with threatened or endangered species and often takes in injured or sick creatures.

Farther down the road cross a bridge over a creek and then enter a corridor of pine plantation before you arrive at Mercer Lake Road and Scotchman Lake Road. Another decision: get back to Highway 70 on Mercer Lake Road or continue through the woods on an unofficial rustic route? Scotchman Lake Road turns to gravel. Be careful with speed as the gravel is not conducive to great control, and your stopping distance is much greater if a deer—or raccoon, beaver, or porcupine—should decide not to look both ways before crossing in front of you.

As you head down Scotchman Lake Road you will see aspen colonies, which can really turn on the color in fall, and then more pine plantation. What you won't see much of is development. Ferns and wildflowers come right to the edge of the road. Cross Adrian Lake Road. At a stop sign go right continuing on Scotchman Lake Road and crossing Camp Nine Road. The lane is a bit sandier here. Just under a mile later look for the signs to **Minocqua Winter Park**. This town park offers some pleasant hikes, but in the winter it becomes a fantastic 45-mile network of well-groomed cross-country ski trails.

A mile later you get a wonderful view of wetlands and see a fire watch-tower up to the left in the distance. Lily pads here will bloom in summer, and it's a lovely view of green and blue on a sunny day. Just past here go right on the asphalt-paved Squirrel Lake Road. It is popular with bikers so be alert.

The road passes close to Franklin Lake on the right where you'll see a boat landing. On your left watch for **Schneider's Pottery Shop**. Dick Schneider had been making (and teaching) pottery for over forty years. His daughter has also taken up the craft. Their workshop and modest show-room are on a half-mile drive on a one-lane, two-rut road through the trees.

Hidden in the deep woods are a few surprises such as Schneider's Pottery gallery.

Just behind the studio and down the hill is Torpy Lake. Despite the appearance of the entry, it is actually very accessible, and there are pull-outs for passing anyone who might be coming out as you are going in.

Drive another mile to WI 70 and go left (west). You could go right, which will take you back to Minocqua as well as Peck's Wildwood Wildlife Park. About 4.7 miles from here, you will come to **Mama's Restaurant**, a reputable eatery specializing in Italian cuisine.

Angela Gentile came from Tortorici, Sicily in 1921 to visit her brother. She ended up getting married and settling in Ironwood, Michigan, until 1954 when,

LAC DU FLAMBEAU NATION

This Ojibwe settlement has been around since the mid-eighteenth century. The abundance of lakes made for a great source of wild rice and fish. The Ojibwe would hunt for fish with spears at night, using torches to light the way. Thus the name "Lake of Torches" was given by the French who first witnessed the practice. In fact, the Ojibwe name is much the same. The Ojibwe never took sides with the French or British and in fact fought in the Civil War alongside Union forces.

The Ojibwe lived among these lakes long before the French traders arrived. Birch bark canoes were common.

after having raised her children, she and her husband James Chiolino bought an old bar near Curtis Lake outside of Minocqua. She began with pizza and gradually expanded into other fare, and the locals soon were affectionately referring to her as Mama. So her restaurant, Bella Vista, eventually took on the name as well. Today some of her children and grandchildren are still directly involved in the successful venture.

Continuing west on WI 70 from Squirrel Lake Road, you'll pass Squirrel Lake on the left, and one mile down the road you will enter the Lac du Flambeau Nation. At CR F, go right. Look for **White Haven Bed and Breakfast** just about a half mile down the road on the left. This little four-room inn sits on fifteen acres on the shore of Whitefish Lake. Beautiful in any season, it is especially cozy in the winter with a large stone fireplace in the great room.

Drive 2.2 miles down CR F and take Thorofare Road on the left. Another 3.2 miles of driving in between lakes will take you to Moss Lake Road where you will go left (west) just over a mile to connect to CR D. Going right on CH D will take you into the town of Lac du Flambeau.

If you are looking for pizza, watch for the **Flame Restaurant**. This eatery with a full bar also has a large display of trophy musky. A screened-in patio affords a view of Long Interlaken Lake.

County D joins Peace Pipe Road where it takes a right angle turn east in town. On your left you will pass the **George W. Brown Jr. Ojibwe Museum and Cultural Center**. Inside are a comprehensive collection of Ojibwe historical artifacts and a diorama of the harvests of the four seasons. A century-old, twenty-four-foot dugout canoe is on display along with an assortment of native bead and birch-bark crafts. Displays dedicated to the French fur traders and a world-record sturgeon caught in one of the local lakes are also here. Watch for periodic workshops and lectures.

Continue on CR D/Peace Pipe Road and you will come to the intersection of WI 47. If you go left, you will see **Lake of the Torches Resort Casino and Bingo,** a decent place to stop for the night. Restaurants on site, however, are mediocre.

Otherwise, go right on WI 47 for 2.8 miles to reach CR H and go left (north). If you are looking for a cutoff, Highway 47 goes all the way back to Highway 51 at Woodruff and Minocqua is just south of there.

Just over half a mile north on your right on CR H is **Waswagoning Indian Village**. Get a feel for what life must have been like for the local Native Americans at this authentic reproduction of an old Ojibwe camp.

Nick Hockings is the real deal. A member of the Lac du Flambeau Band of the Lake Superior Ojibwe, he knows (and teaches) the language. In Ojibwe *wa-swa-goning* means "the place where they spearfish by torchlight." A tour through Wa-Swa-Goning takes about an hour and gives you an up-close, hands-on experience of wigwams and the willow fish traps and birch bark baskets that were part of daily life for the Ojibwe. The twenty-acre compound opens onto Moving Cloud Lake, and the trail passes through diverse forest full of birds and other critters. The gift shop contains local craftwork such as dream catchers.

Wa-swa-goning is a great place to learn about the ways of the Ojibwe of yesteryear.

Continuing north on CH H, you will leave the Nation just as you arrive at US 51. Follow CH H across toward Boulder Junction. **Whispering Pine Resorts** is just outside Boulder Junction and offers four rental cottages with full kitchens on Upper Gresham Lake. The resort has boats and kayaks and rents motors.

When you come to the end of CH H, continue on CH K into Boulder Junction. The village claims to be the Musky Capital of the World (as opposed to Hayward, Wisconsin, which is the Musky *Fishing* Capital of the World!). Take a right at the stop sign to go to Boulder Junction. You will follow a long corridor of pine plantation. This will not be so impressive for fall colors, but great for fresh air.

One of the first properties on the left is **Big Bear Hideaway**, which gleams with varnished wood. Once a collection of stores, it has been converted to eye-catching lodging with names such as Kodiak Grizzly and Polar Bear. Some of the supporting columns in the cottages are actually tree trunks left in their original shapes. A massive wall of lumber like some sort of stockade at the edge of the yard is actually the stockpile for the fireplaces.

Rustic Road 60 heads 13 miles east off of CH M on CH K all the way to Star Lake. The trees of the Northern Highland/American Legion State Forest close in over the road, which winds along past old logging camp sites and some lake vistas. An old saw mill can be seen in Star Lake. Watch for CH K just over a mile south of Boulder Junction on your left if you are heading south.

This a great setup for large families or groups, but couples have cozy options as well.

Boulder Junction itself is a nice little collection of boutique shops and a few restaurants. Pottery fans should be pleased by the work of Bill Karaffa, whose **Firemouth Pottery** workshop and gallery on Main Street shows the range of his creativity. Over ninety artists are represented at **Moondeer and Friends Gallery** nearby.

The finest dining you'll find is the **Outdoorsman Restaurant and Inn**. The dinners tend toward the gourmet, but the breakfasts and lunches offer something for everyone at a reasonable price. The wine list is notable. **JJ's Pub and Grub** is set in a building from the late 1800s, which was also a great place to get a bite. Nothing fancy here, but good, reasonably priced grub. The pizzas are homemade, and they do a popular Friday-night fish fry. If Karaoke is your thing, you can find it here some nights. **Mad Dog Jake's** does up a decent Chicago-style hot dog as well as burgers, sandwiches, and ice cream.

The byway continues south out of Boulder Junction on CR M. If you've never had a **pasty**, stop by **Jan's Bakery and Pasty Parlor** on the right on your way out of town. The pasty was the portable meal made popular by Cornish miners back in the day. It consists of a large pastry pocket filled with meat and vegetables, in the case of northern Wisconsin, meat, potatoes, and perhaps onions or rutabaga. They are good to pack for a picnic as you head out of Boulder Junction. The bakery also sells pie, cookies, sub sandwiches, and coffee to go. Beware: they don't take credit cards.

After you've left Boulder Junction, you have a couple options for a **picnic** on the right. The first is a parking area at North Trout Lake. In 1915 Jack Vilas flew daily forest fire patrols from here in a Curtiss Flying Boat. An historical marker commemorates this as the first time a plane was used for this purpose. There is a boat launch here and some picnic tables. A nicer place but requiring more of a hike is **Cathedral Point**. Continue south on CH M about 1 mile and you will see the sign for the Department of Natural Resources Office on the right. It is an old stone building. The road to the right of it takes you to a parking area. Beyond that it is a short walk through the woods to find a water pump and some picnic tables out on a point that divides Trout Lake into its northern and southern halves. Go right from the water pump and look for some railroad-tie steps down to the water. There are pit toilets along the trail between the parking area and water pump.

If you are up for a great hike, look for Nebish Lake Road just across CH M from the DNR office and Cathedral Point Road. 3.5 miles east on Nebish Lake Road is the parking lot for the **Escanaba-Pallette Lakes Trails.** Four trail loops range in length from 2 to 8.5 miles, taking you through hilly wooded terrain around several lakes.

Continuing south on the byway on CH M, you will come to CH N. You can stay on CH M as a cutoff that would take you directly to US 51 where you can then go left (south) to Minocqua. Otherwise, stay on the byway by going left (east) on CH N and continuing 7 miles to Sayner.

Watch for **Crystal Lake Campground**, which has first-come, first-served campsites, plus a white sand beach. Just across CH N is the parking lot for **Fallison Lake Interpretive Trail**, which has booklets at the trailhead or on the Internet, as well as interpretive signage along the trail. This is hilly terrain with an impressive view of the lake.

In 1924 right here in Sayner, Carl Eliason invented the "motor toboggan" or what the rest of us know as the snowmobile. Check out some more history dating back to the pioneer days of the area at the **Vilas County Museum**.

The Corner Store has been scooping out ice cream for over eighty-three years. This general store has much more than that, however, from camping equipment and bike rentals to beer and convenience items. Find it at County N and Razorback Road just before Sayner. The byway goes right (south) in town at WI 155.

If you're lost (or even if not), stop in at **Sayner Pub Pizza and Sports Bar** and you'll find a giant road map on the ceiling. The bar does handmade pizza and some very big Bloody Marys. They remain open on weekends in the winter, catering to the snowmobilers, skiers, and ice fisherman. Or if you just prefer a coffee break, check out **Colours and Cream Espresso Bar**.

At the south end of town WI 155 heads east to St. Germain. You go right on CH C just about 4 miles until you come to WI 70. Go right (west) here and follow it back to US 51. Right at this intersection is the Whitetail Lodge. The hotel has a pool and a nine-hole, par-three golf course, plus a sports bar and grill. Some rooms have whirlpools and gas fireplaces. Right next door is **St. Germain Golf Club**, a well-reviewed public course.

Boulder Junction's Big Bear Hideaway is an impressive display of woodworking and an excellent place to stop for the night in the Northwoods.

Continuing west on WI 70, the road rides high above small pocket lakes and cuts through the hills. You will pass Little Arbor Vitae Lake on the left and soon after, Big Arbor Vitae on the right. When you reach US 51 go left (south) and you are headed to Woodruff. Right away on your left you will see the gallery of **Art Long** whose **painting and sculpture** have a wildlife theme. Taxidermy was a family business, and his experience with it contributed to his understanding of animal forms.

Woodruff and Minocqua are tourism meccas in themselves with options almost too numerous to list. As a starting/ending point of this byway, I include but a few recommendations.

Woodruff is home to **Fred Scheer's Lumberjack Shows**. The shows are seasonal and showcase professional woodsmen climbing poles, carving wood with chainsaws, racing across logs, and trying to roll each other off those logs. Comedy and music are worked in here so it really is quite entertaining. Call for show times.

Heading south, you can't miss the large Paul Bunyan and his sidekick Babe, the Blue Ox. This large roadside sign marks the seasonal **Paul Bunyan's Restaurant**, which serves lumberjack sized breakfasts and an all-you-can-eat Friday-night fish fry.

In downtown Minocqua try the family-owned **Island Café**, a local institution since 1957 specializing in soups and Greek dishes. Try out some of the local beer at **Minocqua Brewing Company**, a restaurant and pub that offers some upscale pub food for lunch and finer plates for dinner.

Norwood Pines Supper Club on Patricia Lake delivers the quintessential log-built lodge, supper-club experience. The screened-in porch is nice in summer when you might see deer passing through.

Some of the finest accommodations in town are right on the lake at the **Pointe Hotel and Suites**. These condo-suites and guestrooms total sixty-nine, and all have kitchens and lake views. If you are looking for something a bit less commercial, the Chamber of Commerce has a good list of **private homes and cottages** that can be rented in and around the area.

Don't miss the **Min-Aqua Bats**, a free amateur **water ski show** put on three nights a week in summer on Lake Minocqua. This has been going on since 1950, and don't let the word "amateur" suggest it is anything other than the impressive talents of volunteers. Watch for **Beef-A-Rama** the last Saturday in September, a festival of, yeah, you guessed it. Expect a lot of barbeques and street festivities. Check with the Chamber of Commerce for more details.

Minocqua fills up in summer, so plan your trip ahead of time. A few businesses will close down for winter, but the area also enjoys a vibrant snowmobile season (in snowy years). If you—like many others—choose to spend a week up here, the byway is the best way to escape if the hordes of tourists become too much.

IN THE AREA

Accommodations

Big Bear Hideaway, 10490 Main Street, Boulder Junction. Call 715-385-3333. These luxury cottages show gleaming wood and free-form carving. All come with full kitchens, Wi-Fi, and large-screen TVs. Open year round. Web site: www.bigbearhideaway.com.

Blue Lake Pines Resort and Suites, 7650 Blue Lake Pines Road, Minocqua. Call 1-877-644-4322. Open May–Oct. Seven lakeside suites offer kitchenettes, satellite TV, and Internet. Web site: www .bluelakepines.com.

Crystal Lake Campground, 4125 County Road N, Sayner. Call 715-542-3923. This state park offers camping and a white-sand beach.

The Pointe Hotel and Suites, 8269 US 51 South, Minocqua. Call 1-888-356-4431. A collection of sixty-nine condos and rooms with lake views and kitchens. Web site: www.thepointeresort.com.

Whispering Pines Resort, 4780 County Road H, Boulder Junction. Call 715-385-2425. Open May–Oct. These four modern cottages on Upper Gresham Lake come with full kitchens and the resort has boats and kayaks. Web site: www.whispering-pines-resort.net.

Whitehaven Bed and Breakfast, 1077 County Road F, Minocqua. Call 715-356-9097. On fifteen acres on the shores of Whitefish Lake, this inn has four guest rooms with private baths as well as a common fireplace in the great room and a porch overlooking the lake. Open year round. No credit cards accepted. Cash or check. Web site: www.white havenbandb.com.

Whitetail Lodge, County Road C and WI 70 West, St. Germain. Call 1-800-236-0460. Thirty rooms offer comfortable lodging with microwaves and refrigerators. Some have whirlpools and gas fireplaces. A log-built sports bar and grill, a nine-hole, three-par golf course, and mini-golf are across the road. Web site: www.whitetaillodge.com.

Attractions/Recreation

BJ's Sportshop, 917 Highway 51 North, Minocqua. Call 715-356-3900. Rent all sort of bikes here including tandems and child trailers in season, and cross-country skis and snowshoes in winter. State trail passes are for sale here as well. Web site: www.bjssportshop.com.

Charlie's Fine Cheese, 7057 US 51, Hazelhurst. Call 715-356-4518. Open daily year round. Choose from a wide variety of Wisconsin cheeses including aged cheddar, fresh cheese curds (on Thurs.), and other specialty cheeses. Local maple syrup and jams and jellies are also for sale.

Chequamegon's Adventure Bicycles, 301 East Front Street, Minocqua. Call 715-356-1618. Rent a bike for one of the many area trails or rent kayaks and canoes at their second location at 433 East Chicago Avenue. Web site: www.paddlerama.com.

The Corner Store, 3103 Razorback Road, Sayner. Call 715-542-4250. For over eighty-three years, this has been the place to stop for ice cream, but there is much more: get bike rentals, camping equipment, general store items, and beer here.

Fallison Lake Interpretive Trail. Located across from Crystal Lake Campground on CR N west of Sayner, this trail system offers four loops from 0.5 mile to 2.5 miles. Web site: www.vilas.org/hike/hike boulder.html

Firemouth Pottery, 10344 Main Street, Boulder Junction. Call 715-385-2810. Visit the workshop and gallery of Bill Karaffa who makes hand-thrown stoneware with its own unique style of decoration. Web site: fp1.centurytel.net/karaffa.

Fred Scheer's Lumberjack Shows, Lumberjack Village, Woodruff. Call 715-356-4050. Fee. One mile north of Minocqua in downtown Woodruff, see a show of professionals competing at logrolling, sawing, chopping, and various other impressive challenges. Web site: www .scheerslumberjackshow.com.

George W. Brown Jr. Ojibwe Museum and Cultural Center, 603 Peace Pipe Road, Lac du Flambeau. Call 715-588-3333. Fee. Open May–Oct., Mon.–Sat. and Nov.–Apr., Tues.–Thurs. Stop in and learn about the Ojibwe culture and see the world-record sturgeon. Web site: www .ojibwe.com.

Lake of the Torches Resort Casino and Bingo, 510 Old Abe Road, Lac du Flambeau. Call 1-888-599-9200. Over a hundred rooms and suites are on offer at this Northwoods casino complex. Web site: www.lake ofthetorches.com.

Art Long, Artist of the North, 11069 Long Road, Woodruff. Call 715-356-6717. Open daily May–Sept., or by appointment. Located on Highway 51 just south of Highway M, this gallery showcases the painting and sculpture of this local wildlife artist. Web site: www.artlong gallery.com.

Min-Aqua Bats Water Ski Shows on Lake Minocqua. Call 715-356-4549. Check out free water-ski shows throughout the summer on Sun., Wed. and Fri. evenings. Web site: www.min-aquabats.com.

Minocqua Winter Park and Nordic Center, 12375 Scotchman Lake Road, Minocqua. Call 715-356-3309. This not-for-profit town park maintains marvelous cross country ski trails. In the summer these make for some good hiking as well. Web site: www.skimwp.org.

Moondeer and Friends Gallery, 10354 Main Street, Boulder Junction. Call 715-385-2082. Over ninety artists are represented in this gallery. Web site: www.moondeerdesign.com.

Northwoods Wildlife Center, 8683 Blumenstein Road—Highway 70 West, Minocqua. Open year-round, closed on Sun. Tour this animal rehabilitation center and learn about the residents from naturalists.

Peck's Wildwood Wildlife Park, 10094 WI 70, Minocqua. Call 715-356-5588. Open daily, May–mid-Oct. Explore a Northwoods zoo with over 500 animals. Located 2 miles west of US 51 on WI 70. Web site: www.wildwoodwildlifepark.com.

St. German Golf Club, CR C and WI 70, St. Germain. Call 715-542-2614. This public course offers the full eighteen and was recognized by Golf Digest as one of the best places to play. Web site: www.st germain-golfclub.com.

Schneider's Pottery Shop, 8441 Squirrel Lake Road, Minocqua. Call 715-356-6330. Open Tues.–Sun., May–Sept. Watch the father-daughter team of potters do their magic. Shop for some great stoneware and porcelain.

Waswagoning Indian Village, 2750 County Road H, Lac du Flambeau. Call Charlotte 715-588-3560 or Ramona 715-588-1426. Tours are available from 10–4, Tues.–Sat., mid-May–Sept. Fee. Twenty acres of forest along a lake are the site of a re-creation of a traditional Native American village. Learn about the history and culture in this open-air museum.

Vilas County Museum, 217 Main Street, Sayner. Call 715-542-3388. See a collection of exhibits and artifacts from as far back as the late 1800s. Web site: www.vilasmuseum.com.

Dining/Drinks

Colours & Creme Gift Shop and Espresso Bar, 269 Main Street, Sayner. Call 715-542-4123.

The Flame Restaurant, Peace Pipe Road, Lac du Flambeau. Call 715-588-9262. Open daily in season. Call first during winter.

Island Café, 314 Oneida Street, Minocqua. Call 715-356-6977. Since 1957 this local institution has been serving great soups and Greek cuisine. Open for all meals. Web site: www.islandcafeminocqua.com.

J.J.'s Pub and Grub, 10360 Main Street, Boulder Junction. Call 715-385-0166. Open daily for lunch, dinner, and bar food. Good pizza and pub menu. Karaoke is offered three nights a week. Web site: www.jjspub andgrub.com.

Jan's Bakery and Pasty Parlor, 5433 Park Street, Boulder Junction. Call 715-385-9333. Get a traditional pasty or a sub sandwich for the road. The pie and cookies are wonderful as well. Credit cards not accepted.

Mad Dog Jake's, 5505 County Road M, Boulder Junction. Call 715-385-9227. Stop here for Chicago-style hot dogs, ice cream, and more.

Mama's Restaurant, 10486 WI 70, Minocqua. Call 715-356-5070. Mama's is a family business founded by a Sicilian matriarch back in the 1950s. It is very popular for its pasta, steaks, and seafood, and of course, pizza. Web site: www.mamasrestaurant.biz.

Minocqua Brewing Company, 238 Lakeshore Drive, Minocqua. Call 715-356-2600. The brewpub provides the beer, and the restaurant has some fine food to go with it. Open for lunch and dinner. Web site: www.minocquabrewingcompany.com.

Norwood Pines Supper Club, 10171 WI 70, Minocqua. Call 715-356-3666. You might see deer just outside the screened-in porch, but you will definitely find excellent steak and seafood and an extensive wine list. Web site: www.norwoodpines.com.

The Outdoorsman Restaurant and Inn, 10383 Main Street, Boulder Junction. Call 715-385-2826. Expect a full menu serving all meals, but something a bit nicer for dinner. There are also eight basic rooms in the inn. Web site: www.outdoorsmanrestaurant.com.

Paul Bunyan's Restaurant, 8653 US 51, Minocqua. Call 715-356-6270. Open May–Oct. A large Paul Bunyan and Babe the Blue Ox mark this seasonal eatery that serves all meals and has notable breakfasts. Web site: www.paulbunyans.com.

Sayner Pub Pizza and Sports Bar, 310 Main Street, Sayner. Call 715-542-3647. This tavern atmosphere bar and grill has homemade pizza, your favorite Wisconsin sport teams on the tube, and stellar Bloody Marys. In winter it opens for breakfast on weekends. Web site: www.saynerpub.com.

Other

Boulder Junction Chamber of Commerce, 5352 Park Street, Boulder Junction. Call 715-385-2400. Web site: www.boulderjct.org.

Lac du Flambeau Chamber of Commerce, 602 Peace Pipe Road, Lac du Flambeau. Call 715-588-3346. Web site: www.lacduflambeau chamber.com.

Minocqua-Arbor-Vitae-Woodruff Chamber of Commerce, 8216 US 51 South, Minocqua. Call 715-356-5266. Web site: www.minocqua.org.

CHAPTER

11

The Waterfalls of Marinette County

Estimated length: 115 miles
Estimated time: 1 day minimum

Getting There: Take US 141 north to Peshtigo.

Highlights: See various **waterfalls** tumbling through the forests of northern Wisconsin; learn about an amazing tragedy at the **Peshtigo Fire Museum**; eat an **elk burger**; go **whitewater rafting** on the Peshtigo River.

Rivers and rapids cut through rich woodlands that have slowly recovered from a logging rush that had clear-cut much of the area and an infamous fire virtually unknown outside of Wisconsin (and yet is one of the greatest tragedies in state history). Myriad lakes and streams attract anglers and canoe or boat enthusiasts. This is the Northwoods of Wisconsin, perhaps more so than even the other northerly byways in this book. Unlike areas around Hayward, Minocqua, or Bayfield, this county hasn't found a strong commercialized tourism center, and though those other areas are still quintessentially Wisconsin, Marinette County may be as pure as it gets.

The county and its seat, the city of Marinette, take their name from "Queen" Marinette, the daughter of a Menominee princess and a French-Canadian trapper. Born in 1784, she eventually owned a trading post where the city is today. Her birth name was actually Marguerite Chevallier, but

An old church turned museum stands testament to the tragedy of the Peshtigo Fire.

she was better known by the nickname, a shortened version of Marie Antoinette.

White pine was abundant back in those days, and in the 1840s logging became a boom and continued as such for several decades. The excess of it all played a big part in a tragic fire in 1871.

Marinette County is exceptional in its outdoor appeal. With more than a dozen waterfalls, the Pesthigo, Menominee, and Pike Rivers, the vast acreage of lakes, and over 600 miles of trout streams, this is a goldmine of opportunities for hikers, anglers, campers, kayakers, snowmobilers, hunters, and every sort of outdoor recreation enthusiast you can think of. And yet it is still far from being overrun by tourism. The scent of pine in the air, the sounds of rushing waters, and a sense of time stopping make this corner of the Northwoods an attractive destination that is off the beaten path.

In a hiking guide you'll find trails that are easy, moderate, or difficult. This byway might be considered the most challenging. Parts of the route are most definitely living up to the definition of backroads, but this route pays back double in natural beauty. I have used the waterfalls as the backbone of this road trip, which runs a loop through some well forested lanes, a few of which are unpaved.

Peshtigo is 7 miles southwest of Marinette on US 41. Halfway between Marinette and Peshtigo is **Seguin's Cheese**. A wide variety of Wisconsin cheeses—fresh and aged—are available here including cheddar cheese curds. An assortment of local mustards, smoked sausages, salsas and sauces, jams and preserves are on offer, and the store is also an authorized Minnetonka moccasin dealer. Stop for some delectable samples. If you don't buy today, you can always order from Seguin's online.

Peshtigo comes from the Ojibwe word for "river of the wild goose." As you come into Peshtigo, you will cross the Peshtigo River, once a sanctuary and lifesaver for a few lucky souls during a regional disaster. If there's one thing you shouldn't miss, it's the **Peshtigo Fire Museum** housed in an old church on the site of the Catholic church that was destroyed in the blaze. From Highway 41 (French Street) turn left at Ellis Avenue, one block before the traffic light. The museum is straight ahead on the corner of Ellis and Oconto Avenue.

A Catholic priest, Father Perrin, survived the fire. During the rush to escape he failed to find the key to the tabernacle to remove the host and chalice. So he took the entire tabernacle and dumped it in the river, hoping for the best. Days later it was found floating intact. It spent years in an

THE PESHTIGO FIRE

Much has been said and written about the Great Chicago Fire of 1871, which burned for nearly two days, killed perhaps as many as 300 people, and destroyed around 4 square miles of the city. But on that very same night, October 8, little Peshtigo became the center of a conflagration so massive that it crossed state lines in its fury. Deaths are estimated at between 1,200 and 2,400 people; such was the extent of the destruction that no one could ever be sure. Only one house survived thanks to the fact it was newly built with green lumber.

Several factors had created a recipe for disaster. Vast areas of pine had been cut down, and much of the brush left to rot; numerous small fires around Peshtigo; dry hot winds. Being a lumber industry center point didn't help. Even the mattresses were filled with sawdust. As the winds picked up over clear cut lands with no trees to break them, the flames became a firestorm, and 400 square miles were burned all the way up into Michigan's Upper Peninsula.

Two days after the disaster, the news arrived in Madison. Governor Lucius Fairchild and many state officials had already departed for Chicago in response to that city's devastating fire. But Frances, the young wife of the governor, took matters into her own hands and diverted a boxcar of relief supplies destined for Chicago to Peshtigo instead.

unknown location before finally being returned to Peshtigo where it is now kept at the museum. A mass grave in the cemetery next door holds remains of 350 victims.

From Peshtigo begins the waterfall treasure hunt. On Oconto Avenue, go west from the museum and follow it one long block to CR D. You will follow D north about 7 miles to WI 64. Cross the highway to take Leslie Road; on the other side do not follow the curve to the right (Bridge Road), stay on Leslie Road to the left through pines and farmland. Expect plenty of wood lilies along the roads in summer. Just a few miles later, at the end of Leslie Road, you take a right (north) and are on CR W until the village of Crivitz, the "Gateway to the North." Though a small community, it offers sports stores, groceries, gas stations, a few arts and crafts shops, and some restaurants.

Founded in 1883, Crivitz, like so many Wisconsin towns, takes its name from Europe; founder Fredrick Bartels came from a village of the same name in Germany. The **Crivitz Area Museum** has a modest collection regarding local history. When you come to the traffic lights at the intersection of Highway 141, you'll find two places to stop for a bite just across the highway on the right corner. **Crivitz Home Bakery and Gourmet Coffee Café** offers some snacks and java for the road. **Rene's Supper Club** at **Popp's Resort** is a great, old-school supper club set on High Flowage on CR X west of Crivitz. The return route of this loop passes there, so this is a good place for the last meal of the day. Plus the resort has cottages and motel rooms, boat and canoe rentals, and fishing supplies. **The Peshtigo River Inn**, just south of Crivitz on US 141, is a good basic motel with an indoor pool. New ownership has done wonders for its previously sketchy reputation.

Be especially aware of deer crossings because this county is a haven for them; there are more deer per acre in Marinette than in any other Wisconsin county. From Crivitz head north on US 141 another 10 miles to Wausaukee.

The best option for lunch or dinner here is **Newingham's Supper Club**. There's a dining room in the back as well as a large bar and grill area facing the street. This has a characteristic "up north" feel about it. Occasionally you can hear live music here. Other options include the **Chippewa Bar** and **Hoover's Prime Tyme** on Main Street, which are just steps from Newingham's and have decent tavern food. The **Rogers Family Restaurant**, also on Main Street, is a solid breakfast option.

Or if you are just passing through, get a little ice cream at **Blue Eyes Café and Ice Cream Parlor**. This little diner has a walk-up window in summer. They also serve Belgian waffles and gourmet coffee in the morning and pizza, salads, and sandwiches for lunch.

Continuing north on US 141 you have another 9 miles to Amberg. A pull-off to the left is allegedly a scenic view, and there is an historical marker about the Marinette County Forest. The overlook is blocked by trees unfortunately. Ironically, the sign regards how much of the land was once clear cut. After the logging days and during some post-World War I prosperity, many corn farmers were attracted to the area. The Great Depression put the skids on that, and in 1933 reforestation began. Once again there is a modest lumber industry in the county, but this byway shows just how much forest has been restored.

Your first stop will be **Daves Falls County Park** on the left. Don't forget your mosquito protection. All vehicles must pay a daily entrance fee of about $3 ($15 annual). Deposit the money at the self-pay station and post the sticker in your car window. This is good for the entire day at any Marinette County park. You must carry your trash out of here. Facilities include a tiny playground, pit toilets, water, picnic tables, and grills. The

MISCAUNO INN

On October 9, 1905, the **Miscauno Inn** opened for business attracting high-society types all the way from Chicago. At that time, Miscauno Island was known as Holmes Island. The Wisconsin and Michigan Railroad, the builders, spared no costs in making this a luxury destination. The inn centered on a massive fireplace. Silver-plated sconces and Japanese prints adorned the walls, and the chandeliers were from Tiffany. The sophistication of the interiors and the twenty-five guestrooms contrasted the rustic beauty of the Northwoods. But fire destroyed the inn in 1923, leaving nothing more than the fireplace. The Four Seasons Club rose up from these ashes and was built around the surviving fireplace in 1925. Part of its charm comes from imagining that at one time Al Capone may have ducked in here for a little rest and relaxation from the hustle of Chicago.

hike from the parking lot to the falls is up a short hill and down twenty-three hillside steps. Daves Falls is to the right, and a steady boil of whitewater from the Pike River passes through a narrow gate of stone. The river splits into two branches just past the falls.

A footbridge crosses the river, and if you go upstream from the bridge on either side, rugged trails go about 170 yards to the smaller twin upper falls. The left bank is more rugged, with more tree roots, rocks, sand, and some muddy spots in wet weather.

From the park, drive north on US 141 to Amberg. This is a one-horse town with a tiny Main Street just west of the highway; its sole attraction is the small **Amberg Museum** of local history. At one time, granite was king here. In the late nineteenth century, the Amberg Granite Company, owned by William Amberg of Chicago, and the Pike River Granite Company quarried for the abundant stone in the area. At the museum complex, you can see the 1894 town hall and an old house right next to a Mathis school that takes the little one-room schoolhouse concept to the extreme—it is hardly large enough to hold a riding mower. Nearby (as is everything in Amberg) **Julie and Lories Downtown Café** is open daily for all meals. Omelets are the rave here as is the broasted chicken.

Continuing north on US 141 you will drive another 9 miles to Pembine. Be careful when passing on the stretch between Amberg and Pembine. Dips in the road have misled drivers to think the oncoming lane is clear; there were two fatal crashes here just within a week of when I passed through. Half mile north of town is **Amberg Antiques & Sweets**, which specializes in homemade fudge but also offers ice cream and candy.

Your most elegant option for a night's stay here in the Northwoods is at the **Four Seasons Resort**. Just about 2 miles before Pembine in Beecher, head east on CR Z 6.8 miles to Marek Road. Turn right and travel about half a mile to turn left on River Road. A one-lane steel bridge takes you to the hundred-acre Miscauno Island in the middle of the Menominee River, which forms the border between Wisconsin and Michigan. Even if you are not staying at the resort, it's a nice place to see. Stop in for a cocktail at the bar or fresh pizza or pasta and a glass of sangria at Johnathan's Italian Bistro. The resort also has a nine-hole golf course right along the river.

In Pembine you will pass the westbound US 8. You will return here to go west on US 8 to continue the waterfall loop. If you are passing through Pembine from mid-July until about Labor Day, watch for an empty lot on the right just as you come into town. A local vendor (Nancy) typically sells **fruits and vegetables** here each day, mostly from her own garden.

Are you in the mood for elk burgers? **Booka's Bar-B-Que** uses locally raised elk for this low-fat version of a burger. But don't worry, if you are not feeling adventurous, there's a full menu including pizza, barbeque pork, and breakfasts.

The waterfall tour continues as you head north from Pembine crossing the north branch of the Peme Bon Won River. Signs direct you to Morgan County Park, but you need to take the second entry, which is Morgan County Park Road, 1 mile from Pembine. The park and campground are 6 miles down this road, but the entry to **Smalley Falls** is another quarter of a mile along US 141. A small blue sign indicates the falls and a narrow crushed-stone road leads to the right a short distance to a small parking lot. The roughly 250-yard walking trail is marked as a footpath but is not maintained. Watch for tree roots, a bit of mud (in wet periods), and some steep descents for the last hundred feet. One trail goes to the bottom of the falls. A more challenging trail goes up to the right for a great view of the river as it tumbles through a narrow gorge. Exercise caution along the edges as there can be sand or pine needles that could cause one to slip.

Another mile continuing down Morgan County Park Road is the road to **Long Slide Falls**, also on the right. The lane passes through pine plantation to a parking lot. One trail goes to the bottom of the falls, 250 yards away, and the other is short and to the overlook, which again should be approached with great care. Long Slide Falls drops about fifty feet, an impressive sight and a beautiful setting. Backtrack to US 141 and head left (south) to Pembine again to continue the waterfall tour. If you are

Smalley Falls takes a picturesque tumble through a narrow gorge.

considering camping for the night, **Morgan County Park** has thirty-two **camp sites**, half of which can be reserved.

Returning south to Pembine, go west on US 8 about 6 miles to Lily Lake Road. Pass Minnie Lake on the left at about mile 3, and watch for the brown sign for Twelve Foot Falls County Park. Go left on Lily Lake Road.

You'll pass Lily Lake on the left and its small boat landing. Pine plantations line the road, and at just shy of 2 miles you'll go right on Twin Lake Road. Less than a mile from the turn off, a wooden sign points left down the gravel-paved Twelve Foot Falls Road. This will be dusty and can be bumpy in between gradings throughout the year. You'll come into a wide boggy area with lily pads (which blossom in summer) and then some clear-cut areas. Motorcyclists should take care as there are some sandy patches in the road. The first blue sign will read **Eighteen Foot Falls**. The road to these is the roughest of all but thankfully short. The parking area is also small and may be difficult to maneuver in, especially when there are other cars here. The price of admission is another 250-yard hike (plus your daily park sticker—there is no self-pay station here, however).

For a delicious side trip in the fall, keep north on US 141 toward Niagara. At the juncture of US 8 heading *east* take a right and continue for 1.2 miles to Chapman Road (CR R). Follow it 3 miles (following the turns of R) to **Pleasant View Orchard and Bakery**. This is only open to the public from Labor Day until gun deer hunting season in November. The orchard offers apples, cider, fall raspberries, and homemade maple syrup. The bakery is a big draw. The last Saturday of September is Applefest with free horse-drawn wagon rides, live music, and a hearty offering of great food.

The orchard was originally part of the neighboring Rocky Top Ranch next door where you will find **Bjorkman's Horse Outings**. One- and two-hour horse rides are just over $25/hour. Owners Dick and Angie Bjorkman can also arrange covered-wagon rides with picnics or overnight camping, or sleigh rides when the snow is on the ground. Be sure to make an appointment first.

Twelve Foot Falls is less than a mile away as you continue down Twelve Foot Falls Road from Eighteen Foot Falls' entrance. This park is a two-for-one for waterfalls and offers camping and a self-pay station for the park fees. You'll also find pit toilets, picnic tables and grills, and a paved road

Twelve Foot Falls Park offers camping as well as waterfalls such as this, the park's namesake.

Eight Foot Falls is small enough to be enjoyed by swimmers.

and parking lot. The falls are actually visible from the lot, and a trail will take you up close to them heading left along the water. The water tumbles into a wide pool suitable for swimming. Another trail goes right on uneven terrain, following the river to **Eight Foot Falls** where there is another nice swimming hole. Wild blackberries show up in late August along the trail. These falls are both less dramatic than the previous sites, but they are also more accessible and offer swimming and a less intimidating environment for kids.

Returning to the entrance of the park, go left away from the arrow pointing back to Highway 8. This will bring you to Trout Haven Road. Cross this intersection and continue about 1.5 miles to the next blue sign, which will mark **Horseshoe Falls** on your right. Take Marinette County Forest Road 510 to the right and then take another right at a double-rut road into the parking area of the falls. There are no facilities here. It's just a couple minutes' hike through cedars to find where the river tumbles over rocks and bends before you like a horseshoe.

Backtrack to Trout Lake Road (to the left at both intersections) and then go left there as well. Don't drive too fast through here; deer can come out at any time, and the unpaved surface lessens your control and increases your stopping distance. Take your time and enjoy the woods. Fawns will be out by mid-summer.

Drive 2.5 miles to Old County A and go left (south). The canopy closes over the road a bit, and you will cross a one-lane bridge at about 1 mile. The river runs right along the road to your left beyond the trees. Another 3.8 miles takes you to Benson Lake Road, and you can see a small stone marker for Phillipsburg—a 1920s settlement now reclaimed by the forest—to your

WHITEWATER RAFTING

The Peshtigo River has some wonderful stretches of whitewater, but they are not just good for photos. Several area outfitters run river rafting trips along this tumbling waterway. **Kosir's Rapid Rafts** has been in operation since 1975. Rafts take one to four people on about a 5-mile stretch of the Peshtigo that ends right at Kosir's. The outfitter runs a campground and has shower facilities and a restaurant on site. **Wildman Ranch** and **Thornton's** are also reputable outfitters.

The falls may be the star of the show at each park, but the hiking trails often hold their own remarkable beauty.

Strong Falls is the most accessible of the cascades. A picnic area is right next to it.

right. Go right here and continue 7.5 miles to cross Parkway Road and enter **Goodman Park**, which returns you to paved roads. Another sign points you left a mile later into the park. Facilities include restrooms, drinking water, picnic areas, a payphone, and a playground. The Civilian Conservation Corps created this park and built the log shelter in the 1930s, and the Peshtigo River flows right through the middle of it. The park's mowed area goes right to the edge of the river so **Strong Falls** is easily accessible. Just upstream, a walking bridge crosses the water to a boardwalk across a small island in the middle of the river and then on to the other side for hiking trails. The bridge grants a nice view of the falls, but swimming is not allowed. Look for Turk's-cap lilies just off the boardwalk in mid-summer. Jack, one of the park managers, is a great source of stories and local history. The park closes at 9 PM.

The park's rustic cabin rents for around $65 per night with a two-night minimum, and comes with a shower and flush toilet. Up to eight people can stay here.

Returning to the park entrance go right to Goodman Park Road and go right again. This angles down to the unpaved Parkway Road where you will continue to the right and head south to **McClintock Falls**. "Rapids" might be a better description. A couple bridges cross the water above this wide expanse of rapids and lead to hiking trails. The parking lot has a self-pay station, pit toilets, first-come first-serve campsites, and a water pump.

Parkway Road becomes quite serpentine, and the enclosing canopy makes it almost seem like a green tunnel. Fall colors are best here. When Parkway Road meets Eagle River Road, stay right on Parkway and it becomes paved from this point on. A half mile past this juncture, look for Peshtigo River Lane, which will take you about 1,000 feet to **Peshtigo River Supper Club**, which serves lunch and dinner and overlooks the water. Back on Parkway Road continue south. When you arrive at CR C, look to the right to see an ice cream and coffee joint. Going this direction would take you to **Kosir's Rapid Rafts**. Drive left on CR C for a half mile to go right again to continue on Parkway Road.

If the woods become dark and deep, and you have promises to keep (and miles to go before you sleep), take the **cutoff** of CR C, which will take you back to US 141 at Wausaukee. Along the way you'll find **Nimrod Inn Supper Club** just before you reach Athelstane. Gizzard soup is a local specialty, and the environment is seriously "up north."

At Parkway Road, the southern half of the paved **State Rustic Road 32** begins and runs 15.8 scenic miles through forest and along rivers and Caldron Falls Flowage and High Falls Reservoir. There are many places to rent cottages and cabins, and for something modern and comfortable, check out **Peshtigo River Vacation Rentals**.

You will come to CH X on your left and Twin Bridge Park on your right, which has a self-pay station and offers camping, a playground, beach, pit toilets, and a picnic area. Parkway Road continues south, taking you around the south end of High Falls Reservoir, where you will find Veteran's Memorial Park and **Veteran's Falls**. This is on the Thunder River. Camping and picnicking are possible here. A walking bridge goes over part of the falls.

Almost a mile farther along on Parkway Road watch for the sign for **Cookie's Closet**. Cookie has an eclectic collection of "gently used" vintage items and assorted eccentric treasures in a shop set in her renovated garage.

She's only open from spring until deer-hunting season (just before Thanksgiving).

The Rustic Road ends where Parkway Road meets CH W. Go left here and this will take you about 12 miles back into Crivitz. Once in town, follow the signs to US 141. If you're heading back south from this trip on US 41/141, consider a stop at **Luigi's II Pizzeria** in Little Suamico. The deep dish pizza is good enough to inspire Green Bay residents to make the drive north for a meal. If you like cheese, you won't be disappointed. Just be warned that the deep dish takes a little longer to bake. Other items are on the menu such as pasta and burgers.

IN THE AREA

Accommodations

The Four Seasons Resort, N16800 Shoreline Drive, Pembine. Call 715-324-5244. Rumored to have been a haunt of Al Capone's, this elegant resort sits on its own island in the middle of the Menominee River. Web site: www.thefourseasonsclub.com.

Goodman Park. Call 715-732-7530. The park rents a rustic cabin with a flush toilet and shower. Reservations require a two-night minimum stay, and up to eight people can be accommodated. Rates start around $65 per night.

McClintock Falls, just south of Goodman Park on Parkway Road. Call 715-732-7530. Camping is on a first-come, first-serve basis.

Morgan County Park, near Pembine. Call 715-732-7530. The park has thirty-two campsites, half of which can be reserved ahead of time. Go north of Pembine and take Long Slide Road or Morgan Park Road east.

The Peshtigo River Inn, W7842 Airport Road, Crivitz. Call 715-854-9800. This is a decent motel with an indoor pool just south of town on US 141. Web site: www.thepeshtigoriverinn.com.

Peshtigo River Vacation Rentals, Crivitz. Call 1-800-505-0485. A collection of ten condos along the Peshtigo River just south of the Caldron Falls Flowage. Web site: www.peshtigoriverrentals.com.

Popp's Resort, W11581 County Road X, Crivitz. Call 715-757-3511. Lakeview cottages and motel suites as well as boat and canoe rentals and fishing supplies. Web site: www.poppsresort.com.

Attractions/Recreation

Amberg Antiques & Sweets, US 141, north of Amberg. Call 715-759-5343. Shop for antiques and try some homemade fudge.

Amberg Museum, Amberg. Call 715-759-5698. A collection of historical buildings including a one-room schoolhouse.

Bjorkman's Horse Outings at Rocky Top Ranch, W5994 Chapman Road, Niagara. Call 715-251-4408. Saddle up a horse for an hour or two or take longer covered-wagon rides (or sleigh rides in winter). Overnight trips are possible and groups are accommodated. Call for an appointment first. Web site: www.horsefun.net.

Cookie's Closet, W11810 Chesapeake Run, Crivitz. Call 715-757-9489. Located in a renovated garage, this shop sells a variety of vintage and eccentric items. Open May–Nov., Wed.–Sun. or by appointment.

Crivitz Area Museum, 204 Oak, Crivitz. Call 715-854-3278. Open May–Sept., Wed.–Sat., 12–4.

Kosir's Rapid Rafts, W14073 County Road C, Silver Cliff. Call 715-757-3431. Enjoy the whitewater of a 5-mile stretch of Peshtigo in rafts for two to four people or single-person "funyaks." Three scheduled trips run on Sat., and two trips per day Sun.–Fri. Web site: www.kosirs.com.

Peshtigo Fire Museum, 400 Oconto Avenue, Peshtigo. Call 715-582-3244. Open May–Oct. Donations welcome. See a collection from the past 150 years and learn the story of the tragic 1871 fire.

Pleasant View Orchard and Bakery, W6050 Chapman Road, Niagara. Call 715-856-5815. Only open to the public from Labor Day to hunting season in Nov., Pleasant View sells apples and late-season raspberries, and the bakery is outstanding. The last Sat. of Sept. is Applefest, an old-fashioned family-oriented festival. Events include free horse-drawn wagon rides, face painting, live music, and grilled food. Web site: www.pleasantvieworchard.com.

Seguin's Cheese, W 1968 US 41, Marinette. Call 1-800-338-7919. This family-owned roadside store halfway between Marinette and Peshtigo has been a mecca for Wisconsin cheese and a variety of other delicious local products for over thirty-five years. Minnetonka moccasins are also sold here. Web site: www.seguinscheese.com.

Thornton's Rafting Resort and Campgrounds, W12882 Parkway Road, Athelstane. Web site: www.thorntonsresort.com. This outfitter runs 5-mile rafting trips on the Peshtigo and has campsites as well.

Wildman Whitewater Ranch, N12080 Allison Lane, Athelstane. Call 715-757-2938. Get out on the Peshtigo River for some whitewater fun in river rafts.

Dining/Drinks

Blue Eyes Café and Ice Cream Parlor, 626 Main Street, Wausaukee. Call 715-856-6085. Get some ice cream from a walk-up window or stop in for Belgian waffles for breakfast. Lunch includes pizza, burgers, sandwiches, and salads.

Booka's Bar-B-Que, N18398 US 141, Pembine. Call 715-324-6001. Try a local, low-fat elk burger or play it safe with some good pizza or barbeque pork.

The Chippewa Bar, 803 Main Street, Wausaukee. Call 715-856-6699. Another option for tavern eating or a beer with the locals.

Crivitz Home Bakery and Gourmet Coffee Café, N6813 US 141, Crivitz. Call 715-854-7944. For a light breakfast and a cup of Joe.

Hoover's Prime Tyme, 816 Main Street, Wausaukee. Call 715-856-5999. A bar and grill that serves pizza.

Julie and Lories Downtown Café, N15087 Dutton Street, Amberg. Call 715-759-5304. The omelets are famous as is the broasted chicken. This café is open daily for all meals and offers a few vegetarian selections as well as a Friday-night fish fry.

Luigi's Pizza Palace II, 1326 West Frontier Road, Little Suamico. Call 920-826-5955. Located just over a mile east of US 41/141 and Sobieski

Corners taking County Road S, Luigi's is an Italian pie legend. Expect the deep dish pizza (recommended) to take a while and offer plenty of cheese.

Newingham's Supper Club, 722 Main Street, Wausaukee. This is the best option for variety for lunch or dinner. There's a dining room in back and a large bar and grill area facing the street. Occasionally there is live music here.

Nimrod Inn Supper Club, N12808 County Road AC #A, Athelstane. Call 715-856-5168. Great steaks and seafood and the Northwoods menu includes a few regional specialties such as gizzard soup!

Peshtigo River Supper Club, N10907 Peshtigo River Lane, Crivitz. Call 715-757-3741. Offers a full menu for lunch and dinner in a casual Northwoods tavern environment overlooking the water. Web site: www.peshtigoriverresort.com.

Rene's Supper Club at Popp's Resort, W11581 County Road X, Crivitz. Call 715-757-3511. Open daily for dinner and for lunch on weekends, Rene's specializes in steaks. Web site: www.poppsresort.com/dining.php.

The Rogers Family Restaurant, 1236 US 141, Wausaukee. Call 715-856-5982. This is a good spot for breakfast in particular.

Other

Marinette County—Tourism Director, 1926 Hall Avenue, Marinette. Call 1-800-236-6681. Web site: www.marinettecounty.com.

Wisconsin Welcome Center—Statewide information, 1680 Bridge Street, Marinette. Call 715-732-4333. Web site: www.travel wisconsin.com. Open May 1–Oct. 31.

If the Lake side is rough, go to the Green Bay side for calmer water.

CHAPTER

12

Door County

Estimated length: 95 miles

Estimated time: 2.5 hours minimum, but even better for a long weekend

Getting There: From Green Bay take WI 57 north to Sturgeon Bay.

Highlights: See the dunes at **Whitefish Dunes State Park** and the caves next door at **Cave Point County Park**; visit **lighthouses**; eat at a **traditional fish boil**; pick cherries and sample wines; take the ferry to historic **Washington Island**; hike through **Peninsula State Park**; see a movie at an old-time drive-in; shop at boutiques and galleries in several lakeside towns.

The Door County Peninsula is popular not just for its beauty and the abundance of shoreline—it has Lake Michigan to the east and Green Bay to the west—but also its accessibility. Right up Interstate 43 from the Fox River Valley, Milwaukee, and Chicago, the peninsula is a quick drive and yet seems a world away. Perhaps best known for its cherry production or as the thumb of the mitten that is Wisconsin, Door County's name has an origin that is anything but inviting.

The Native Americans—specifically the Ho-Chunk (Winnebago) and Potawotami tribes—had already settled the area before the French arrived who were led first by Jean Nicolet. As the French fur traders began coming by boat, they passed through the strait between the tip of the peninsula and the Potawatomi Islands, most notably Washington Island. They gave the unpredictable waters of the passage the name "La Porte des Morts" or Death's Door. The Native Americans were forcibly removed in the 1830s as pioneers from Europe came for timber, farming, and commercial fishing.

The peninsula's limestone bedrock is part of the massive Niagara Escarpment that spans from Wisconsin to the falls of the same name. This underlying rock combined with a climate tempered by the lake creates excellent conditions for fruits, especially cherries. More than 2,200 acres of cherry trees make the equally impressive 1,000 acres of apple trees look small.

Though the towns along the route bustle with tourism in the summer, Door County maintains a laid-back spirit, and the natural beauty of the place is no small contributor. State and county parks are numerous and offer forested bluffs, sandy beaches and dunes, boreal and hardwood forests, as well as streams and some wetlands. The shipping and commercial fishing industries were often threatened by a dangerous shoreline and the temperamental lake, so lighthouses are also in abundance.

The best time to go depends on your fancy. Summer is delightful, of course, but the apple and cherry blossoms of late spring are a sight to behold as are the fiery colors of autumn. Winter does slow down the tourism trade, but with a blanket of untouched snow, the peninsula is a wonderland destination for winter sports or a romantic fireplace-centered getaway.

If the towns of Door County are your primary focus, you can simply make a loop of WI 57 heading north to WI 42 at Sister Bay. There you can either continue north to Gills Bay and Washington Island or return south on WI 42 along the Green Bay side, which will lead you back to Sturgeon Bay. The byway as written here, however, includes a few extra backroads and the natural wonders along the way as well.

As you head north from the bridge in Sturgeon Bay watch for CR T at just under 2 miles. Take CR T to the right (east) and follow it through farmland about 3 miles where it enters forest. Cross Brauer Road and CR T also becomes **State Rustic Road 9**. For the next 6.7 paved miles this heads northeast through sand dunes and forest, crossing trout streams along the way, and then rounding Whitefish Point to head north-northwest. Lakeshore property obstructs some of the view of Lake Michigan, but there are a couple of boat landings where you can stop to have a look.

A great place to stay for the night is coming up on your right. **Glidden Lodge Beach Resort** sits on the loveliest beach in Door County. From here you could actually walk to Whitefish Dunes State Park along the sand. The one- to three-bedroom suites come with kitchens, whirlpools, and gas fireplaces, and the views include the sunrise over the lake. When CR T reaches Bark Road past the resort, go right. Bark Road goes just about a half mile to an outlet to the beach and boat landing. Continue north on Cave Point Drive, which is more or less straight across but slightly to the left. Follow this and you are actually entering Whitefish Dunes State Park. When you come to an intersection with CR WD, take a hard right on Schauer Road to find parking and the visitor center.

Whitefish Dunes State Park is the most visited day-use park in the state. Visitors enjoy a stroll along the sandy beach and along boardwalks through the dunes or trails through beech forest. The visitor center has exhibits chronicling the geology and ecology of the area. A fine layer of creeping plant life holds the dunes in place, and visitors are instructed to walk only in designated areas. A reconstruction of a village in the woods honors the Native Americans who once lived here. In addition to the

Whitefish Dunes State Park has the peninsula's finest beach.

attraction of its natural beauty, this park is a good place for a swim or a pick up game of volleyball.

Nestled within the state park is a smaller county park, and a spectacular sight at that. **Cave Point County Park** sits along the shoreline of Lake Michigan north of the visitor center as you continue on Schauer Road. Stop here and have a look at the limestone sea caves that were formed by the incessant pounding of Lake Michigan's waves. The caves are in the water

See what years of waves have done to the coastline at Cave Point County Park.

and can be seen from points that jut out from the mainland. You can also climb down to walk along the rocky shore. Kayaking trips often come here in the summer season.

Schauer Road continues north through the park; at Cave Point Road go right and it will follow the lakeshore north to rejoin WI 57 right outside of Jacksonport.

Founded in 1869, **Jacksonport** was once a hub for shipping timber. A sign welcomes you to the "quiet side" of Door County, and it's true—relatively speaking, the Lake Michigan coastline doesn't get as congested with tourists in high season. Watch for Lakeside Park that has a Wisconsin Maritime Trail marker that recalls a couple of shipwrecks just off-shore where there was once a pier. You will see an anchor and capstand from one of the vessels. The maritime trail offers many land-based markers along the shores of both Lake Michigan and Superior that commemorate the sailing life. A whole Web site is dedicated to them.

On your right as you enter town is **Square Rigger Lodge and Galley**, which does a traditional fish boil and in season serves good breakfasts and lunches. The seasonal motel has basic, clean rooms, and the beachside location is nice. Cottages closer to the water are also on offer. Shoppers should check out the refur-bished 1860s log home that is now the **Jacksonport Craft Cottage**. Arts and crafts by over a hundred artists are on display, and you will also find Amish quilts here.

Continuing north on WI 57, the next village is **Baileys Harbor**. In 1848 the same year the state was founded, Captain Justice Bailey took shel-ter from Lake Michigan's October wrath. His exploration of the shore led

THE FISH BOIL

Admittedly it does sound like an unpleasant swimmer's rash, how-ever, the fish boil is a Door County culinary tradition and a bit of a spectacle. Originally intended to feed big groups of local lumber-jacks and fisherman, the boil became commercialized and is now offered at a handful of restau-rants. The idea was to cook a large amount of whitefish steaks in a pot of salted water with sweet onions and new potatoes boiling over a wood fire. The oils from the fish that give it that "fishy" taste would leach out into the water and float on top. To remove these, the boilmaster needed to make the kettle boil over. And so he did, by dousing the fire with kerosene! The resulting conflagration engulfs the kettle, and the water foams over the edges taking the unwanted oils with it. The fish is removed and served with plenty of melted but-ter. Even if you don't like fish, you should consider this mild variety. At the very least, get a photo of the flaming boil over.

to lumbering and quarrying by winter. The harbor that takes his name became the first community and county seat of Door County. An assortment of shops offers places to linger, and when you are hungry head over to the **Sandpiper Restaurant**. This seasonal eatery is famous for its breakfasts and is another site for a fish boil. If that's closed, you can always count on **Harbor Fish Market and Grille** for being open. Located right on the water, this restaurant offers a little bit of everything in a casual environment. Dinner tends to be a bit more upscale.

If you need a bed and breakfast, consider the **Blacksmith Inn on the Shore** in the heart of town. Two buildings house fourteen rooms with water views. Another full house is available as well. The property is Travel Green–certified and the attractive interiors, and third-floor balconies with hammocks make this a perfect escape.

WI 57 continues north and just as you are leaving town, watch for Ridge Road, which is **State Rustic Route 39.** Take this out and back 2.5 miles each way to see some pristine lakeshore. This road passes through **The Ridges Sanctuary**. Back on WI 57 go north less than a mile to CR Q and go right. This will take you to the sanctuary's entrance.

Created in 1937, this is the oldest non-profit nature reserve in the state and 5 miles of trails and boardwalks take you through a very special collection of wildflowers, boreal forest, and wetlands. Naturalists guide **hikes** and offer weekly lectures in summer and guided snowshoe hikes are offered from January to March. You can see the carnivorous pitcher plant here and a very rare species of dragonfly. The sandy ridges that give the reserve its name alternate between wet areas known as swales. This curious land formation represents 1,200 years of lake activity and shows the varying shorelines. Two **range lights** for lake navigation are within the sanctuary as well.

Follow CR Q past the park and in a couple miles you will see Moonlight Bay on your right. Cana Island Road, which is also **State Rustic Road 38,** is on your right soon after. Follow this to **Cana Island Lighthouse**. You can park your car at the end of the road and cross a narrow isthmus to get to the island. The lighthouse has a small museum inside and you can climb to the top for a scenic view from May through October.

Backtrack to CR Q and go right following it just about 7 miles to WI 57. Go right here and after 2 miles the highway meets WI 42 at Sister Bay. A left turn will take you back south on the Green Bay side. Otherwise go right and follow WI 42 to the top of the peninsula.

Sister Bay was established in 1912 by Norwegian loggers, and that is reflected in its Scandinavian theme. The remarkable thing about Sister Bay

CANA ISLAND LIGHTHOUSE

Built in 1869 with Milwaukee's characteristic Cream City brick, this postcard example of a lighthouse is now encased in protective steel plates and painted white. The black two-story lantern houses a third-order Fresnel lens from Paris, France. The tower was built to replace the light-house at Baileys Harbor and was once fueled by whale oil, kerosene, and acetylene before finally receiving electricity. The island was so low that the lake frequently swept over it, and in 1902 top soil was brought in. Today

The Cana Island Lighthouse is a short walk away along a narrow causeway.

there is a modest forest cover around the yard. It was only recently that vistors were allowed to enter the tower.

is the community bought out a downtown waterfront resort and tore it down to double the size of the city park. Shoppers can expect some galleries and shopping areas throughout the village.

If you are looking for ethnic-themed gifts (and more) stop at the gift shop at **Al Johnson's Swedish Restaurant and Butik**. Your first thought might be, "hey, you don't see a building with grass growing on the roof very often." True enough. Even rarer is one with goats grazing on it. What started as a practical joke by a friend became a tradition, and you can see them keeping the roof trimmed during the growing season. The pancakes are legendary as are the lingonberries that go on top of them. Swedish meatballs are another specialty, and salmon or pork chops are fine options as well.

WASHINGTON AND ROCK ISLANDS

Just across "Death's Door" lie two marvelous escapes from mainland life. **Washington Island** offers a breather from tourism development. Sure, you'll have attractions such as the Maritime and Farm Museums and hotels and campgrounds to extend your stay, but the feel of the place is quintessentially small town America. Long inhabited by Native Americans followed by French explorers, the island is best recognized now as an enclave of Icelandic culture. Check out the wooded stave church or the short, stocky Icelandic horses. The shoreline shows dunes in some places and the smooth-cobblestone Schoolhouse Beach is a nice, if chilly, place for a swim. If you leave your car on the mainland you can rent bicycles or mopeds or board a trolley tour such as the Cherry Train or Viking Tour Train. If you are going only for the day, it is best to take a morning ferry.

Another ferry on the northeast coast departs for **Rock Island**, which has no vehicles whatsoever. **Rock Island State Park** there offers the remotest camping you will find in the state.

Washington Island makes a great day away from the peninsula and shows this pebbled beach.

Little Sister Resort is a collection of chalets and cottages on the smaller harbor to the south of town. Here you'll also find indoor/outdoor seasonal dining at **Fred and Fuzzy's Waterfront Bar and Grill.** This casual spot is perfect for a sunset and a burger. The menu offers wraps and sandwiches (a grilled three-cheese sandwich is a fine choice) and an assortment of fried goodies such as cheese curds. The whitefish pâté is fabulous.

The next community north is Ellison Bay. A local institution, the **Viking Grill** was the first place to offer a commercial fish boil, and the tradition continues. Don't forget dessert: Door County cherry pie. You can get breakfast and lunch here as well. Here's a restaurant alternative: learn to cook your gourmet meal before you eat it. **Savory Spoon Cooking School** occupies the town's old schoolhouse, and Chef Janice Thomas has over twenty years of experience in a variety of culinary backgrounds. Learn how to make some pretty incredible dishes and then eat them. A shop onsite sells specialty items.

Follow the highway once again about another 5 miles north to Gills Rock. You can see a fishing tug and learn about the history of commercial fishing at the **Gills Rock Door County Maritime Museum**. Exhibits also cover shipwrecks and lifesaving, and there is a gift shop onsite. Tired of being behind the wheel? Climb aboard the **Island Clipper**, a passenger ferry to Washington Island. For the **car ferry** to Washington Island, continue 3 more miles up to Northport.

Continuing on the byway on the peninsula, backtrack down WI 42 and continue south past Sister Bay until you reach **Ephraim**. This is another marvelous place for a sunset. The village's **South Shore Pier** also offers a variety of water recreation including Jet Skis, kayaks, sailboats, boat excursions, parasailing, pontoon rental—you name it. You will find it at the bend in the road at the center of town. Right across the street on your left is **Wilson's Restaurant and Ice Cream Bar**, a landmark in Ephraim since 1906. The burgers, sandwiches, and salads are all fine, but the ice cream is what steals the show. They make their own root beer and the various sundaes and ice cream concoctions are legendary. Old-school diner tables and booth jukeboxes add to the experience.

Southward out of town you will pass **Peninsula State Park Golf Course** on your right, one of the most frequently played courses in Wisconsin. Just past it is Shore Road that will take you into the remarkable **Peninsula State Park.** This is sort of the backdoor of the park. The office is at the other end in Fish Creek, and this is where you can purchase your required state park sticker or check into your campsite. Also just outside the park near the office are **Nor Door Sport and Cyclery** and **Edge of Park**, two good places to **rent bikes** for the fantastic trail system inside the park. The former rents **cross-country skis and snowshoes**, while the latter also rents **scooters**.

As far as state park's go, this may be the best in terms of variety of offerings. In fact, it is the only one with a golf course of its own. Despite the fact that there are 468 campsites, reservations are a good idea in high season. The drive through the park is scenic enough as it is, but it'd be a shame not to stop for a spell to try one of the many outdoor activities such as hiking on the park's 20 miles of trails, biking, fishing, boating, or swimming at sandy Nicolet Beach. Winter is no less active with plenty of opportunities for cross-country skiing, snowshoeing, sledding, and snowmobiling. You are likely to see deer and wild turkeys as well as a variety of other birds and critters including foxes, coyotes, and porcupines. Shore Line Road takes a lower route through the park with access to cobblestone beaches, while Skyline Road offers loftier views of Green Bay including a seventy-five-foot observation tower atop the 180-foot Eagle Bluff. Consider a visit to the **Eagle Bluff Lighthouse** as well.

Take to the lake and kayak the shoreline.

Door County has several wineries.

And as if all that wasn't enough, did I mention live entertainment? **American Folklore Theatre** makes its summer and fall home at an outdoor theatre inside the park. Works are purely original and include plenty of music and merriment with such past hits as *Lumberjacks in Love* and a musical about ice fishing. The troupe has garnered a lot of critical acclaim and plenty of hearts over the years.

If you stay on WI 42, heading past Shore Road and bypassing the park, you will come to **Skyway Drive-in Theatre** where you can watch the latest double features from your vehicle and eat popcorn with real butter.

Follow the highway southwest past the state park to where it turns west passing the park entrance before crossing Fish Creek and entering the town of the same name. Starting already in the late nineteenth century, **Fish Creek** was really the early bird in the tourism industry as well-heeled travelers from Milwaukee and Chicago once took steamships up to Door County for natural air-conditioning. The town has preserved some of that past and shows dozens of Victorian structures.

The oldest continuously operating inn in Door County is **The Whistling Swan Inn**. It was constructed in 1887, but it has only been in Fish Creek since 1907. That year the structure was dismantled on its original site in Marinette, Wisconsin, and hauled across the ice of Green Bay to be put back together. The inn is quite elegant, and the **Whistling Swan Restaurant** offers more upscale gourmet dining experiences.

White Gull Inn and Restaurant is one of the few places that offer the fish boil year-round. Breakfast here is a real treat, especially the cherry-stuffed French toast. One of the better shopping districts, **Founders Square**, is near Whistling Swan Inn at the corner where WI 42 bends left at Spruce Street.

Scottish-born Alexander Noble moved to Fish Creek in 1863 where he lived and worked as a blacksmith and postmaster. **Noble House Historic Home** was the first stick-built home in Fish Creek and operates as a museum showing many of the original furnishings from the late nineteenth century. If you're around town in the evening, stop down at **Sunset Park**; just as the sun slips below the horizon, an audience generally applauds the show.

Back on the byway, take WI 42 south as it heads up the hill out of town through a rock cut in the bluff. South of Fish Creek about a half mile is **Orchard Country Winery and Market**. Stop in and sample the wines and the wide variety of cherry products including salsas and sauces and the delicious snack, dried cherries. You can also pick your own fruit. Cherry sea-

Pick your own cherries in Door County.

son runs from about mid-July through August and apples are ready in September and October, but the winery and market are open year-round. Tours are put on hold from November through April, but in winter you can join sleigh rides. The winery is also the starting point for the **Door County Trolley**.

Scenic tours, lighthouse tours, winery tours, and even a spooky ghost tour are on offer with the red-painted trolley. Expect some highly informative and humorous narration from the guide.

Just about 2 miles south of Fish Creek, watch for Peninsula Player Road. If you go left (east) the road will take you to a great little sidetrack for creative types: **Hands On Art Studio**. It looks like a small farm, but all the buildings house studios for various media. You can pay a nominal studio fee for the day to work on pottery, mosaics, metal and glass work, and much more. The only additional costs are certain materials. It's loads of fun, and staff members double as art instructors. The build your own **sandwich bar** is a good lunch option, and many will enjoy the friendly farm animals.

In the opposite direction on this road is another theatre in the woods. **Peninsula Players** provide professional entertainment amid cedar forest along the shores of Green Bay.

Continue down WI 42 to the last town on the byway, **Egg Harbor**. The story of this village's name smacks of a local gag on the unsuspecting traveler, but apparently historical evidence exists. It has to do with a food fight. In 1825 French traders led by Commodore Pierce Roulette were paddling to Mackinac Island (Michigan) when they were ordered to put ashore. The tradition is that the commodore lands first. When other paddlers decided to egg him on by beating him to shore, the commodore refused to have egg on his face, and his crew started bombarding the other paddlers with their omelet supply.

And as if that wasn't enough of an eggsample of this community's commitment to the name, stop in at **Dovetail Gallery and Studio**, which

A fish boil is a Door County tradition and a bit of fireworks.

specializes in egg art. Resident artist Kathleen Mand Beck has international renown for her intricate etched egg art designs. Also on site is a small museum of egg art from around the world and an actual dinosaur egg.

If it's time for a cold one, stop in at **Shipwrecked Brew Pub**, where you'll find a menu that combines pub fare, salads, and a few finer entrees with a selection of in-house beers. The spirits behind the bar aren't the only ones here. Many are the reports of resident ghosts, and the staff will be happy to tell you about them. This is one of several places in the state with an Al Capone connection.

Expect some very fine eats at **The Bistro at Liberty Square,** which is open for all meals daily. Stop in just for gourmet coffee or a full breakfast; consider the cherry-covered French toast. Paninis, salads, and wraps are great lunch options, and dinner is strong on steak and seafood as well as pasta. The wine list offers pairing suggestions and The Board Room in back hosts tastings on Saturdays. The Italian dishes on the dinner menu are notable.

If you choose to make Egg Harbor a stopping point for the night, you have some good options. **Egg Harbor Lodge** on the north end of town sits on a bluff overlooking the water. All rooms have water (and sunset) views, and there is a pool and whirlpool onsite. **The Landmark Resort** is the largest resort in Door County and offers suites with full kitchens on a wooded property. Some rooms have water views. If you are looking for something a bit more personal, consider **Door County Lighthouse Inn Bed and Breakfast**. The inn is built to look like a lighthouse, and the innkeepers can help you set up tours to the ten lighthouses in Door County.

You have now reached the final stretch of the byway, and hopefully you are doing this around sunset. Heading south on CR G, which becomes CR B, you will follow the Green Bay shoreline, which offers a few nice stopping points as you make your way back to Sturgeon Bay. **Old Stone Quarry Park** just south of Little Harbor offers great views of the water, and you can see Sherwood Point Lighthouse and Potawatomi State Park across Sturgeon Bay. In winter time this is an access point to drive on the ice for ice fisherman and those feeling daring. The park includes a boat launch with a safe harbor, restrooms, fishing off the dock or seawall, as well as picnic tables and a pavilion. From here CR B follows the shores of Sturgeon Bay into town where you can connect with Business Highways 42/57 to head south.

IN THE AREA

Accommodations

Blacksmith Inn on the Shore, 8152 State Highway 57, Baileys Harbor. Call 920-839-9222. This green-certified bed and breakfast offers fourteen rooms in two houses, all with water views. Rooms offer private baths, whirlpool tubs, and gas fireplaces, and some third-floor balconies come with hammocks. Rates can drop drastically in winter. Web site: www.the blacksmithinn.com.

Door County Lighthouse Inn Bed and Breakfast, 4639 Orchard Road, Egg Harbor. Call 1-866-868-9088. This inn is built to look like a lighthouse and offers five rooms with varying amenities that might include a double whirlpool, fireplace or an outdoor deck. The innkeepers can help you arrange lighthouse tours. Web site: www.dclighthouseinn.com.

Egg Harbor Lodge, 7965 Highway 42, Egg Harbor. Call 920-868-3115. Set on a bluff overlooking the water at the north end of town, all rooms have balconies or patios with a view of the sunset over the water. The hotel has a pool and whirlpool. Some rooms have double whirlpool baths and a large suite offers a kitchen. Web site: www.eggharborlodge.com.

Glidden Lodge Beach Resort, 4676 Glidden Drive, Sturgeon Bay. Call 920-746-3900. One- to three-bedroom suites look out over the lake and the finest beach in Door County. Units come with full kitchens, gas fireplaces, and whirlpools. Web site: www.gliddenlodge.com.

The Landmark Resort, 7643 Hillside Road, Egg Harbor. Call 1-800-273-7877. This is the largest resort in Door County, and its buildings lie serpentine through the woods. All suites offer water or woodland views from balconies or patios and a full kitchen, and the property has a fitness center, game room, and indoor pool. Web site: www.thelandmark resort.com.

Little Sister Resort, 10620 Little Sister Road, Sister Bay. Call 920-854-4013. Set on a small bay just south of Sister Bay, this collection of chalets and cottages is tucked into the woods. If you are looking for the summer-by-the-lake vibe, this place has it. Web site: www.littlesisterresort.com.

Square Rigger Lodge and Galley, 6332 State Highway 57, Jacksonport. Call 920-823-2404. This simple motel with clean, spacious rooms caters well to families and sits on the shores of Lake Michigan. The restaurant does a great fish boil. Cottages are also for rent closer to the water. Web site: www.squareriggerlodge.com.

Whistling Swan Inn, 4192 Main Street, Fish Creek. Call 920-868-3442. This bed and breakfast is one of the most elegant places to stay and the longest running inn in Door County. The building was moved here across the ice from Marinette back in 1907. The onsite restaurant is top-notch gourmet. Web site: www.whistlingswan.com.

Attractions/Recreation

American Folklore Theatre, Peninsula State Park, Fish Creek. Call 920-854-6117. Located within the state park, this open-air theatre offers evening entertainment from June–Oct. Most of the works are original, and all of them include music and laughs. Web site: www.folklore theatre.com.

Door County Trolley at Orchard Country Winery. Call 920-868-1100. The red trolley is as humorous as it is fascinating. Join some wonderful guided tours through all the scenic places or some themed rides to lighthouses, wineries, dinners, or haunted places. Web site: www.door countytrolley.com.

Dovetail Gallery and Studio, 7901 State Highway 42, Egg Harbor. Call 920-868-3987. Check out this unique collection of etched egg art and see examples of this unusual medium from around the world in the egg museum. Web site: www.dovetailgallery.com.

Edge of Park, Inc., Park Entrance Road, Fish Creek. Call 920-868-3344. This is the only place to rent a moped in Northern Door County. They can also supply you with a variety of bicycle options and safety equipment, including a tandem recumbent bike. Web site: www.edgeof park.com.

Gills Rock Door County Maritime Museum, Wisconsin Bay Road, Gills Rock. Call 920-854-1844. Web site: www.dcmm.org/gillsrock.html. Open May–Oct. Fee. Climb aboard an old fishing tug boat and learn a bit about life on the waves. A variety of exhibits also address shipwrecks and lifesaving.

Hands on Art Studio, 3655 Peninsula Players Rd. Fish Creek. Call 920-868-9311. This farm-cum-art-camp is a creative wonderland. For a nominal fee use the entire grounds all day and just pay for some of your materials. Instructors are on site as is a build-your-own sandwich bar. Web site: www.handsonartstudio.com.

Jacksonport Craft Cottage, 6275 State Highway 57, Jacksonport. Call 920-823-2288. Web site: www.jacksonportcraftcottage.com. Open daily May–Oct., and on weekends or by appointment in winter. Over a hundred artists are on display in this refinished 1860s log cabin and Amish quilts are also for sale.

Orchard Country Winery and Market, 9197 Highway 42, Fish Creek. Call 920-868-3479. Here is a great place for pick-your-own cherries in July and Aug. and apples in Sept. and Oct. The winery offers tours and tastings, and the market sells a wide variety of delicious cherry-related products and much more. Tours run from May to Oct. Web site: www.orchardcountry.com.

Noble House Historic Home, Highway 42 and Main Street, Fish Creek. Call 920-868-2091. Open daily for tours except on Mon., 11–4, mid-June–mid-Oct. Weekends only mid-May–mid-June. Fee. This 1875 Greek-revival farmhouse is now a museum showing many of its original nineteenth-century furnishings. Web site: www.doorcountycottage.com/noblehouse.

Nor Door Sport and Cyclery, 4007 State Highway 42, Fish Creek. Call 920-868-2275. Open Mon.–Sat., 10–5, Sun., 10–3. Rent a variety of bikes and equipment including children's bikes, helmets and trailers, as well as cross-country skis and snowshoes in the colder months. They also have some good bike-route maps on their Web site. Web site: www.nordoorsports.com.

Peninsula Players, W4351 Peninsula Players Road, Fish Creek. Call 920-868-3287. This fine wooden pavilion in the woods along Green Bay offers a variety of quality plays throughout the season. Web site: www.peninsulaplayers.com.

Peninsula State Park, 9462 Shore Road, Fish Creek. Call 920-868-3258. A state park fee applies. Four-hundred and sixty-eight campsites make this the mother of all parks, but the endless options for recreation are even more stunning. Hiking, biking, boating, swimming, kayaking, golfing, and cross-country skiing are a few activities on the list, but there is also the open-air American Folk Theatre. Web site: www.dnr.state.wi.us/org/land/parks/specific/peninsula.

Peninsula State Park Golf Course, Fish Creek. Call 920-854-5791. Enjoy eighteen holes set in the woods of the state park. This is one of the state's most played courses. Reservations are recommended. Web site: www.peninsulagolf.org.

The Ridges Sanctuary, County Road Q, Baileys Harbor. Call 920-839-2802. Boardwalks and hiking trails pass through remarkable terrain formed by hundreds of years of a shifting shoreline. Several rare species can be found here and birders will be impressed. Two range lights can be seen as well as some pristine protected beach area. Guided tours and presentations are common throughout the year. Web site: www.ridge sanctuary.org.

Savory Spoon Cooking School, 12042 State Highway 42, Ellison Bay. Call 920-854-6600. Open June–Oct. Chef Janice Thomas studied at Cordon Bleu in Paris and with other great chefs around the world. To study (and ultimately eat) for an hour or two, check the online calendar for upcoming classes. Web site: www.savoryspoon.com.

The Skyway Drive-In Theatre, 3475 State Highway 42, Fish Creek. Call 920-854-9938. Enjoy a double feature from your car and have popcorn with actual butter on it. Web site: www.doorcountydrivein.com.

Whitefish Dunes State Park, 3275 Clark Lake Road, Sturgeon Bay. Call 920-823-2400. A state park fee applies. With a beautiful beach and fragile dune system, this is the state's most popular day-use park. Learn more about the ecosystem and geology at the visitor center, have a swim in Lake Michigan or hike (or ski) through the beech forest and dunes. Web site: www.dnr.wi.gov/org/land/parks/specific/whitefish.

Dining/Drinks

Al Johnson's Swedish Restaurant and Butik, 10698 North Bay Shore Drive, Sister Bay. Call 1-800-241-9914. This is the restaurant famous for having goats grazing on its grassy roof. The gift shop inside is also quite popular, but be sure to come here for a hearty breakfast of Swedish pancakes with lingonberries or lunch and dinner with Swedish meat-balls. Open year-round, but the goats have the winter off. Web site: www.aljohnsons.com.

The Bistro at Liberty Square, 7755 State Highway 42, Egg Harbor. Call 920-868-4600. Part of a nice shopping complex, this restaurant is open for all meals. Look for cherry-smothered French toast at breakfast or the crab cakes later in the day. The wine list is marvelous and user friendly for those who aren't necessarily experts. The Italian items on the menu are notable. The Board Room in back hosts some pretty outstanding dinners and opens to a fine art gallery. Web site: www.libertysquare shops.com.

Fred and Fuzzy's Waterfront Bar and Grill, located at Little Sister Resort, Sister Bay. Call 920-854-6699. Set under the trees along a small bay this casual hangout has a varied menu of sandwiches and wraps and is an excellent place for a cold one.

Harbor Fish Market and Grille, 8080 State Highway 57, Baileys Harbor. Call 920-839-9999. Breakfast options include Door County cherry pan-cakes and some takes on eggs Benedict. Though a casual restaurant, the dinner menu tends to go a bit more upscale. Look for weekly lobster boils. Web site: www.harborfishmarket-grille.com.

The Sandpiper Restaurant, 8177 State Highway 57, Baileys Harbor. Call 920-839-2528. This seasonal restaurant is another great option for the fish boil, and the breakfasts and lunches are extremely popular. Web site: www.sandpiperfishboil.com.

Shipwrecked Restaurant, Brewery, and Inn, 7791 Egg Harbor Road, Egg Harbor. Call 920-868-2767. Dine on very good pub fare and salads and a few finer entrees, and wash it all down with one of the several house-brewed beers. A host of ghosts allegedly occupy the building, and there is an Al Capone connection to the property. Web site: www.shipwrecked microbrew.com.

Square Rigger Galley, 6332 State Highway 57, Jacksonport. Call 920-823-2404. Set along Lake Michigan, the restaurant does a popular fish boil and good hearty breakfasts. Web site: www.squareriggerlodge.com.

The Viking Grill, 12029 State Highway 42, Ellison Bay. Call 920-854-2998. This is the original Door County fish boil, but the menu offers all meals and quite a nice variety, from complete breakfasts to supper-club dinners. Web site: www.thevikinggrill.com.

Whistling Swan Restaurant, 4192 Main Street, Fish Creek. Call 920-868-3442. If you are looking for something a bit more upscale than a fish boil, stop in here for delectable options such as andouille-encrusted snapper or Australian lamb loin. Web site: www.whistlingswan.com.

Wilson's Restaurant and Ice Cream Parlor, 9990 Water Street, Ephraim. Call 920-854-2041. Since 1906, this institution has been serving its own root beer and some wickedly decadent ice cream concoctions. A lunch menu is also available. Web site: www.wilsonsicecream.com.

Other

Door County Visitor Bureau, 1015 Green Bay Road, Sturgeon Bay. Call 920-743-4456. Web site: www.doorcounty.com.

Washington Island Ferry, Northport. Call 920-847-2546. From Dec. to Mar. the ferry doesn't run as often, but May–Oct. it sails several times a day, in fact, every half hour in peak season. Web site: www.wisferry.com.

Wisconsin's Maritime Trails. Web site: www.maritimetrails.org.